INDIA PARTITIONED
The Other Face of Freedom

——————— • ———————

Volume II

Edited by

MUSHIRUL HASAN

LOTUS COLLECTION
ROLI BOOKS

This edition first published 1995
Revised and enlarged edition 1997
Fourth impression in 2005

The Lotus Collection
An imprint of
Roli Books Pvt. Ltd.
M-75, G.K. II Market, New Delhi 110 048
Phones: ++91 (011) 2921 2271, 2921 2782
2921 0886, Fax: ++91 (011) 2921 7185
E-mail: roli@vsnl.com; Website: rolibooks.com
Also at
Varanasi, Bangalore, Jaipur and the Netherlands

ISBN: 81-7436-011-5
Rs 595 for the set of two volumes

Typeset in Galliard by Roli Books Pvt Ltd and
printed at Syndicate Binder, New Delhi

'These savageries pass as much in the outside world as in India under the name of communal trouble or Hindu-Muslim rioting. But these expressions have become the cliches of a stale journalese, which convey no real sensation of the phenomenon they purport to describe. Nor am I able to suggest a better alternative. I have weighed nearly all the words and phrases which the murderous ferocity of man, as distinct from his warlike ferocity, has contributed to the vocabulary of European peoples: massacre, pogrom, lynching, fusillade, noyade, St Bartholomew, Sicilian Vespers, Bloodbath of Stockholm, Bulgarian atrocities, Armenian massacres, Belsen, genocide, etc., etc., but find all of them inadequate. Their vividness has worn off. Instead of evoking horror, they would rather throw a veil of historical respectability on spectacles of mass murder, rotting corpses, gutters choked with human bodies emitting stomach-turning stench.'

Nirad C. Chaudhuri, *Thy Hand, Great Anarch!*, p. 835.

—1948, Krishen Khanna

Contents

Preface   9

The Heart Divided   13
MUMTAZ SHAH NAWAZ

A Diary of Partition Days   27
GANDA SINGH

Love is Stronger than Hate   87
KHUSHDEVA SINGH

Oranges and Apples   113
INTERVIEW WITH KAMLABEHN PATEL

We are Still Theirs   124
INTERVIEW WITH AMRIK SINGH OF DOBERAN VILLAGE

Only One Junoon   137
INTERVIEW WITH SIMRET SINGH OF THAMALI VILLAGE

Humiliated and Harassed They Left   145
SHORISH KASHMIRI

In the Shadow of Freedom   158
ANIS KIDWAI

Hindu-Muslim Social Relations 1935-47:
A Personal Perspective   172
ISHTIAQ HUSAIN QURESHI

From the Valley of Jamuna to the Valley of Hakra   184
MASUD HASAN SHAHAB DEHALVI

My Ordeal as a Citizen of Pakistan   196
JOSH MALIHABADI

Delhi in Mourning   207
KAMALADEVI CHATTOPADHYAYA

The Ganges in Mourning   213
ARUNA ASAF ALI

The City of Djinns   222
BADRUDDIN TYABJI

Who Killed India?   231
KHWAJA AHMAD ABBAS

So Freedom Came   255
D. F. KARAKA

The Birth of a Nation   264
WILFRED RUSSEL

A Limb Cut Off   272
INTERVIEW WITH LAKSHMI SAHGAL

A Quick Look at Pakistan   280
A. D. MANI

I Say Unto Waris Shah   287
AMRITA PRITAM

GLOSSARY   290

Preface

The first volume encapsulated three overarching themes: the Muslim League's mobilization campaigns, the meanings attached to the 'two-nation' theory, the bloody legacy of partition and the nightmare of millions uprooted from their homes and separated from family and friends. Official records do not reflect their pain and agony, their fear and afflictions, their dismay and disillusionment. Creative writing does.

This volume has a much wider 'source' base, drawing on published diaries, poems, excerpts from autobiographies, post-partition reflections, accounts of riots in Punjab, Delhi and Bombay and four unpublished interviews. They reveal the pressures and the circumstances that led people to migrate to Pakistan, their experiences of living in that country, the vivid and nostalgic memories of their homeland and the scale and depth of Hindu-Muslim-Sikh violence in north India. Taken together, this anthology underlines, among other things, two crucial points. First, the varied individual and collective experiences; second, the complex nature of the Pakistan movement itself. Surely, the sense of a popular Muslim upsurge with religious underpinnings is apparent; yet the movement neither embraced all segments of 'Muslim society' nor was the Muslim League's agenda understood by them in much the same way. It was interpreted in several different ways and, for that reason, conveyed different meanings to individuals and groups. In sum, the suggestion in some quarters that the Pakistan movement was a linear and monolithic movement is not quite vindicated by this collection.

One does not, likewise, discern a 'Hindu', 'Sikh' or 'Muslim' viewpoint. Most writers and poets speak a language that would make sense to the 'elites' as much as the 'subalterns', the 'Hindus' as well as the 'Muslims', the urban dwellers and the rural folks. Most of them invoke symbols of unity rather than discord. They dwell on pan-Indian values and traditions which bear the hallmark of the country's composite and syncretic development. And when religious idioms are pressed into service the purpose is to soothe rather than inflame passions. They are outraged, in equal measure, by the divisive effects of militant Hindu nationalism and the two-nation theory. In sum, the intensity of their reactions, the locale of their stories, the carefully-woven themes, and the delineation of characters convey the unmistakable message that India's partition was an epic human tragedy, a man-made catastrophe brought about by cynical and hot-headed politicians who lacked the imagination to resolve their disputes and the foresight to grasp the implications of division along religious lines.

Social scientists may well raise their eyebrows and ask: How can such magisterial conclusions be drawn from fiction, poetry and autobiographies? Students of literature may express similar doubts. Some might have reservations about the selection, the arrangement and the sequencing of the materials. Sceptics may even question the utility of this exercise.

My preface to volume one underlines the reasons for undertaking this project. The choice of stories, poems, interviews, eye-witness accounts and autobiographies reflect my own preferences and my concern to locate the hitherto neglected theme of partition outside the magisterial debates on nationalism and communalism. There is, however, no attempt to impose a perspective or a historical structure. Rather, the effort is simply to draw attention to 'The Other Face of Freedom', to explore shared memories, shared symbols and shared experiences of India's composite and collective past. These volumes serve, above all, as a reminder of how partition cruelly displaced millions, divided India's past, wrecked its civilizational rhythm and unity and left behind a seemingly constant legacy of hostility, bitterness and rancour between the peoples and governments of India and Pakistan.

Thanks to Ritu Menon for notes on Kamaladevi Chattopadhyaya and Aruna Asaf Ali; to Urvashi Butalia for her note on Begum Anis Kidwai; and to Mr L.Deevani of the Nehru Memorial Museum and Library for biographical information on A. D. Mani, Ganda Singh and D. F. Karaka.

A special word of gratitude to Krishen Khanna, renowned artist, for his drawings, included as frontispieces. Dating back to 1947, they are of historical value and represent a document of the times.

September 1996   M.H.

Acknowledgements

The editors and the publisher are grateful to the following copyright owners for permission to reproduce texts. Every endeavour has been made to contact copyright owners and apologies are expressed for any omission:

To Vikas Publishing House Pvt. Ltd. for 'Who Killed India' by Khwaja Ahmad Abbas from *I am Not an Island*, New Delhi, 1977, pp. 276-99; to the *Patriot*, New Delhi, for the extract from *Inner Recesses Outer Spaces* by Kamaladevi Chattopadhyaya, Delhi, 1986, pp. 306-10, 313 and from *Fragments from the Past* by Aruna Asaf Ali, New Delhi, 1989, pp. 171-9; to Roli Books for excerpt from *Memoirs of an Egoist* by Badruddin Tyabji, Delhi, n.d.; to National Book Trust for 'Azadi ki Chaon Mein' by Begum Anis Kidwai, Delhi, 1980, pp. 5-21; Ms Nighat Khan for excerpt from *The Heart Divided* by Mumtaz Shah Nawaz, Lahore, A. S. R. Publications, 1990, pp. 412-27; to Shaan-i-Hind Publishers for excerpt from *Yaadon ki Baraat* by Josh Malihabadi, Delhi, 1992, pp. 284-98; to Chattan Limited for 'Boo-i-gul, Naala-i-dil, Dood-i Chiragh-i Mehfil' by Shorish Kashmiri, Lahore, 1972, pp. 509-13, 517-20, 521-3, 526-9, 530-4; to *Journal of Indian History* for *A Diary of Partition Days* by Ganda Singh, Delhi, 1960, pp. 205-80; to Guru Nanak Mission, for 'Love is Stronger than Hate' by Khushdeva Singh, Patiala, 1973, pp. 11-41; to Maktaba Ilhaam for 'Wadiye Jumna Se Wadiye Hakra Tak' from *Delhi ki Bipta* by Masud Hasan Shahab Dehalvi, Bahawalpur, 1987, pp. 5-6, 12-24; to Thacker and Co Ltd for 'The Birth of a Nation' from *Indian Summer* by Wilfred Russell, Bombay, 1951, pp. 123-30; to Victor Gollancz Ltd, for 'So Freedom Came!' from *Betrayal in India* by D. F. Karaka, London, 1950, pp. 35-43; to Hitavada Publications for 'A Quick Look at Pakistan' by A. D. Mani, Nagpur, 1948; to Sahitya Akademi for the poem 'Aj Aakhan Waris Shah Nu' by Amrita Pritam, *Modern Indian Literature*, New Delhi, 1992.

Sometimes I wonder if we are not perpetual refugees — belonging nowhere

—*1948, Krishen Khanna*

The Heart Divided

MUMTAZ SHAH NAWAZ

Mumtaz Shah Nawaz (1912-48), or 'Tazi' as she was affectionately known, was Sarojini Naidu's 'adopted spiritual daughter'. She was the granddaughter of Sir Mohammad Shafi, a leading Punjabi politician. Unlike the family's loyalist traditions, she identified with socialist ideas. She corresponded with Jawaharlal Nehru, wrote socialist poetry during the years 1939 to 1942, attended a few Congress sessions, and maintained close contact with socialist groups. Her disillusionment with the Congress began with the Quit India movement. She was drawn into the Muslim League and undertook to organize Muslim women in Delhi and Punjab.

The novel *The Heart Divided* focuses on the period 1930 to 1942, 'weaving the many dimensions of those turbulent years and the painful ambivalence of those who lived through them'. Its first draft was completed in March 1948 but was published several years after the author's death in a plane-crash. 'Those who know Mumtaz,' commented her brother in his preface to the novel, 'have often wondered how she would have reacted to the "iron curtain" which had grown up by then between India and Pakistan. It was not what she had envisaged in the closing chapters of *The Heart Divided*.'

The great controversy began in India, the controversy that was to mould the destiny of the country and affect the lives of millions of people, for the Lahore resolution of the Muslim League was the most talked of, discussed, applauded and maligned subject of the day. Congressmen were up in arms against the proposed vivisection of 'Mother India' and the Congress leadership was emphatically against any such move. The Hindu press denounced partition in strong terms and some of the papers abused the League leadership while most of them called the League plan 'nothing short of

From *The Heart Divided* (Lahore: A. S. R. Publications, 1990), pp. 412-27.

Pakistan.' Muslim India gratefully accepted the definition, and with each day that passed, the demand for Pakistan was voiced by a larger and a larger number of people.

Zohra returned to Amritsar with anguish in her heart. It seemed to her as if all that had been built up through the years with slow and laborious efforts was crashing around her and she could not reconcile herself to it. Her girlhood had been strongly influenced by the National Movement of 1930 and patriotic fervour had become a part of her being. She had loved and idolized India as the motherland for which each of her sons and daughters must live and die. Now she was face to face with a demand for its partition and the demand came from her own people, the ones she loved and cherished, from those whose integrity she could not question, from people like her father and her uncle, Saeed and Habib. She was profoundly unhappy and could not find an interest in anything. Even her work became distasteful to her and she turned away from it with a feeling of nostalgia. Each day she sat for many hours in her room thinking deeply about things and arriving at no conclusion. Who was right and who was wrong? She had seen for herself the tremendous political and anti-imperialist awakening among the Muslim people, and no one could deny that it had become a great force. And yet this force demanded separation. Theirs was a patriotic fervour reminiscent of the days of 1930 and yet it was a fervour for Pakistan. Pakistan, the name was stranger for her and did not arouse a deep tenderness like the word 'India'; yet for millions of people it had already become the promised land and she could see that the adherents of the new idea were growing daily.

She began to read carefully both the Congress and Muslim League newspapers and in either she found little to console her. They seemed to be abusing each other more and more, and vied with one another in intolerance and prejudice.

Then a strange thing began to happen. She noticed that the Muslim students in her own college were avoiding her. At first she thought that it was just her imagination, but soon whispers of 'Miss Jamaluddin is anti-League' and 'she hates the thought of Pakistan, she's Congress, you know' came to her ears. As if to counteract this attitude, the Hindu and Sikh girls, and a very few 'nationalist' Muslims began to pay her greater attention, but to her the attitude of this group was as deplorable as that of the other. 'Ya Allah' she thought, 'what are we coming to? This division has entered all our hearts, this hatred is spreading. Where shall it lead us? Where can it lead us?' And she was more miserable than ever.

She tried to study the speeches of the leaders, she cried to read each and every book she could lay her hands upon, but still she found no answers to the questions that haunted her mind. If the Muslim League was reactionary and pro-British, how had it roused the patriotic fervour of the Muslims and why was it rescuing the Punjab Muslims from the clutches of today's Unionists? If the Congress was truly national and non-communal in its outlook, then why were the Muslims leaving its fold at the very time when their political consciousness was growing by leaps and bounds? On the other hand if the League was truly patriotic, why was it strengthening the foreigners' hands by demanding partition?

She could find no reply to these questions and with each day that passed, the anguish in her heart grew more intense.

Meanwhile, the war in Europe was no longer phoney. The Fascist hordes had let loose all their fury, overrun the Netherlands and broken into France and the whole world seemed to tremble with apprehension.

And then she met Ahmed.

She went one Sunday afternoon to the house of Professor Ilmuddin and found him entertaining some guests to tea.

'Come in, come,' he said cordially when he saw her standing at the door.

'Ah! I'm sorry. I didn't know you had a party.'

'Come right in, my dear, and meet my friends. We're all delighted to see you. Now let me present my friends,' and he introduced her to all his guests except one about whom he said, 'and surely you know Ahmed Hussain?'

Zohra looked up to see a face that was remarkable more for its rugged strength than its beauty.

'I—I don't think I. . .' she began.

'You wouldn't remember,' said the young man with a smile, 'you were only about that high,' his hand was two feet from the ground and she laughed.

'Really?'

'His father worked with yours for many years,' said Professor Ilmuddin.

'He was Sheikh *Saheb*'s head clerk, and I, the boy who sometimes came to play with, Habib. Now do you remember?'

'Oh yes, of course, I do and once when—'

'Once when one of Habib's friends pulled your hair, I came to the rescue.'

'We're old friends then,' she said and sat down near him. 'But what have you been doing all these years?'

'Among other things, I was teaching at a college in Lahore, before I got a better job here.'

'Were you? But—but didn't you ever come to the house?'

'I did. I came to pay my respects to Sheikh *Saheb* several times.'

'But—but—I—we—never met you.'

'Now I wonder why?' He was smiling again. 'Perhaps it was because it's all very well for children to play together, but a head clerk's son is not quite the company for the daughter of a rich landholder!'

His tone was light but she flushed.

'What nonsense!' she said spiritedly. 'On the contrary, perhaps the young intellectual snob did not think the landholder's daughter worth meeting!'

'Touché!' he bowed. 'I'm sorry,' he said. 'I stand corrected. Shall we call a truce?'

'Yes, let's!' she smiled again. 'Long ago I forgot all that nonsense about who's who and who's what!'

They both laughed and he passed her some cake and that was how their friendship began.

He came to see her at the college and they talked of many things. A few days later, he invited her to tea at his house and she met again the dear old lady with snow-white hair, his mother. She remembered her so well, invariably thrusting a sweet or two into her hands whenever she used to call on her many years ago. His mother insisted on calling her 'Zohra *Bibi*' and she flushed and begged her to call her by name. 'I'll call you Auntie if I may,' she said, and the old lady was delighted.

Ahmed and his mother had rented half a bungalow. There was a little lawn on one side bordered with orange and eucalyptus trees and here they sat on wicker chairs after the hot sun had gone down. Those were the days of Dunkirk and the talk inevitably turned on the War.

'The world is changing before our eyes,' said Zohra. 'No one knows what the coming months will bring?'

'One thing is certain,' he said, 'that Britain is up against it and if she wishes to survive she must try to rally around her the freedom-loving people of the world.'

'I think that the freedom-loving people of many countries already sympathize with her.'

'That's partly true, but Asia's vast resources of men and material and American and Russian help can only be won if she gives up imperialism.'

'What about us? We don't, we can't sympathize with Hitler and Mussolini!'

'We don't, but we must be free before we can help the others.'

'Ahmed, where are you?' they heard someone calling and a moment later three young men walked out on the lawn.

'There you are,' said one, 'I've looked in every room.'

'Let me introduce you to Miss Zohra Jamaluddin.'

'Ah! So this is the young lady Rajindar talks so much about.'

'Oh, do you know Rajindar?' asked Zohra.

'I do, and my name is Prakash and this is Yusuf and this—but surely, you know Vijay?'

Zohra looked at the last-named for the first time and gasped for he reminded her so much of—'Vijay!' she exclaimed, 'not—not—Mohini's little brother?'

'The very same. How are you Zohra *Apa*?'

'Oh, Vijay, I'm so happy to meet you again.'

'I too.'

'Ahmed,' said Prakash, 'we came to ask you to be sure to come to the meeting on Sunday. Perhaps you would like to come too?' he asked turning to Zohra.

'What's it all about?'

'It's a meeting in Chhehartta for the workers there. A trade union meeting, but some students are coming also, Vijay among them.'

'I'd love to come. Perhaps you will be good enough to take me, Ahmed?'

'Certainly, but you'll have to come in a *tonga*. I don't own a car.'

'I like *tongas*.'

'Miss *Saheb*,' said the college maid coming up to her at 4 o'clock on Sunday afternoon.

'There's a man waiting for you outside. A man in a *tonga*. He—he says you are going out with him,' she added doubtfully.

'Yes, that's right. Tell him to wait. I won't be a minute.'

'There you are,' said Ahmed as she came out of the gate. 'Come on, princess, my one-horse vehicle awaits you!'

'Don't call me princess in that tone. I know you don't mean it as a compliment!'

'I certainly don't!'

'Is that so? Well, Professor, since your intellectual highness condescends to take out a—a—'

'A spoilt little girl!'

'A spoilt little girl—she may teach you a thing or two!'

'I'm sure she will.'

They both laughed and he helped her into the tonga.

'To tell you the truth,' he said gently, 'you were a sort of princess for me in the days gone by. When you were about seven years old, you ruled all the little boys with your rosy cheeks and naughty eyes.'

'You too?'

'I was one of your most faithful adherents. A little older than most of the others, I used to stand on one side, awkward and tongue-tied, aching for some opportunity to protect you and to show you how brave I was but you were quite merciless. Oh, Ah—mad you would say, in your lisping voice, you always stand in a corner like one who's been punished and you are so big and dark—just like a big bear.'

'Did I really?'

'Oh yes! And so many other things. You were terribly spoilt, and yet it needed but the sight of a cheeky youngster's hand upon your dark curls for me to rush to your rescue!'

'After a few years you disappeared.'

'I was fifteen when I went to college, and soon after I'd taken my degree, my father died.'

'Ah! And then?'

'But for your father's kindness. I would not have been able to continue my studies. Sheikh *Saheb* is a wonderful man.'

'Yes he is, in so many ways . . . Only nowadays. . . .'

'Nowadays what?'

'Oh I don't know, it's . . . it's just these wretched political matters. . . .'

He looked at her closely. 'You sound unhappy about something Zohra.'

'I am unhappy, very unhappy!'

'Tell me.'

'It's come into everything, just everything the hatred and the division. . . . Oh Ahmed, you can't imagine what it's like seeing my own family! . . . There was a time when we had so many Hindu friends. In fact when we first came out of *purdah*, there were more non-Muslims at our social gatherings than Muslims. . . . And now . . . why we are even meeting them less . . . less and less.'

'I know.'

'Then coming to the political side—when they talked about safeguards for Muslims one could sympathize, although I always felt that it was overdone. . . . But now. . . . Complete division. . . . Pakistan! It doesn't make sense somehow. . . . And yet, they have awakened the Muslims, and in the Punjab they are becoming anti-imperialist for the first time since 1919.'

'That is true.'

'And they have a faith and a fervour that is remarkable.'

'Also . . . there's something else. . . .'

'Yes?'

'I've always been with Congress and loved and admired it, but in recent years there have been so many sins of omission and some of commission towards the Muslims.'

'We can't deny that.'

'No, we can't.'

'And not just that, the ministries left a great many election pledges unfulfilled; their agrarian policy has been very half-hearted and inadequate for the peasants and their attitude towards the workers, especially in Kanpur and Ahmedabad, deplorable.'

'All this is very true.'

'More and more Muslims have left them and now even the younger Muslims are leaving. Just imagine the girls in my college have begun to shun me because I'm Congress.'

'You poor dear, how dreadful for you.'

'I wouldn't mind but for the fact that the Hindu and Sikh girls have "taken me up" and it is as if a battle were raging over me! But above all, it's the confusion in my mind that's worrying me. I'm all in a muddle.'

'So are a great many people, Zohra. Perhaps I can help you.'

'Oh please, if you only would!'

'Well, no time is as good as now and we have another half an hour before we reach Chhehartta. I'll try to explain a few things.'

'Please do.'

'What is it you want most for India, freedom and greatness, is it not?'

'Yes.'

'And the unity of the country?'

'Yes.'

'But that means the unity of the people, does it not? For mere geographical unity means nothing. In that sense the whole world is a unit, a Europe or an Asia. Am I not right?'

'Quite right.'

'Nor does history have any frontiers. Kabul was a part of India for a long time and on the other hand northern India and the Deccan have seldom been under one government.'

'That's so.'

'Well then it's the unity of the people that matters.'

'What would you rather have—a people who have the right to make new frontiers, who may even make them, and yet peace and harmony continues, or that the country remains geographically one by force and the people continue to fight among themselves?'

'Oh I wouldn't want either. I'd like the country to remain one and the people to be united also.'

'But that cannot happen by force or coercion. Tell me, are the people united today?'

'No.'

'Yet the country is geographically one. Then why are the people disunited? Can you blame only the Muslim League for this?'

'No it's . . . because the leaders on both sides . . . are . . . are always quarrelling . . . if only the, could be truly national. . . .'

'Truly national. . . . There you have an idea, Zohra. Let's examine it. What is nationalism? Love for one's homeland?'

'I suppose so.'

'Do the Muslims feel it any less than the Hindus?'

'I suppose not.'

'The trouble is that in India nationalism has begun to mean thinking and living according to the Congress and in that way only. We are apt to forget that those who think and live differently also love their homeland just as much.'

'I don't quite see.'

'Let me put it in a different way. India is vast and has many peoples, many cultures, religions and languages.'

'Yes.'

'If we tried to impose a single culture or way of life on all those people, it would be disastrous . . . just like taking the colours and designs out of a lovely carpet and making it a single colour. The people would resent it and rebel against if for each section of people in this land is anxious to preserve its own language, culture, traditions and way of life. Therefore India is a multinational State.'

'A what?'

'A multinational State. A state with a great many slogans. Not merely political awakening, because the more politically awakened a people become, the more they are desirous of developing their own arts and industries and propagating their own way of life.'

'I see, I see now.'

'That is why you are confused. The Congress awakened the people, a great majority of whom were Hindus, and it was but natural that their art, their language, and their philosophy develop and come into greater prominence. The Muslims began to feel that their language, culture and religion would be swamped, and so when the Muslim League brought them political consciousness, they began to do all that they could to develop their own art and literature. They also had the natural fears of a minority and kept demanding safeguards so as to preserve their own way of life and combat their impotence. The Hindus resented this for they thought the Muslims were putting impediments in the way of freedom— hence the clash.'

'I begin to see. But how can unity come about?'

'It could have come about if some political party had presented the people a great social ideal and worked boldly for it, some system by which the lot of the common man could have been improved. That would have at least reduced the glaring inequalities and made the rich less rich and the poor less poor. And also some system by which each section of the people could have voluntarily united and yet had the liberty to live and develop in its own way. The Congress should have done this, but it has failed miserably.'

'And?'

'And the rise of the League and the demand for Pakistan is a consequence. Let me explain it historically. After the so-called

Mutiny of 1857, the Muslims, who took a major part in it, were a crushed and beaten people.'

'My father told me all that long ago and also how the Hindus first took to education and trade and industry. . . .'

'Industry and trade. . . . There's the crux of it. The trading class among the Hindus took to it first in the ports of Bombay, Calcutta and Madras; then it began to spread and new industries were opened up in fresh places. But invariably the existing industrialists and traders or their friends and relations were the ones who began in the new place and took control of the trade and industry there as well, for they had the backing of the great banks and the existing industrialists. Others who tried to come it were generally wiped out in no time.'

'And so?'

'And so a certain class of people, mostly Hindus, and that too one class of Hindus, some Parsis and others from Bombay and Calcutta control the whole trade and industry of the country.'

'I see.'

'The Muslims among others are hardly in it and they resent this. Some of them have dared to come in, but a very few have succeeded for it's impossible to compete with the established concerns. The Muslim feudal lords in the north and east see the growing power of the industrialist and are afraid. The Muslim worker has a natural resentment against the owner. The Muslim middle class seeing no openings for its young men in trade and industry, has turned to the services, but there again the Hindus who took to Western education earlier came in first and they invariably help their relations or friends to get in; then the Muslim demands safeguards and percentages and the Hindu resents this . . . and so on . . . So the Muslims are dissatisfied, the rich, the middle class and the poor . . . and when a political party arises that says it will safeguard their rights, they flock to it.'

'So many things become clear now.'

'Good. The Muslims demand safeguards and to counteract the growing power of the others, they demand more and more safeguards. The Hindus instead of letting them have what they want, to satisfy them once and for all and thus to allay their suspicions, are resentful and . . . the result, a clash again. The Muslims begin to think that they will be swamped and lose their identity in this vast land or worse still that they will become a "lower caste".

Whether their feelings are justified or not is another matter; the fact remains that's what they think. They also remember that there are vast tracts in this country where they are in a majority and they demand the separation of these tracts, lands where they may live in their own way and develop their own arts, and industries without being dominated or ruled by anyone—their reasons, as you have seen, are cultural and economic as well as religious. And there you have the cry for Pakistan which is an expression of the freedom-urge of the Muslim people.'

'You've explained it all very well. But there are one or two things. To begin with you say India has many nations. Does religion make a nation?'

'Of course, most Muslim say it does, but to my way of thinking, religion is one of the factors that makes a nation; language, culture, habits and so many other factors also count.'

'Would you make nationality territorial?'

'I would for cultural units.'

'And you would give each nationality the right of self-determination?'

'Yes.'

'Then shall we put it this way that the people of northwestern and northeastern India could demand Pakistan.'

'That would be certainly more logical.'

'And so the people of Rajasthan, UP, Bihar and others could all demand separate states.'

'Yes, where they form cultural units they could.'

'Then the whole of India would be split up.'

'Of course not. If it was worth their while to stick together, they would.'

'How would you decide.'

'By a people's plebiscite.'

'I see. Then if the plebiscite in some areas, goes in favour of Pakistan those areas would form Pakistan.'

'Yes.'

'But all would vote, not only Muslims.'

'Yes. But in effect in the areas, where they are in a majority, the will of the Muslims would count.'

'They would break away from India.'

'Not necessarily. If India was generous and had vision and made it worth their while to stay, and if the Muslims were wise enough to see the advantages of remaining united, they would not break away and there would be a free Pakistan in a free India. . . . Otherwise . . .' he shrugged his shoulders. 'You can't keep people together by force. They must have the right of self-determination.'

'What should we do now?'

'All true patriots must strive for unity between the two great national organizations—the Congress and the League, and unity can only come about on the basis of self-determination.'

'Do many people like you think this way?'

'Some, and we are trying to convince others.'

They had turned into a side road and now they began to pass through a tiny *bazar* of small houses and shops.

'Here we are,' he said, and helped her down from the *tonga*.

At some distance on either side of the *bazar* and in front could be seen factory buildings. It was obvious that they had been built anyhow, without any planning. The smoke that arose from the chimneys sank towards the earth again in heavy waves and mingled with the dust and the heat. They walked down the street and then they saw a large open place to the right of them. It was barren, bereft of any grass or trees and not very clean. The dust was flying around in little eddies and garbage heaps dotted it. But at some distance ahead of them, a large number of people had collected and over their heads flew a red flag. They had come to the meeting.

'Are they all communists?' she asked.

'By no means, what makes you think so?'

'The red flag—' she began.

'Is the labour flag over the world?' he smiled. 'You forget the British Labour Party . . . !'

'But here?'

'Some are communists, others are socialists, many are Congressmen and there are some Muslim Leaguers as well. All are workers, and belong to the trade unions.'

It was unlike anything she had ever seen before, there was none of the pomp and show of Congress meetings with their elaborate loudspeaker arrangements and their smart men and women volunteers. There was no decorated *pandal* like those in which League meetings were held and no long line of cars belonging to the visitors. Some thousand workers had gathered together and a few students had joined them. Half a dozen chairs were grouped round a table at which the president was sitting and the flagpole had been fixed in the ground. But the strangest thing of all was the zeal on the faces of the Leaguers. Nowhere had she seen this look of rapt attention, this oblivion to all else, as she saw on the faces here and in the eyes that were brimming over with the hope of the hopeless.

They made their way round the crowd and one of them vacated his chair for Zohra. A few heads were curiously turned in her direction and that was all. The rest were absorbed in the song that a worker with a curiously sweet voice was singing and when he came to the chorus they all joined in.

North and South and East and West
We'll keep our banner flying.
This song shall be upon our lips
When on the scaffold dying. . . .

Then the President rose to speak and she hardly heard the first part of his speech for the words of the song were still ringing in her ears, but after a while his strong voice penetrated her consciousness.

'We build the loveliest houses, but we live in hovels, and we weave the finest silk, but our wives and children are clad in rags. . . .'

She could see again the workmen, almost naked, with only dirty loincloths tied around them, laying brick upon brick of her new home in the June heat . . . and she could hear again the cry of a beggar woman in December. . . . 'My child is dying of cold, *Bibiji*, for my husband earns only 8 annas a day— a warm piece of cloth, for the love of Allah. No schools for our children, no hospitals for our sick, no old-age pensions. Work, work, work from morning to night, twelve hours, thirteen hours and we are tired— so tired.' She shuddered to think of bodies that had no leisure and minds that knew no recreation. 'All we make is a rupee a day, and no work on Sundays, and now the prices are rising—rising. . .' he continued.

'A rupee a day? she thought, and may be a wife and children to feed! It would not even fetch enough bread . . . and what about salt, sugar, oil and cloth?'

'Are there no labour laws as in other lands, no maximum hours of work?' she whispered to Ahmed who stood near her.

'Very few, and the war is an excuse for the abeyance of even those.'

'But all this does not discourage us brothers,' the worker president went on, 'for there are so many of us. So many of us the whole world over. We are a majority, we workers, we tillers of the soil and hewers of the wood, we who build and weave and construct—and in other lands the workers are winning their battle for a decent life, and the right to the fruits of their toil. And we, we too must unite and close our ranks and rise and demand our rights and then nothing can stop us for we shall build a new world, brothers, a new world where hunger, want and ignorance are no more.'

The whole gathering broke into a triumphant song, 'We shall build a new world,' they sang and their eyes shone as if it were a new dawn.

There were many speeches, poems and songs, and it was almost dusk before they began their journey back to Amritsar. She was very silent, for her mind had been to the full that day.

'A new land—Pakistan!' said the Leaguers.

'A new India—Free India!' said the Congressmen.

'A new world!' cried the workers. . . .

And she thought of Iqbal's words:

'Change alone hath stability.'

Her eyes were thoughtful and he smiled and let her think.

A Diary of Partition Days

GANDA SINGH

Ganda Singh (1900-87) is considered a doyen of Sikh history. A professor of Khalsa College, Amritsar, Ganda Singh became Director, State Archives, PEPSU (1950-6). Founder-Principal of Khalsa College, Patiala, he later set up the Department of Punjab Historical Studies in Punjabi University, Patiala, in 1963. Among his numerous publications are *Banda Singh Bahadur* (1935), *The Sikhs and Sikhism* (1959), and *The Sikhs and Their Religion* (1974). In 1967, he started a quarterly *Punjab: Past and Present*. This is an edited version of his diary. Spellings of persons and places are standardized. The unedited version is available in the first edition of *India Partitioned: The Other Face of Freedom*.

I wrote this diary during the most eventful days of the present century, seen from the Punjab. The upheaval that the country saw immediately before and after its division in 1947 is unparalleled. From what I heard from several first-hand secret sources in 1946 and 1947 of the activities of the Muslim Leaguers of Amritsar and Lahore, I felt that something extraordinary was about to happen. This prompted me to be more regular in recording day-to-day events and in greater detail.

Some indications of coming events came from the speeches of the League leaders. As early as the beginning of April 1946, Malik Sir Firoz Khan Noon said that 'the havoc which the Muslims will play will put to shame what Halaku did' (*Tribune*, Lahore, 11 April 1946). And Halaku (Hulagu) Khan is known to the history of the world as one of the most cruel and remorseless destroyers of life and property. Sardar Abdur Rab Nishtar said in August 1946, seven months before the bloodthirsty dagger was actually unsheathed, that 'Pakistan can only be achieved . . . if need be, and opportunity arose, by shedding the blood of others. Mussalmans are no believers in the

Reprinted from the *Journal of Indian History*, no. 112, part 1, April-August 1960.

creed of *ahimsa*. We will do just as the situation demands' (*Tribune,* Lahore, 18 August 1946). And according to Raja Ghazanfar Ali's statement (31 August 1946), they were to wait 'until the fire order comes from Quaid-i-Azam Jinnah'. On 4 September, Khan Iftikhar Husain Khan of Mamdot, President of the Punjab Provincial Muslim League, appealed to the Muslim lawyers 'in the name of Islam and Pakistan . . . to cast aside all thoughts of personal occupation, business and profit, and as shock troops of the Muslim League spread out all over the province, in every village, *qasba*, town and city, to do preliminary spade work of propaganda without which no revolutionary upsurge and determined struggle is possible' (*Dawn,* 5 September 1946). Even the Quaid-i-Azam, Mr. Mohammad Ali Jinnah, thought of civil war as an effective method of coercing his adversaries to agree to the demands of his Muslim League.

Preparations and training for a bloodbath, therefore, continued in full swing in the autumn and winter months of 1946 and the fire order was given in December, as a trial to begin with, in the north-western district of Haripur Hazara. This was predominantly a Muslim area and a stronghold of the Muslim Leaguers. There could, therefore, be no doubt about the success of the fire and sword operations there against the negligible minorities of Hindus and Sikhs who were taken unawares. Encouraged by their successes in the north-west, the Leaguers opened their offensive in central Punjab in the cities of Amritsar and Lahore in March 1947. Considerable parts of these cities were burnt down in a few days. The contagion soon spread to other places as well, and by the time the division of the country was declared in August, sword and fire had done incalculable harm to life and property in the urban as well as rural areas. As the Muslim Leaguers were found not to understand any language other than that of sharp steel, the Hindus and Sikhs of Punjab were left with no alternative. And this had the desired effect, although a little too late. There were appeals and conferences for peace and promises of protection to the minorities. It, however, took some time before the refugees could go unscathed to their destinations.

The diary given in the following pages starts from 1 April 1947 and ends on 16 January 1948, with a gap of three months—June, July and August—when I was too busy at the refugee camp in the Khalsa College, Amritsar (where I was a lecturer in history), to squeeze in any time for it. As it is, I hope, it will be of considerable help to students of history when a close and critical study of this period is undertaken.

For purpose of reference, the following abbreviations have been used in the diary:

API	Associated Press of India
CM, CMG	*Civil and Military Gazette,* Lahore
HT	*Hindustan Times,* Delhi
INC	*Indian News Chronicle,* Delhi
St.	*Statesman,* Delhi
Tr.	*Tribune,* Lahore, Ambala

Patiala   GANDA SINGH
5 December 1959

Tuesday, 1 April 1947

Two butchers Sadiq and Taj, who were dressed as Nihang Sikhs wearing artificial beards and moustaches and armed with spears, murdered Chanadin, a big landlord of Mandeke in the jurisdiction of the Burki. They confessed their crime and produced the artificial beards and moustaches used by them to look like Nihang Sikhs. . . .

Meetings were held in different parts of the country, particularly in the district of Jalandhar, to mourn the loss of an eminent Sikh, Babu Labh Singh, who was murdered by Muslims while he was appealing to people to maintain peace and order and to resume normal work.

Wednesday, 2 April 1947

Sardar Ishar Singh Majhail, MLA, and Giani Gurmukh Singh Musafar, who had toured the affected and disturbed areas in Rawalpindi and neighbouring districts, urged upon the deputy commissioner of Rawalpindi the necessity of restoring confidence among the minority communities. They were also successful in composing the differences among the local Sikhs.

Sardar Partap Singh, Giani Gurmukh Singh and Dr Lehna Singh invited the attention of Mr Plumb, DIG in charge of investigations, to the havoc caused by Muslims in Chauntra police station in the Attock district and asked for immediate investigations in that area.

Qazi Ataullah, speaking in the Frontier Assembly, remarked: 'I feel that certain British government officials in the NWFP are in an unholy alliance with the Muslim League.' 'These British officials,' he continued, 'have been giving full access to the Pir of Manaki and certain other League elements and are carrying on League propaganda in the tribal areas.'

Six persons were killed and 20 injured as a result of the attack by green-uniformed Muslim Leaguers on Hindu and Sikh passengers at Gorazai railway station, 17 miles from Kohat towards Rawalpindi.

Thursday, 3 April 1947

Nine Hindu and Sikh members of the Central Assembly from the Punjab sent a letter to Pandit Jawaharlal Nehru requesting him to forward it to the Viceroy and HMG. 'The only way out of the present deadlock is to partition the Punjab into two provinces,' said the letter, adding that 'it is no longer a long-term constitutional issue but an urgent and immediate administrative problem which should have the first priority.'

Mr Virendra, MLA, asked the secretary of the Punjab Muslim League, Mian Mumtaz Daultana, in a statement, 'If the Muslim is prepared to negotiate on the basis of two ministries in the province, one for the Muslim majority area, and the other for the non-Muslim majority area, as at present, the Punjab will either have two ministries or none at all.'

Sardar Ujjal Singh, MLA, said: 'Division of Punjab is the only remedy now and we all agree on that issue.'

In a meeting of the Punjab Assembly Panthic party, with Sardar Swaran Singh as its leader, there was complete unanimity on the question of the division of the Punjab. The Governor was urged 'to take necessary steps to remove the inadequate representation of the minorities in the police now that 6,000 constables are to be recruited in the additional police.' The party protested against 'the heavy, inequitable and unjust collective fines' in Multan demanding that 'only the aggressors be punished and not the aggrieved'.

Malik Firoz Khan Noon, in a press interview, demanded the division of the armed forces and military equipment, and also ordinance factories.

A bill aimed at nullifying forcible conversions and marriages was introduced in the council of state by Mr S.K. Roy Chowdhry.

of other parties and that they cannot have Pakistan without the confidence of the minority communities. 'As the Muslim League is the largest party in the legislature, the duty for restoring order in the province rests more on its shoulders than on any other. It is the duty, therefore, of the Muslim leaders as a first step to make an all-out effort to have the abducted women promptly restored to their families, to induce those in the possession of loot to voluntarily hand it over to the authorities, and to make generous personal contributions for the relief of riot victims, not only of one community but of all communities.'

Friday, 11 April 1947

'We are determined to see that Punjab is divided, because only with such a division can there be reciprocal protection and not in the imposition of a communal ministry. . . . Punjab will never agree to a partisan communal ministry. Mr Ghazanfar Ali talks of provocation—what provocation? The flashing of the solitary sword when thousands of swords had been flashing for 34 days before the ministry fell! Coercion was the order of the day,' said Dewan Chaman Lal at Calcutta.

Saturday, 12 April 1947

The *Times*, London, said in an editorial: 'The Muslim League attempt to seize power in Punjab, admittedly the nodal point of Pakistan, has so far broken down in the face of Hindu and Sikh opposition. If persisted in, it seems likely to reinforce the growing demand for the division of the province into Muslim and non-Muslim areas.'

'Open propagation of coercive methods and adoption of unconstitutional means by the Muslim League to capture power has resulted in the creation of a very unhappy situation. Some thousands of innocent persons have been killed and a still larger number have become homeless. Property worth crores of rupees has been destroyed. . . . Under the circumstances, we support whole-heartedly the proposal for the partition of Punjab, and, as a first step in the direction, demand the immediate setting up of two ministries in the province.' Lala Bhimsen Sachar and Sardar Swaran Singh (*CMG* 15).

Sunday, 13 April 1947

'The Pakistan demand of the Muslim League is a negative demand,' said Pandit Jawaharlal Nehru at the Jallianwala Bagh Day meeting at New Delhi. Continuing he said, 'How can this problem be solved? It can either be done through mutual agreement or by a fight. There is no other course. No political aim can be achieved by coercion and intimidation.' (CM 15).

The Hindus and Sikhs of Calcutta, through Lala Karam Chand Thapar, presented to Sardar Swaran Singh a cheque for one lakh of rupees for relief work.

Five hundred Sikhs from all parts of Punjab took a pledge in fron of the Akal Takht, Amritsar, to fight Pakistan.

'If, as desired, we have but to divide our country, we have also to consider the question of division of those areas where the Hindus are in a majority, as we have to divide Bengal and Punjab . . . the Congress will have to see that the majority community does not force the minority to remain with it,' declared Dr Rajendra Prasad (CMG 15).

Monday, 14 April 1947

Baba Kharak Singh in a statement said: 'I am a staunch advocate of Akhand Hindustan. . . . Should, however, partition become inevitable and be unfortunately thrust upon us, I would plead for adequate safeguards and legitimate protection for the non-Muslim minorities living in the territories proposed to be partitioned.' (CM 15).

Master Tara Singh condemned the criticism levelled at the Maharaja of Patiala by the Muslim press for his saying at the ceremony of presenting new colours to the 1st Patiala Sikh Infantry that his army belonged to the Panth as the Panth belonged to his army and that 'the State forces should always be prepared to defend a righteous cause during critical times ahead'. It was a mere reiteration of historical fact. The Phulkian states, Patiala, Nabha and Jind, were governed by the sole principle: 'What is mine is yours,' declared Master Tara Singh.

Sardar Patel appealed to the Muslim League to settle the question of Pakistan and partition with fellow-countrymen, addressing a meeting at Bombay. If this question was not settled peacefully and amicably, he declared, then the only way it could be settled was by taking recourse to violence and bloodshed. Such a course would lead to mutual slaughter and all-round destruction, and, hence, it would benefit no one (*CM* 16).

Tuesday, 15 April 1947

The following communique was issued from the Viceroy's house, New Delhi:

'On His Excellency the Viceroy's initiative and at his special request, Mahatma Gandhi and Mr Jinnah signed the following declaration and authorized its publication:

"We deeply deplore the recent acts of lawlessness and violence that have brought the utmost disgrace to the fair name of India, and the greatest misery to innocent people, irrespective of who were aggressors and who were victims.

"We denounce for all time the use of force to achieve political ends and we call upon all the communities of India, to whatever persuasion they may belong, not only to refrain from all acts of violence and disorder but also to avoid both in speech and writing, any incitement to such acts." (sd.) M. A. Jinnah (sd.) M. K. Gandhi.'

The general council of the Frontier Majlis-i-Ahrar, through a resolution, condemned in unequivocal terms the hooliganism and goondaism prevailing in the Frontier Province (*Tr* 18).

Wednesday, 16 April 1947

In a meeting held at Amritsar, the Shiromani Akali Dal, through a resolution, expressed the opinion that the partition of Punjab was the only remedy to end communal strife in Punjab and for purposes of determining boundaries, it suggested the appointment of a Boundary Commission which could keep in view the question of population, landed property and protection of historical and religious buildings.

The second resolution condemned the Muslim League's and the Muslim papers' demand for the banning of the *kirpan*.

The third resolution congratulated the Maharaja of Patiala for affording timely relief and shelter to refugees.

Mir Makhdum Husain Qureshi in a statement at Lahore said: 'On behalf of my co-religionists, I assure the Hindus and Sikhs in Multan division that the Muslims would always protect their lives and property and that they need have no fear and distrust now. I shall advise them to stick to their ancestral hearths and homes rather than resort to migration, which would create more trouble and unrest (*Tr* 18). . . .

Friday, 18 April 1947

Master Tara Singh, Giani Kartar Singh and Sardar Baldev Singh met the Viceroy, Lord Mountbatten. They are understood to have demanded division of Punjab with the river Chenab as its boundary, and veto power for the Sikhs in respect of questions affecting Sikh interests as is given to the Muslims. They also urged substantial increase in the percentage of Sikhs in the police force (*CM* 19).

According to a statement of Qazi Ataullah, Revenue Minister of Peshawar, a Muslim student from Punjab held a conference with the Muslim Leaguers of Dera Ismail Khan and then incited the Muslims to set fire to the shops and houses of the Hindus and plunder their property, if they could not do anything else. Immediately after this inflammatory speech that young man began to set fire to Hindu shops with the help of local boys. An Afghan tribe also took part in murder and loot *(Prabhat* 19). . . . .

Tuesday, 22 April 1947

Sardar Swaran Singh and Lala Bhimsen Sachar sent a representation to Pandit Jawaharlal Nehru demanding immediate division of Punjab into two or three autonomous provinces saying 'that in the existing circumstances we are not prepared to cooperate with the Muslim League for forming a single ministry for the whole of Punjab.' Pinning the responsibility of the recent violence and rioting in Punjab on the Muslim League, they said: 'These dreadful events of the last month and a half have conclusively proved that any government in which the Muslim League is the dominant partner will not inspire confidence and will fail to protect the minorities' (*Tr* 23).

'We cannot submit to be ruled by those who have committed or caused to be committed these inhuman atrocities in Punjab and, therefore, demand that immediate steps be taken to divide Punjab into two, and, if necessary, into three autonomous provinces' (*CM* 23).

'There can be no solution on the basis of Pakistan,' and 'bloodshed can stop if Jinnah is sincere', said Mr Ali Zaheer in a statement at Sultanpur (Oudh) (*CM* 23).

Wednesday, 23 April 1947

Baba Kharak Singh in a statement to the press said: 'If the Muslim League is really anxious to win the confidence and cooperation of the non-Muslims in Punjab, let its leaders come forward and do something tangible in condemning the recent disturbances. The Khalsa is big enough to forgive and forget, but under no circumstances will the Sikhs submit to injustice and humiliation' (*CM* 24). . . .

Thursday, 24 April 1947

Feeling that the Viceroy is determined to play fair, Mr Jinnah appealed 'to the Muslims generally and Muslim Leaguers in particular, to maintain peace and order so as to give the Viceroy every opportunity to fully understand the situation' (*CM* 25).

According to Sardar Mangal Singh's statement at Ludhiana, 'it will be suicidal for the Sikhs to go anywhere near the tempting offers that the Muslim League leaders are making to the Sikhs' (*CM* 25). . . .

Saturday, 26 April 1947

News from Jalandhar—seven persons including the son of the Muslim sub-inspector in charge of the Sadar police station have been arrested in connection with the murder of Babu Labh Singh on the 6th March while going about on a peace mission (*Tr* 27).

The SGPC and the Shiromani Akali Dal sent the following telegram to the Viceroy, Pt. Nehru, Sardar Patel and Sardar Baldev Singh:

'Numerous reports of police interference with *kirpan*, the religious symbol of the Sikhs, received. Great resentment prevailing. The Sikh community can under no circumstances tolerate such interference with this fundamental religious right' (*Tr* 27).

Syed Ali Zaheer in a statement to the press at Lucknow said: 'Every honest man knows that the Muslim League and the British policy pursued in the past are directly responsible for the present state of affairs. The riots were and are the direct result of the direct action resolution of the Muslim League and they began on 16 August 1946' (*CM* 27).

Sardar Mangal Singh, MLA, said that before 1925, India had nine provinces, which were later on made into eleven. So division meant readjusting of boundaries. 'For the maintenance of peace this is essential,' he declared (*CMG* 27).

News from Rawalpindi—A number of *lambardars*, *inamdars*, military pensioners and *zaildars* are among the 1,371 persons so far reported to have been arrested in Jhelum district.

These include Yakub, a big landlord and *zaildar* and the first *inamdar* of Ghoog, the worst affected village in the Nila police station of Chakwal sub-division; a *lambardar* of Warval, another village in the Nila police station, two *subedars* of Chak Mamlok in the Chakwal police station; a *lambardar* of Bhin village, Zaildar Mohammad Bux of Dhudial and Aslam of Dhumal Kamal.

Sunday, 27 April 1947

An Ahrar worker of Amritsar condemned the Muslim agitation against the *kirpan* and said that it was un-Islamic to interfere with the religious beliefs of other people (*Ajit* 30). . . .

The Frontier Finance Minister, Mr Mehr Chand Khanna, gave the total figure of 400 killed, 150 wounded, 50 places of worship and 1,600 shops and houses burnt and looted, over 300 persons forcibly converted, 50 abducted since the commencement of atrocities in December last in Hazara (*CM* 30). Not a single Muslim was killed in the riots (*HT* 30). . . .

Monday, 28 April 1947

The third preliminary meeting of the Constituent Assembly opened with Dr Rajendra Prasad as President.

Khan Abdul Ghaffar Khan, on the eve of the viceregal visit, made a sensational allegation against the Frontier Governor, Sir Olaf Caroe, both at a press conference and a public meeting at Charsadda: 'Sir Olaf Caroe was alleged to have sent for his ministers on or about 11 March and advised them to join the Muslim League, in which he would give them all support' (*CM* 3 May).

Tuesday, 29 April 1947

The Viceroy visited Kahuta, a Muslim-riot affected town in Rawalpindi district.

Mian Mumtaz Daultana suggested a conference of three communities of Punjab to discuss methods of restoring peace in the province and of tracking the criminals (*HT* 1 May, *CM* 30).

A deputation of the Hindu-Sikh Minorities Board, with Sardar Partap Singh and Rai Bahadur Dina Nath and five others, presented a memorandum to the Viceroy pinning the responsibility of the riots and all the bloodshed upon the Muslim League's direct action (*Ajit* 1 May).

The executive committee of the Punjab Provincial Hindu Mahasabha resolved that in case some of the provinces of India were to be separated, Punjab and Bengal should be so divided as to leave law and order and defence in the hands of the central government. It further resolved that communal disturbances should be checked and that an enquiry committee be set up to enquire into the causes and effects of the riots (*Ajit* 2 May).

Wednesday, 30 April 1947

Lady Mountbatten visited the riot-affected areas of Amritsar.

Mr Jinnah, in a statement, denounced the demand for the partition of Punjab and Bengal as 'a sinister move, actuated by spite and bitterness,' and demanded the division of the defence forces for himself. (*CM* 1 May). While pleading for the division of India in his statement, he opposed the division of the provinces (*HT* 2).

Dr Rajendra Prasad in an interview declared that if there was to be a division of India then it should be as complete and as thorough as possible, including the division of Punjab and Bengal, so that there might not be left any room for contention or conflict. 'If that requires division of the defence forces, that should also be brought about, and the sooner the better' (*HT* 2 May).

Dr Mubarik Ali Khan, general secretary of the India Muslim League of America, in a letter to Dr Aranha, President of the General Assembly, wrote: 'On behalf of the India Muslim League of America that . . . the United Nations take up the question of who is responsible for death by violence of thousands who might have lived to see a genuinely free India'—Reuter (*CM* 2 May).

Thursday, 1 May 1947

Mian Mumtaz Daultana, general secretary of the Punjab Muslim League and Sardar Shaukat Hayat Khan, secretary of the Punjab Muslim League Committee of Action, resigned their respective offices with the ostensible object of concentrating on relief operations in the riot-affected areas (*CM* 2, *Tr* 3).

Lady Mountbatten visited the riot-affected areas of Amritsar city. A young cameraman ventured to suggest to Her Excellency 'that Mr Jinnah should be asked to tour the riot-affected areas in Punjab and NWFP as Mahatma Gandhi was doing in other parts of India' (*CM* 3).

Referring to the continuance of violence in NWFP, Punjab and other places, Mahatma Gandhi 'held that it was not open to Jinnah Saheb to plead that his followers did not listen to his appeal in the face of his claim to the undisputed Presidentship of the Muslim League which represented the vast bulk of the Muslim population. Was the British Government to yield to the force of arms rather than the force of reason?' he asked.

Thirty influential tribesmen of Waziristan made an emphatic declaration that the tribal people do not support Mr Jinnah's move for Pakistan and that they welcomed the appointment of the Tribal Area Sub-Committee of the Constituent Assembly (*HT* 2).

Friday, 2 May 1947

Although the original draft of the Constitution of India was being framed in English, it was announced by Dr Rajendra Prasad, the President of the Constituent Assembly, that he would get it translated into the national language.

Sardar Swaran Singh, Lala Bhimsen Sachar and Sardar Harnam Singh saw the Governor, Sir Evan Jenkins, at Lahore and placed before him a Hindu-Sikh plan of partition, dividing the province in such a way as to ensure the solidarity of the Sikhs and an equal distribution of provincial assets, including a share in canal colonies. (*CM* 3, *Tr* 3).

The Government of Punjab 'forfeited a document purporting to contain instructions issued by the Muslim League for the establishment of Pakistan by direct action and violent methods and supposed to have been given out by an ex-Muslim Leaguer, and described variously as a circular and a letter.'

The document, according to the forfeiture order, is likely to promote feelings of enmity between different classes of His Majesty's subjects—API (*CM* 3).

Chaudhary Lahiri Singh, Sir Tek Chand, Giani Kartar Singh, Sardar Ujjal Singh, Mr Prithvi Singh Azad, Dewan Chaman Lal and Dr Gopi Chand Bhargava, met the Congress Working Committee to place before them their demand for the division of Punjab (*Tr* 3).

Saturday, 3 May 1947

In a statement Master Tara Singh said, 'the partition of Punjab must be based on the consideration of the population of the Muslims and non-Muslims and the property held by them' (*CM* 4, *Tr* 5).

At a meeting organised by the National Muslim Committee of Great Britain, Chaudhary Akbar Khan, president of the India Workers Association, criticized the policy being pursued by Mr Jinnah and the Muslim League and said, the history scarcely provided another instance in which a section of the community had lost all reason (*CM* 4). . . .

Badshah Khan of Frontier in a statement said that in his opinion 'the British plan seemed to be to help the Muslim League in the Frontier Province in order to make the Frontier and a part of Punjab a buffer state between Russia and India' (*Tr* 4).

Dr Khan Saheb in a statement at Peshawar said: 'It has come to my knowledge that an absconder accused of violence in my bungalow case has been presented to the Viceroy in a deputation of the Muslim League and the man has been sent by air to Mr Jinnah. I am going to make an official investigation as to how this has been done' (*Tr* 5). . . .

New Delhi—Mahatma Gandhi regretted in the prayer meeting that no definite and tangible move in the direction of peace on the part of Mr Jinnah was noticeable so far. Or else how could communal disturbances still continue in areas where the followers of Jinnah were predominant (*Tr* 5). . . .

Sunday, 4 May 1947

Dr Saifuddin Kitchlew, while presiding at the meeting of the Punjab Provincial Congress Committee, observed: 'I must say that the Congress policy of appeasement and its desire to placate the Muslim

League has resulted in giving so much strength to the Muslim League. As it happens the generosity of the Congress has been regarded by the League and Mr Jinnah as a weakness of which they have taken full advantage.'

While reiterating its faith in the unity of India, the PPCC resolved that if the anti-national and undemocratic demand of the Muslim League is to be accepted and India is to be partitioned, then that part of Punjab which desires to remain with the Indian Union should be entitled to exercise its inalienable right to do so (*Tr* 5).

Monday, 5 May 1947

At the annual function of the Jat College, Rohtak, the Maharaja of Patiala, the Maharaja of Bharatpur, Sardar Baldev Singh, Giani Kartar Singh, while criticizing Mr Jinnah's demand for Pakistan and his attitude towards the riots supported the claim of the Jats for a separate province (*Tr* 7).

Mr Firoz Khan Noon in a statement to the press said: 'We Muslims are not willing to surrender one inch of the Punjab territory.'

Mr R. K. Sidhwa, Congress leader of Sind, had an interview with Pt. Nehru and pressed the demand of the Hindu minorities of Sind to be taken outside Pakistan and to amalgamate seven towns of Sind consisting of the Hindu majorities into one separate division (*Tr* 7).

Acharya Jugal Kishore, general secretary of the Congress, and Dewan Chaman Lal, who had been sent to survey the Frontier situation, reported to Pandit Jawaharlal Nehru that Sir Olaf Caroe was responsible for encouragement to the law-breakers in the province and that he should be removed from governorship (*HT* 6). . . .

In a very challenging and outspoken statement, Khan Abdul Ghaffar Khan accused Sir Olaf Caroe of 'an open conspiracy with the Muslim League to bathe the province in blood'. 'I am afraid the Governor's nefarious deeds will lead to a most unimaginable bloodshed and carnage in my province for he seems to be bent upon making the Pathans fight amongst themselves. . . . It is dishonest on the part of the present Governor to give a political status to the communal movement of the Muslim League whose followers have been indulging in the murder of innocent men, women and children,' said the Khan at Peshawar (*HT* 7).

Tuesday, 6 May 1947

Mahatma Gandhi and Mr Jinnah met at New Delhi. They discussed two matters. They could not agree on the division of India into Hindustan and Pakistan. Mahatma Gandhi was opposed to it while Jinnah insisted on it. According to Mr Jinnah's statement they agreed 'that we must do our best in our respective spheres to see that the appeal of ours is carried out and we will make every effort for this purpose (*Tr*, *CM* 7).

Ban on the publication of the *Prabhat* (Lahore) for three months was imposed under the Punjab Public Safety Act in connection with the "Anti-Pakistan Number" of the paper (*Tr* 7).

In reply to a question Mahatma Gandhi said: 'It would be a good thing if the British were to go today—13 months mean mischief to India. I do not question the nobility of the British declaration. I do not question the sincerity of the Viceroy, but facts are facts' (*HT* 7).

The Frontier League leaders in consultation with Mr Jinnah decided not to call off the civil disobedience movement in that province (*CM* 7).

Sardar Aurangzeb Khan, a former premier of the Frontier province who was arrested at Mardan under Frontier Criminal Regulations, was sentenced to six months, rigorous imprisonment in default of security (*CM* 7).

A book *Rape of Rawalpindi*, being a collection of photographs of the happenings in Rawalpindi district compiled by Prabodh Chandra, MLA, on behalf of the Complaints Section of the Punjab Riots Sufferers Relief Committee, was proscribed (*Tr* 8).

Wednesday, 7 May 1947

A collective fine of Rs 30 lakh was imposed by the Governor of Punjab on the Muslims of Rawalpindi district, excluding the areas within the municipal and cantonment limits of Rawalpindi and the municipal limits of Gujjarkhan, with a few other exemptions (*Tr*, *CM* 8).

Mr Jinnah appealed to the Muslims in general, and the Muslim Leaguers in particular, to remain peaceful, in a statement on the Frontier situation (*Tr* 8). . . .

Thursday, 8 May 1947

The genesis of the *Zalme-Pakhtoon* (Young Afghans) was explained by Khan Abdul Ghaffar Khan, the leader of the non-violent Khudai-Khidmatgars, as 'a strong reaction among the Pathans to Muslim League violence', and an organization believing in armed defence of non-violent people against violence and terrorism. 'Its object is defence and not offence.' The Khudai-Khidmatgars are wedded to non-violence, declared the Khan (*CM* 9). . . .

Friday, 9 May 1947

The division of India, a reactionary step, 'which no one welcomes outside the ranks of the Muslim League' 'throws away the chief boon of political and economic unity which British rule had brought to the people of India,' said the *New Statesman* and *Nation*, London (*CM* 10).

There was a setback in the communal situation in Amritsar where five persons were killed and eight injured as a result of stray stabbings (*CM, Tr* 10).

Sardar Atma Singh, ex-chairman of the Sheikhupura municipality, in a statement to the press, protested against the rumoured inclusion of Sheikhupura district in the Pakistan areas. More than half the land in the district belongs to the non-Muslims and more than 50 per cent revenue is paid by the Sikhs and the Hindus. The entire industry and business belongs to them. The house-property in the towns is almost entirely theirs. Nankana Sahib, the birthplace of Guru Nanak, with an estate of about 800 squares of land, is like Mecca to them. They have seven high schools, while Muslims do not have even one. The population figure of the Muslims is false and inflated, as in many other places.

Saturday, 10 May 1947

Stabbings continued in Amritsar.

A crowd of 200 Muslims fell upon a funeral party of about a dozen Hindus including a woman (of Kucha Kamboan, Katra Sher Singh) outside Daimaganj, when the latter were returning home after disposing of the body of a child and massacred seven of them in cold blood, dashed their bodies against the wall of an *Idgah* mosque, and then set them on fire with petrol. One woman and three men, who had also been injured, escaped during the confusion.

'I was shocked to see such a ghastly tragedy and never in my life had I seen such a crime,' said a police official to the API.

The district magistrate imposed a fine on the locality (Nawankot), where the ghastly tragedy took place, at the rate of Rs 20 per adult residing in the area with a view to awarding immediate compensation to survivors of the deceased. The number of people affected by this order is estimated at 9,000 (*Tr* 11).

Sardar Ishar Singh Majhail, going in a jeep to Jhabal, was attacked by an armed Muslim mob at the Bhagtanwala railway crossing between 3.00 and 4.00 p.m. Sardar Ishar Singh warded off the attack with his *kirpan* and escaped when his driver backed the car and returned to Amritsar (*Tr* 11).

The Viceroy invited Pandit Jawaharlal Nehru, Mr M. A. Jinnah, Sardar Vallabhbhai Patel, Mr Liaquat Ali Khan and Sardar Baldev Singh to a meeting at his house at New Delhi at 10.30 a.m. on Saturday, 7 May, to present to them the plan which the His Majesty's Government has made for the transfer of power to Indian hands.

The representatives of the Indian States, who were on the States Negotiating Committee, were also invited for a meeting the same afternoon (*Tr* 11).

Sardar Swaran Singh declared that the Sikhs were determined not to remain under Muslim subjugation and reiterated the demand of the Hindus and Sikhs for the division of Punjab along the natural boundary of the Chenab to ensure a fair distribution of the population, property and provincial assets (*HT* 12).

On account of the communal atmosphere in the Aligarh, Muslim University, the UP government permitted the Dharam Samaj and Barahseni Intermediate Colleges of the town to be affiliated to the Agra University for degree classes (*HT* 12).

Chaudhary Hamidullah Khan, acting President, All-Jammu and Kashmir Muslim Conference Party in the Kashmir Assembly, in a statement, urged the Maharaja to immediately declare Kashmir an independent state and to convene its own Constituent Assembly in order to frame a constitution for the people of the State according to their own liking (*Tr* 12). In this, the Chaudhary assured full cooperation of the Muslims.

Hindus and Sikhs of Gurdaspur, in a number of telegrams to Mr Bhimsen Sachar, urged him to exert pressure on the authorities in England and India not to include Gurdaspur in the proposed Pakistan, 'as it is not a Muslim majority district' (*Tr* 12).

Sardar Shaukat Hayat, in a statement, tried to explain how the division of Punjab would benefit neither the Hindus nor the Sikhs and urged them to remain in Pakistan, 'and if non-Muslims are unhappy after a trial in Pakistan, there can be room for the exchange of population' (*Tr* 12).

Mr Shankarrao Deo, secretary of the Congress, addressing a public meeting at Dadar, declared that if India were to be divided, the Congress would insist on the division of Bengal and Punjab to the end (*HT* 12).

Sunday, 11 May 1947

To avert the partition of Bengal, Professor Humayun Kabir, MLC, suggested to Premier Suhrawardy to have a bill, or at least a resolution passed, accepting joint electorates for the province and inviting the Congress party to join his cabinet on the basis of equality (*Tr* 12). . . .

Speaking at Nahaqqi, in Peshawar *tehsil*, Khan Abdul Ghaffar Khan said, 'Now that the British are leaving India for good it behoves all of us, whether red shirts or green shirts, poor or rich, to hold a united *jirga* and chalk out a programme common for the welfare of the entire Pakhtun race (*Tr* 13).

Monday, 12 May 1947

Amritsar witnessed regular pitched battles in which a large number of country-made bombs were used. There were nine cases of arson. 18 persons were reported to have been arrested in connection with the cold-blooded murder in the Daimganj area (*Tr* 14).

Qazi Ataullah, Revenue Minister, declared at Peshawar 'that the Frontier Province would be an independent sovereign state devoid of any influence of either the so-called Hindustan or Pakistan' (*Tr* 13). . . .

Wednesday, 14 May 1947

Riot madness returned to Lahore, leaving 11 killed and 17 injured (*Tr* 15).

Reported from Indore that 35 Central India states, with the exception of Bhopal and Indore, decided to enter the Constituent Assembly (*Tr* 16).

Thursday, 15 May 1947

Amritsar and Lahore continue to be in the grip of communal riots.

According to the leading article of the *Tribune* (Lahore), the Muslim demand for Pakistan is based on fictitious census figures.

The district magistrate, Lahore, banned the holding of Jor Mela at Lahore in connection with the martyrdom of Guru Arjan on account of riots in the city (*Tr* 16). . . .

Sikh National College, Lahore, searched. Some rifle and pistol cartridges were recovered. A pistol was recovered from outside the premises. Half a dozen students were taken into custody (*Tr* 16, 17). . . .

In a confidential circular, the Provincial Muslim League asked the Leaguers not to work with Hindus on peace boards (*Tr* 17).

The partition of Sind was demanded in a letter of the president of All-India Hindu Sangha to the Viceroy, saying that the districts of Nawabshah, Hyderabad, Tharparkar and a part of Karachi be amalgamated with Jodhpur state (*Tr* 17).

Mr Prithvi Singh Azad, in his memorandum to the Punjab Governor, urged the division of Punjab along the river Chenab (*CM* 19).

Friday, 16 May 1947

The riot situation in Lahore deteriorates, with several stabbing cases and numerous devastating fires.

Reports published that some *badmashes* of Amritsar had sent the *goondas* of Lahore some bangles (and also *mehndi*, according to rumours in Amritsar) to wear. This incited the Lahore *badmashes* to reindulge in stabbing and arson, said the district magistrate of Lahore (*Tr* 17).

Mr Suhrawardy's talks with Mr Jinnah regarding Bengal failed. With a rebuff, Jinnah uncompromisingly disapproved of any arrangement in Bengal on the basis of joint electorates. Suhrawardy was asked to resign if he could not carry on the fight for Pakistan, as Jinnah wanted (*CM* 17, *Tr* 17).

At the instance of the Viceroy, Maharaja Yadavindar Singh of Patiala had talks with Mr Jinnah regarding Sikh-Muslim compromise, based on partition. Mr Jinnah, as usual, remained uncompromising and adamant. He repeated his usual verbal assurances and guarantees, and wanted the Sikhs to accept his word, which, of course, could not be done after the inhuman brutalities committed by the Muslims in the minority areas of north-west districts and Multan and DIK (*Tr* 18).

Saturday, 17 May 1947

Stabbings and arson continued in Lahore.

Sunday, 18 May 1947

Stabbings and arson continued in Lahore and Amritsar. . . .

Monday, 19 May 1947

A plan for the rehabilitation of thousands of victims of Muslim cruelties, estimated to cost the Punjab government Rs 10 crore, is under consideration of the Governor, as reported in the press (CM 19).

Wednesday, 21 May 1947

Nawab Muhammad Khan Jogazai, member of the Constituent Assembly from Baluchistan, Khan Abdul Samad Khan, president of the Anjuman-i-Watan, Maulvi Abdulla Jan, president of the Jamiyat-al-ulama, sent telegrams, protesting against the inclusion of Baluchistan in Pakistan without previous reference to the people (*CM* 23).

Thursday, 22 May 1947

Reported from New Delhi, in connection with Sir Eric Mieville's talk with Mr Jinnah, that Mr Jinnah agreed to the partition of Punjab and Bengal with Lahore as capital of Pakistan and Calcutta a free port (*CM* 23).

Mr Kotu Ram, Frontier MLA, in a statement at Bannu, welcomed the proposal for an independent sovereign Pathan republic comprising of the Pushto-speaking people of NWFP (*Tr* 25).

Friday, 23 May 1947

According to Dr Rajendra Prasad, Mr Jinnah's demand for a corridor to link up north-east and north-west Pakistan areas was untenable (*CM* 25).

Dewan Chaman Lal offered a plan to the Muslim League for the unity of Punjab, in an interview with the *Globe*, on the basis of joint electorates, equal representation for Muslims and non-Muslims in the Cabinet and services, premiership by rotation for three years, socialistic [*sic*] distribution of big estates among the peasantry, guarantee of fundamental rights to minorities, etc (*CM* 25).

Addressing a press conference at Calcutta, General Mohan Singh said that in case of Pakistan being established, the present Indian army must be divided to eliminate fifth-columnists from Hindustan's army (*Tr* 25).

According to a report published this day, 'Muslim Leaguers in the United Provinces have been collecting arms manufactured for them in certain Indian states, and have, for some time, been making hectic preparations. Besides, there has been a large-scale infiltration of Pathans, disguised as labourers or contractors, into the province.' This revelation was made by Mr Purshottamdas Tandon, Speaker of the UP Assembly (*Tr* 25). . . .

Saturday, 24 May 1947

According to Sir Akbar Hydari, the Governor of Assam, 'Assam should remain as it is with its centuries-old continued communal cordiality' (*Tr* 25).

An ASI of Police, Giani Gurcharan Singh, was stabbed while on duty in Hall Bazar, Amritsar, by Muslim *goondas* in the presence of Muslims police constables (*Tr* 26).

Dr Shyama Prasad Mookerji, addressing the Hindus of Dacca, denounced the agreement reported to have been reached between Mr Sarat C. Bose and Mr Abdul Hashim, the Muslim League leader, for a free state of Bengal. This was a sinister move, said Dr Mookerji, to grab the whole of Bengal for Eastern Pakistan which would thus virtually be established in the province, which the Hindus would never accept (*Tr* 26, *CM* 27).

Sunday, 25 May 1947

Sardar Baldev Singh, in an interview at New Delhi, said that if India was to be partitioned, the division of the Army was inevitable. 'When the Army is divided, the Pakistan state will have to find funds to pay for all the Muslims in armed forces. This will be a big drain on Pakistan finances and its pinch will be felt by the Muslim masses who, at this stage, do not understand the implications of the division of India.'

Referring to the unnatural solicitude of Mr Jinnah for the Sikhs, Sardar Baldev Singh continued, 'Punjab was and is the homeland of the Sikhs. A Sikh prince ruled over the territory whom the British took under their tutelage as a minor. Punjab should, therefore, be restored to the Sikhs' (CM 27).

Monday, 26 May 1947

Pandit Gopinath Kunzru, vice-president of the UP Hindu Mahasabha, warned the provincial government to reduce the number of the Muslims in the police to their due percentage on the basis of population within three months, otherwise the Hindu Mahasabha will have to resort to some direct action, including satyagraha (CM 27).

Sardar Baldev Singh visited Lahore and said that adequate military was being sent to Punjab to stop riots. A deputation of seven women of Sareen Mohalla, arrested under the Arms Act, complained to him of the foul language used by a certain Muslim official in dealing with them, and, weeping bitterly, made shocking allegations against a magistrate.

He was also told by Principal Niranjan Singh of the Sikh National College of Lahore how the students during the search of the College, were made to stand in the sun the whole day without being allowed even to take their meals.

In the course of a statement, Sardar Baldev Singh said that the division of Punjab was inevitable, that Mr Jinnah's demand for a corridor could not be accepted, nor could Lahore be allowed to go to Pakistan (Ajit 28, CM 28).

An informal conference of Forward Bloc members held in Calcutta adopted a resolution supporting the move for the partition of Bengal and Punjab (Tr 28).

Tuesday, 27 May 1947

Jathedar Udham Singh said that the Sikhs had lost faith in the sincerity of Mr Jinnah and his followers after what they had done in the so-called Pakistan in the western districts of Punjab. Nothing could satisfy the Sikhs but the division of the province, declared the *Jathedar* (*Ranjit* 28).

Wednesday, 28 May 1947

Allama Mashriqi issued a statement at Patna asking the people to revolt against Mahatma Gandhi and Mr Jinnah and to start a revolution against the British.

Additional troops, including a portion of the 4th Indian Division from southern India, began pouring into Punjab to cope with the situation arising out of the Viceroy's conference with Indian leaders on June 2 and thereafter (*CM* 29).

Reported from Nainital that thousands of Muslim criminal nomad tribesmen had been infiltrating from Punjab into the Saharanpur district of the UP and settling there under the patronage of Muslim League zamindars (*Tr* 29).

According to Giani Kartar Singh, the division of Punjab with only twelve districts for the non-Muslims, comprising Ambala and Jalandhar divisions and Amritsar district, would not satisfy the Sikhs and that they 'would have to fight before the Boundary Commission' (*Tr* 30).

Thursday, 29 May 1947

Reports published that 20 villages in Gurgaon district have been burnt down by rioters (*Tr* 31).

Mr Jinnah's demand for a corridor is fantastic nonsense and can never be conceded by the rest the country, said Master Tara Singh (*Tr* 31).

Pandit Jawaharlal Nehru visited Lahore to see for himself the riot-affected areas and had discussions with the political leaders of Punjab, including Tara Singh and Giani Kartar Singh, and had talks with the Governor.

15 August 1947

India was declared to be independent.

26 August 1947

Muslim refugees, helped by local Muslims, attacked non-Muslims at Bahawalnagar, inflicted 445 casualties and looted Hindu shops. (Other towns affected by Muslim attacks on non-Muslims, being Hasilpur with 348 casualties including 11 Muslims, the city of Bahawalpur with 147 casualties including 21 Muslims and Christians, Mandi Sadiqganj, Khairpur and Udhampur, with casualties under 1,000) (*CMG* 22 Nov.).

7 September 1947

Over 100 Sikhs, men, women and children were massacred at the instigation of Mahfuz Husain, sub-inspector of Police, in the village of Wanieke Tarar in the district of Gujranwala, according to the statement of Lala Sunder Das Narang, dispenser of the place (*Ajit* 14 Dec).

Wednesday, 10 September 1947

Muslims carried out mass conversion of Hindus and Sikhs, forcible marriages and organized loot in Lilla in Jhelum district and in the surrounding villages of Pind-Dadan Khan *tehsil*. The Muslim *Pir* called Shahzada was responsible for the marriages of a number of Brahmin girls to Muslims. The converted Hindus and Sikhs were made to eat one meal at his house (*Tr* 10 Sept).

Six or seven thousand people of the *kafilas* were killed at Bhambipur, about 2,000 at Mandi Pirmahal and 7,000 at Kamalia by Muslim mobs of Pakistan, according to Lala Des Raj Puri, *zaildar* of Toba Tek Singh. According to him, a *kafila* of Hindus and Sikhs staying at Chak. No. 301, Gugera Branch, was brought in front of the house of Toba Tek Singh, DSP, about 400 women and girls were taken away, people were robbed of their property and then sent to Hindustan in a special train. Muslim *goondas* seated in the train killed a large number of Hindus and Sikhs and threw them in the Ravi (*Tr* 18 Nov.).

Sunday, 28 September 1947

A British Major, lately of the Indian Signal Corps, was arrested at Bombay and brought to Jabalpur. A number of fire-arms and ammunition were recovered from his kit. . . .

The people have recovered from Jabalpur a large number of unauthorised arms and ammunition and road mines (*HT* 30).

A Hindu-Sikh convoy from Sargodha arrived at Lyallpur (*Tr* 9 October).

An organized mob of about ten thousand armed Muslims, with army vehicles and civilian buses to carry away looted property and kidnapped women, attacked Mianwali town. Killing and looting continued for several hours (*St* 14).

Monday, 29 September 1947

Mr Jethanand Raghumal, a member of the Sind Provincial Congress Committee, told the *Hindustan Times* correspondent at Jodhpur that men, women and children coming from Sind were being subjected to brutal indignities by the over-zealous Pakistan officials who were vying with one another in stripping them of all their valuables. There have been many instances where babies have been deprived of their cradles and feeding bottles (*HT* 30).

Mr Sri Prakash, India's High Commissioner, met Mr Jinnah and requested him for a declaration that Pakistan was not a theocratic state, nor would it be governed by Islamic laws. This step, Mr Sri Prakash is reported to have said, was necessary to restore confidence in the minds of the minorities UPI—(*HT* 30).

Tuesday, 30 September 1947

Nawab Akbar Ali Khan, *rais* and zamindar of Pandrawal, a village on the border of Aligarh and Bulandshahr districts, was arrested for collecting all Muslims of the place in his *garhi*, raising a false alarm of attack by non-Muslims and having in his possession a large quantity of arms and ammunition (*HT* 4).

The Hindu-Sikh convoy on its way from Lyallpur to Jaranwala was attacked by Muslims. Thirty were killed and 29 wounded (*HT* 5).

Seven Sikh prisoners after their release from Lahore central jail were attacked and murdered by Muslims (*HT* 5).

Wednesday, 1 October 1947

Mr Jayaprakash Narayan, speaking at a meeting in Bombay, said that the people of Hyderabad should agitate for the removal of the Nizam from the throne not because he was a Muslim but because he had betrayed the trust of his people (*St* 3).

The government of West Bengal has decided to establish Bengali as the official language of the province (*St* 3).

The refugee camp at the Khalsa College, Lyallpur, was attacked at night (Oct. 1-2) by a Muslim mob armed with bren-guns and other automatic weapons, with about 600 casualties . . . (*Tr* 9).

Thursday, 2 October 1947

A Hindu-Sikh convoy coming from Tandlianwala under the escort of Indian Army troops was attacked by Muslims armed with bren-guns and other fire-arms. An Indian, Major Ram Singh was killed and some soldiers wounded (*St*, 3, *Tr* 10).

The Arya School Lyallpur refugee camp, housing mostly Hindus, was attacked by Muslims, inflicting about 300 casualties and kidnapping 15 girls (*Tr* 9 October).

The number of killed and wounded is reported to be 50 and 40, with 20 girls taken for good, and many more forcibly taken, misused and returned (*HT* 13).

Friday, 3 October 1947

In response to Sardar Patel's appeal to the Sikh community, it began organizing a volunteer corps in East Punjab to ensure the safe passage of Muslim refugees to Pakistan, expecting similar treatment for the Hindu and Sikh emigrants from that dominion (*St* 5).

Addressing a gathering at Srinagar, Sheikh Mohammad Abdullah, president of the All-India States People's Conference and Kashmir National Conference, said: 'I never believed in the slogan for Pakistan . . . I did not believe in the two-nation theory. . . . My personal conviction will not stand in the way of Kashmir taking an independent decision in favour of one or the other dominion. Our choice should be based on the welfare of four million people living in Jammu and Kashmir State . . .' About Pakistan he said: 'What have four and a half crores of Muslims in India gained through it? I sympathize with them in their plight. Pro-Pakistan elements in India started their "Direct Action" in Noakhali and inflicted sufferings on non-Muslims there. This was followed by revenge in Bihar. Later Hindus and Sikhs were killed in NWFP and West Punjab which was followed by killing of Muslims in East Punjab and Delhi. For all this Mr Jinnah's two-nation theory is responsible' (*St* 5).

Congress leaders and legislators of western Pakistan, in the course of a statement issued at Delhi said: 'The swift and tragic march of events and their climax in western Pakistan have forced us to realize that in western Pakistan, life, in any sense, has become impossible for the Hindus and Sikhs. The plain fact is that they are not at all wanted there and any attempt on their part, under any material or ideological impulse, to return to their hearths and homes is bound to lead to a repetition of the horrors they have witnessed and experienced. . . . There can be no going back. . . . Pakistan pales into insignificance before the ineffably barbarous nature of the atrocities perpetrated on them. It is a slur on animals to call the perpetrators beasts.' In the end six suggestions have been made by them for consideration by the government (*HT* 4).

Jathedar Udham Singh Nagoke appealed to the Shahidi Dal and other Hindu and Sikh organizations to allow the Muslim refugees to proceed safely to Pakistan (*Punjab* 5).

Muslim soldiers accompanying a Muslim convoy in camp at Amritsar killed two Sikhs and one Hindu. Five kidnapped Hindu women and a Hindu boy were rescued from their possession (*HT* 7).

Saturday, 4 October 1947

In a statement, Syed Nausher Ali, a Nationalist Muslim leader of Bengal, said: 'A section of Muslims in the Indian Union has followed a suicidal policy for a long time. . . . I am afraid, if the Muslims continue in the way they have so far, the result will be that Muslims will practically cease to exist in the Indian Union' (*HT* 5).

Qadiani Muslims attacked a Sikh village in the neighbourhood (*HT* 13).

A non-Muslim convoy from Bahawalpur heading for Jodhpur was attacked near Rahimyar Khan on the Bahawalpur-Jaisalmer border by the military escort of Bahawalpur State on the night of the 4 October and 5 October. The number of casualties is said to have been very heavy—over 2,000—with some 700 girls kidnapped (*HT* 13).

Sunday, 5 October 1947

To solve the shortage of land and house property left by the

Muslims in India for the rehabilitation of Sikhs and Hindus arriving from Pakistan, Master Tara Singh urged upon the government to arrange for the vacation of Muslim lands and houses in the adjoining parts of the UP and Delhi provinces, asking the Muslims of those areas to go to Pakistan and take possession of the extra land and house property left by the Sikhs and Hindus there (*HT* 6).

Accompanied by Miss Jethi Sipahimallani, Hasan Shahid Suhrawardy and Choudhry Khaliquzzaman visited Keamari harbour where they saw for themselves how Hindu and Sikh evacuees were searched and deprived of their valuable belongings. Mr Suhrawardy said it was silly to subject people bent upon leaving to all that trouble (*St* 6).

The Government of India refused to recognize the accession of Junagadh to Pakistan, and disagreed with claims of Pakistan to Babariawad and Mongrol (*HT* 6).

Appealing to the Indian Muslims to help the Hindu and Sikh refugees from Pakistan, Ehtisham Mahmud Ali, MLA from UP, said, 'Notwithstanding the solemn pledges of loyalty given by the League leaders, I make bold to say that a coterie of self-seeking leaders is still playing a double game of keeping one eye on Hindustan and the other on Pakistan. The millennium for which the Muslim rank and file were made the tools of unscrupulous League leaders has turned out to be a mirage and the Muslim masses who were fed by them with the gospel of hatred and animosity towards the majority community, find themselves in a state of utter helplessness and are confronted with the grim realities of the situation' (*HT* 7). . . .

Monday, 6 October 1947

The Government of India in a communique said that they consider 'that the stationing of Junagarh forces in Babariawad and Mongrol, both of whom have acceded to the Indian dominion, is an unjustified and provocative act of aggression' and desired these forces to be withdrawn (*St* 6).

Jathedar Udham Singh Nagoke appealed to the Hindus and Sikhs of East Punjab to allow safe passage to the outgoing Muslim convoys to avoid retaliation (*St* 9).

Tuesday, 7 October 1947

Mr Adam Adil of Bombay, in a letter published in the *Hindustan*

Times, appealed to the Muslim League leaders not to bother about the Muslims of Hindustan, and said 'Will the Jinnahs, the Zafarullahs, the Noons, the Isphahanis give up their attempt to convert these poor, unprotected, and innocent Muslims in Hindustan into a community of fifth-columnists and allow them in peace to play a worthy role which shall ensure their safety and security?' (*HT* 7).

A conference of the representatives of Pakistan and India held at Lahore. The Pakistan Premier requested the Indian ministers not to send to Pakistan Muslims from Delhi and other provinces. The Indian ministers reiterated the policy of the Indian government that they could not, in the circumstances, force Muslims, who were eager to leave, to stay on against their wishes. They were free to choose (*St* 8).

Mr Liaquat Ali Khan, Pakistan Premier, said at Lahore that he considered any conflict between Pakistan and India suicidal. Continuing, he said: 'I still consider it a disgrace to Pakistan that in certain parts of West Punjab, the majority should have failed to do their duty to protect the minorities. Nor is the name of the Frontier Province, or for that matter of Baluchistan and Sind, entirely unsullied (*St* 8). . . .

Mr V. D. Savarkar justified the retaliation of the Hindus and Sikhs saying in the course of a statement: 'When the government was found weak, was it was not wrong that millions of Hindus and Sikhs, prompted by the instinct of self-preservation, rose in arms in East Punjab, in Bharatpur, in Alwar, in Patiala and in Delhi itself and retaliated. If Pandit Nehru and his colleagues are still safe, they owe it to this brave band of Hindus and Sikhs' (*HT* 8).

The Pakistan government justified the accession of Junagadh to Pakistan, and asked the government to withdraw their troops from the neighbourhood of Junagadh (*St* 9).

In the absence of security and protection for Hindus and Sikhs in Lahore, Dr C. H. Rice, Principal, Forman Christian College, Lahore, has asked the Hindu and Sikh staff of his College not to return to Lahore to resume their duties (*Tr* 9).

In his reply to a deputation of Karachi businessman, Mr Ghulam Muhammad, Pakistan Minister of Finance, said: 'I most categorically assure you that Pakistan is a secular, democratic and not a theocratic State . . .' (*HT* 9).

The Pakistan government was reported to have supplied arms and ammunition to Muslim convoys passing through East Punjab under the pretence of supplying them with wheat which was used as a cover (*Ajit* 8).

The Hindu and Sikh population of Makhdumpur, Jodhpur, Rampur and Kach-khu was reported to have been completely wiped out.... Hindu and Sikh villagers around Khanewal were being attacked. All the young girls of devastated villages have been kidnapped (*Tr* 9).

Reported that a Sikh platoon saved about 6,000 Muslim residents of the village of Dhankot, 33 miles from Delhi (*Tr* 10).

Wednesday, 8 October 1947

Mr S.K. Abbas, general secretary of the All-India Shia Conference, appealed to the Muslims in general, and Shias in particular, to abstain from cow slaughter on the occasion of *Bakr Id* (*HT* 8).

Daulat Ram, a refugee from Qadian, reported that Muslims of Qadian shot four Sikhs going from Qadian to Harchowal (*Ajit* 19).

A Sikh and Hindu evacuee train was attacked at Montgomery by Muslims (*CM* 19).

Thursday, 9 October 1947

The Hyderabad state delegation, headed by the Nawab of Chattari, arrived at New Delhi to resume negotiations with the Government of India on that state's accession to the Indian dominion (*St* 10).

The *Ajit* (Amritsar) published the gist of a secret circular issued by the council for Direct Action of the Muslim League calling upon the Muslims to wipe out Hindus and Sikhs from the villages and towns in Pakistan and to take possession of their lands and property (*Ajit* 10).

Mr Charan Singh, the UP Parliamentary Secretary, in a statement at Lucknow said that the complete exchange of population or unqualified denunciation of the two-nation theory by the Muslim Leaguers were the only two solutions of the present trouble. Continuing, he said, 'there is no other middle path; not all the efforts of our Nehrus and Pants can bring peace to this unfortunate land. If Leaguers believe that they acted rightly in working for the achievement of Pakistan, they must voluntarily pack up for Pakistan today; or circumstances will compel them to do so tomorrow.

Whether Pakistan is ready to receive them is none of our business'
(*HT* 12).

Friday, 10 October 1947

Baluchi sepoys of the military escort of a Muslim caravan shot four
Hindus and Sikhs near Jalandhar Railway Station and got mixed
up with their comrades to avoid detection (*Khalsa Sewak* 12).

'Are these murders sanctioned by Islam? Is this butchery allowed
by Islamic laws? Is this killing of women and children in accordance
with the rules of *Shariat*? Well, I dare say, these acts are against Islam
and Shariat.' Letter by Sheikh Akbar Husain, Ravi Road, Lahore,
(*CMG* 10 October).

Anti-Pakistan Day was observed at a mass meeting of Muslims
held in Juma Masjid after the Friday prayers. Some of the speakers—
staunch supporters of the League—confessed that they had been
betrayed and misguided by the wrong leadership of Mr Jinnah. The
policy and creed of the League had been mainly responsible for the
bloodshed in West Punjab and unrest all over the country. . . . *They
admitted that the atrocities perpetrated on the non-Muslims in the West
Punjab were ten times more than what had been done in East Punjab
and Delhi against Muslims.*

Mr Ahmad said that Mr Jinnah, by exploiting the religious
sentiments of the Muslims of India and in alliance with the British,
had realized his objective. . . . (*HT* 11).

Sardar Abdur Rab Nishtar, in an interview, said that Pakistan
could only be destroyed by God or by the senseless action of
Muslims who were responsible for disturbances in Pakistan (*Tr* 11).

According to an official communique, a Muslim mob attacked
village Dakala (Karnal), killing six Hindus. Muslim villagers round
about Swani (Hissar) attacked Hindu villagers, killing 26 and
wounding one. Muslim troops killed some Hindu-Sikh refugees and
abducted 4 women and 2 children near Dera Baba Nanak. Nine
abducted Muslim girls and 2 children were recovered in Jalandhar
district (*Tr* 11). . . .

Saturday, 11 October 1947

According to today's lead article in the *CMG* (Lahore), 'despite
ministerial assurances, searches of refugees continue; their

exploitation has not ceased, and their property is in great jeopardy (not, be it noted, in bylanes or isolated areas but in the main streets of the busiest towns). Members of the minority community are not safe, and even where they are endeavouring to carry on they receive constant and pointed reminders of their insecurity. . . . The public has lost confidence in the police as guardians of law and order; and citizens no longer feel that they may have redress at the hands of officers and officials for the misdeeds of the rank and file.'

Reported that armed looters, more with the desire of looting the property of the Hindus and Sikhs than anything else, were at large in the Frontier province. Officials refused to carry out the orders of the Premier in the interest of Hindus and Sikhs (*HT* 12).

'If the ultimate solution of the minority problem is to be mass exchange of population, let it be taken up at the Government plane . . .' said Mr Jinnah (*St* 12). . . .

Sunday, 12 October 1947

'Non-Muslims cannot reconcile themselves to the paper assurances of protection given to them by Pakistan leaders. . . . The value of these assurances is writ large on thousands of murders, abductions, forced marriages, burnt houses and maimed children. . . . The conclusion is irresistible that Mr Liaquat Ali Khan is not prepared to own or face the consequences of decisions to which he has been a willing party,' said Sardar Vallabhbhai Patel in a rejoinder to the Pakistan Premier in reply to the latter's statement. The representatives of the Government of India to the Lahore Conference of 5 October, also repudiated the misstatement of the Pakistan Premier (*HT* 12, *St* 12). . . .

Lady Mountbatten concluded her two-day tour in East Punjab, during which she saw for herself the pitiable state of victims coming from Pakistan. At the Indo-Pakistan border, she complained to the Pakistan authorities of the searches carried on and property snatched by them. She learnt that Muslims from across the Pakistan side made 27 raids and 16 minor attacks on the Indian villages with the help of Pakistan Police, Army and National Guards (*HT* 13). . . .

A large quantity of arms and ammunition recovered from two Muslim zamindars of Shahjahanpur and Tajpur, and gun-powder from *Mauza* Jalali, Aligarh district (*HT* 13).

Refuting Mr Jinnah's allegations, Mr Girdhari Lal Puri, deputy speaker of the Frontier Assembly, in a statement at Bombay said that the Frontier minorities had shown no disloyalty to their government while the latter had failed to protect them from the Muslim criminals (*St* 18).

Monday, 13 October 1947

A notice put up by the Muslim University authorities that Pakistan officials were coming to Aligarh to recruit officers for Pakistan, increased the public suspicion regarding the loyalty of the Muslim intelligentsia and caused tension in the locality, strengthening the demand for the disorganization of the Muslim League (*HT* 14).

A report published that about 500 of a Hindu-Sikh convoy of 2,400 refugees bound for east Punjab had been killed near Jhelum, a large number being wounded (*HT* 14). . . .

Tuesday, 14 October 1947

Khan Abdul Ghaffar Khan in public meetings in Peshawar area is asking the Red-Shirts to unite and get ready for any emergency (*CMG* 15).

Four east-bound lorries of Hindus and Sikhs were attacked by Muslims who were repulsed by escort (*CMG* 15).

Mr H. J. Khandekar, MLA, president of the All India Depressed Classes League, asked the Harijans not to follow the advice of Mr Jogendra Nath Mandal, Pakistan Labour Minister, calling upon them to wear a distinguishing green badge with a crescent and star. He advised the Harijans to migrate to the Indian dominion at once by whatever means possible (*CMG* 15).

A large quantity of arms, ammunition, stolen railway and other government property was recovered from Pakistan-bound Muslims at Allahabad railway station. Six Muslims including a woman were arrested (*Tr* 14).

Reported that 10,000 to 12,000 are accommodated in Mianwali camp where the day's meal consists of one barley chapatti, and a bit of dry onion. Water is hopelessly scarce, a pitcher of water costs Rs 50 (*St* 14).

Prof Abdul Majid Khan of Punjab called upon the Muslim Leaguers of India to liquidate the Muslim League of their own accord and join the Congress *en bloc*. He said: 'Those Muslim Leaguers, who are still in India, should either immediately migrate to Pakistan or give a clear indication of their unswerving loyalty to the Indian dominion. It is the duty of Indian Muslims to repent sincerely for their past anti-rational and anti-national activities and be prepared to defend the freedom of India to the last (*St* 14). . .

The UP government announced that Hindi in Devanagari script will be the official language of the province (*HT* 14).

Wednesday, 15 October 1947

A refugee Muslim train from Lalamusa was attacked at Shahdara near Lahore by Muslim militarymen, killing ten and wounding as many Sikhs and Hindus. At Lalamusa itself property of some of the refugees was looted by Muslims (*Tr* 16).

An armed gang of Muslims in military uniform, armed with two sten-guns, a bren-gun and revolvers, came in a military truck, overpowered the sentry of the Signals Section near Delhi civil secretariat, and took away 27 army revolvers, 10 rifles and cartridges (*HT* 17, *Tr* 17).

The Pakistan government was reported to have cut off the water supply of the Hindu and Sikh refugee convoys from the canal subjecting them to incredible hardships in their journey from Balloki Headworks and Khem Karan (*HT* 17).

Criticizing the aggressive propaganda launched by the Pakistan government against Kashmir giving false news over the radio, a press Note issued by the Kashmir government says that 'the truth is that thousands of people armed with modern weapons from Pakistan are raiding Poonch territory. Petrol, salt and wheat coming to the state from Rawalpindi have been stopped. Adjoining feudatory states are being put up to issue threats of secession, as well as armed intervention in the internal administration of the state. When representations are made to the Pakistan government, summary denials are wired back. The world will judge whether it is Kashmir or Pakistan that is behaving aggressively towards the other—API (*St* 17, *HT* 20).

Thursday, 16 October 1947

The West Punjab police arrested Rai Anwar Khan Kharal, MLA, Rai Shahadat Khan, Unionist MLA, and Col. Dara (INA), Salar-i-Suba

National Guards, Olympic hockey player and a student of the Government College, Lahore, on a charge of abducting non-Muslim women (*Pakistan Times-Indian News Chronicle*, 18). . . .

Mr Abid Ali Jaffarbhoy of Bombay, in the course of his reply to the complaints of Choudhry Khaliquzzaman and other Leaguers issued at Bombay, said that 'the behaviour of Indian Muslims is not much changed. They still look to Jinnah Saheb for guidance and to Pakistan for protection. They have not liquidated the Muslim League in India. They try to minimize the atrocities on Hindus in Pakistan and exaggerate similar happenings in Hindustan.' He suggested that such of the Muslims who sincerely feel that it is not possible for them to become genuinely loyal to the dominion of India should leave the country immediately.

According to Mr Parsram V. Thehlramani, MLA, 'Nearly 400 Sikhs were killed in Nawab Shah district of Sind last month, 20 persons were killed and several injured when a branch line train was derailed between Nawab Shah and Mirpur Khas, over 50 Hindus and Sikhs were stabbed in running trains and many were injured when thrown out of trains in one month. Looting, forcible occupation of locked houses and lands owned or held by Hindus, and forcible conversion of Sikhs to Islam, are multiplying day after day' (*Tr* 17).

Friday, 17 October 1947

Lala Bhimsen Sachar said at Amritsar: 'It is Muslim assassin's dagger, supported by police and military bullets, that compelled the Hindus and Sikhs to run away from Pakistan for sheer self-preservation. . . . The Muslim League leaders and the Muslim League government could never be absolved of the responsibility for utter ruin of Hindus and Sikhs in West Punjab. . . . The Muslim League had been working according to a plan and it is sinful to pose the role of injured innocence.' He termed the statement of Mr Jinnah suggesting 'that the tragic migration of the Hindus and Sikhs from West Punjab was the outcome of a plan hatched to ruin the Pakistan State,' as amazing and most outrageous (*Tr* 18, *INC* 19).

Reports received from Lahore are that those non-Muslims who go to Lahore banks to cash cheques or otherwise draw money from them are stabbed outside the bank precincts as soon as they come out (*Tr* 18). This is in spite of the assurances of the Pakistan government to non-Muslims in general and bank employees in particular.

Report(s) published that Pakistan troops engaged in escorting Muslim refugees to their dominion have been encouraging Muslim refugees to loot the countryside and abduct Hindu and Sikh girls. The troops have been annoying civilians and adopting a threatening attitude towards Indian troops (*HT* 18). . . .

A large number of daggers, spears, knives, airguns, etc., were recovered from the Muslims of five big *mohallas* of Aligarh (*HT* 20).

Saturday, 18 October 1947

Over 11 tons of live and empty cartridges and about 25 maunds of lead pellets were recovered from Muhammad Ismail Cutchi Seoni, a prominent Muslim Leaguer, member of the local peace committee and a cloth merchant of Jabalpur (*INC* 19, *St* 19, *HT* 19).

Mr Shams-ul-Haq, former deputy mayor of Calcutta, and R. Muslim in a statement suggested that Muslim minority in the Indian Union should 'most emphatically repudiate the two-nation theory and have no allegiance whatsoever to the Muslim League which should be liquidated at once.' They appealed to Maulana Abul Kalam Azad, Maulana Husain Ahmad Madani and other Muslim leaders to take the reins of the Indian Muslims into their hands (*CMG* 19).

Report published of about 260 abducted Hindu and Sikh girls recovered from Pakistani Punjab through the efforts of Mridula Sarabhai (*HT* 19).

Hindu and Sikh refugees were searched and deprived of their belongings at Lala Musa by Pakistan military and police. A few girls were kidnapped and handed over to local villagers (*CMG* 21).

Giani Kartar Singh, president Shiromani Akali Dal, sent a telegram to Mahatma Gandhi saying that the Sikhs should be consulted at the time of talks regarding the settlement of the minorities problem between India and Pakistan in view of some problems peculiar to the Sikhs, particularly with regard to their demand for Nankana Sahib—UPI (*HT* 21). He has asked for Nankana Sahib to be conferred the status of Vatican City in Rome (*CMG* 23).

Sunday, 19 October 1948

Sardar Partap Singh, minister, warned the Sikhs, with particular reference to the Maharaja of Patiala, against any schemes or scheme for the establishment of Khalistan (*Tr* 20).

According to Sardar Ishar Singh Majhail, minister, in a speech at Banga, 'the two-nation theory is the root cause of our present trouble and devastation. The originators of the theory would have to take away the Muslims, not only of East Punjab but from other parts of the Indian Union as well' (*Tr* 20).

A Muslim young man was found lurking about with suspicious intentions in the premises of the residence of Maulana Abul Kalam Azad in New Delhi. On the arrival of a guard on duty, he took to his heels and was ultimately arrested and handed over to police. He gave his name as Aziz Ahmad belonging to Chak No. 55/21 in the Police jurisdiction of Okara in West Punjab (*HT, Ajit,* 21).

The Council of the Sind Muslim League (Karachi) by a resolution recommended that the Constitution of Pakistan should be socialistic (*CMG* 21).

Mr Autar Narain complained to Raja Ghazanfar Ali Khan that while the DC and SP (Jhelum) were cooperating in restoring confidence in the minorities with a view to resettling them in their old homes, petty officials were out to sabotage the movement. He cited the mysterious disappearance of a Sikh woman with two children from a camp and the fact that an evacuee was robbed of Rs 200 by a military picket (*CMG* 21).

Fourteen Hindus and Sikhs were killed and 4 injured in a Muslim raid at Dajal in Dera Ghazi Khan district (*Tr* 26).

General Mohan Singh, Cols. Niranjan Singh and Gurbakhsh Singh Dhillon announced their decision to organize Desh Sewak Sena, with headquarters at Majitha House, Amritsar (*Tr* 21).

Monday, 20 October 1947

In reply to a deputation of Amritsar traders and industrialists, the East Punjab Governor, Sir Chandulal Trivedi, assured them that the East Punjab Government had no prejudice against Amritsar in the consideration for the selection of a capital (*CMG* 21).

The government of Kashmir has complained to the Governor-General and Premier of Pakistan, in a telegram, about the unfriendly attitude of Pakistan towards Kashmir in not allowing the working of the standstill agreement and creating difficulties. It added, 'If unfortunately this request is not heeded, the Kashmir government fully hopes that the Governor-General and Premier of Pakistan would agree that Kashmir would be justified in asking for friendly assistance—Reuter (*CMG* 21).

From one house in Ahmadiya colony in Monghyr (where various kinds of arms and ammunition were recovered), a 248-page manuscript of a book containing full diagrams and illustrations for the manufacture of various types of fire-arms was discovered—API (*Tr* 21).

Mr Mehar Chand Mahajan declared that 'people who wish to sabotage the existing government (of Kashmir) and substitute a parallel government of their own will undoubtedly be treated as rebels and, if caught, will share the fate that meets all rebels' (*Tr* 21).

The Patiala government categorically refuted the wrongful charges levelled against it by Mian Iftikhar-ud-Din, West Punjab Minister for Rehabilitation, after his hurried visit to the state and gave detailed information about the Muslims in the various refugee camps in the state (*HT* 22).

Tuesday, 21 October 1947

Mr Muhammad Saadat Ali of Lahore contradicted the 'categorical assurance' of the Pakistan Minister regarding 'Pakistan is a secular, democratic and not a theocratic state,' and said that this assurance 'has absolutely no support of the Muslims.' Continuing, he writes in his letter (*CMG*, Lahore, 21 October) that 'ever since Mr Jinnah undertook to fight out our case, he has on occasions without number, proclaimed emphatically that Muslims were determined to set up a state organized and run in accordance with the irresistible dictates of the Islamic *Shariat*. . . . They (the Muslims) were promised resurgence of Islam. . . . If secularization were our sole aim, India need not have been partitioned, for India undivided would have a much greater power. We raised this storm for partition because we wanted to live as free Muslims and organize a state on Islamic principles. . . .'

Two cannons, one of American manufacture, two pistols, a cartridge-making machine, a number of daggers and a cart-load of earheads were recovered from a Muslim locality at Bareilly, including the houses of the religious head of a Muslim sect and the *salaar* of the Muslim League National Guards. Six persons, including the religious head, were arrested—API (*CMG* 22).

Minister Ishar Singh Majhail announced that living accommodation in East Punjab would be controlled and 'rationed'.

·The Pakistan government denied Kashmir's allegation and threatened the grave consequences of the present policy of the state (*Tr* 22).

Raids from across the border were made on some villages in Amritsar district (*St* 24).

General Mohan Singh and Col. Niranjan Singh laid the foundation of the Desh Sewak Sena (National Service Corps) at its headquarters at Majitha House, Amritsar, with a pledge of service to the country. General Mohan Singh will be the Senapati (Commander in-Chief) and Col. Niranjan Singh the Chief of Staff (*CMG* 23).

Wednesday, 22 October 1947

Frontier Premier, Khan Abdul Qaiyum Khan, in a broadcast speech at Peshawar, called the supporters of the Pathanistan movement enemies of the Muslim nation and Pakistan and told them that they would be treated as such (*CMG* 23).

A Panthic Conference was held at Patiala at the invitation of Maharaja Yadavindar Singh. Sardar Patel deplored the vilification of the Sikhs by interested propagandists from abroad. He appealed to the Sikhs for support to the government in maintaining peace in the country true to their braveness. Maharaja Yadavindar Singh warned his community against cries of Khalistan or Sikhistan (*St* 23 *HT* 23).

Sardar Vallabhbhai Patel, who attended the Panthic conference, said in the course of his speech that he was gratified at the Sikh response to his appeal for peace, and deplored the vilification of the Sikh studiedly and systematically carried on abroad by interested parties. . . .

A Muslim mob attacked the Bombay Mail carrying Hindu and Sikh evacuees to India (*Tr* 26).

Over 2,000 tribesmen, armed with rifles, bren-guns, machine guns and flares entered Kashmir territory in military trucks at night and burnt Muzaffarabad town and looted it.

Malik Firoz Khan Noon appointed Special Representative of the Quaid-i-Azam, GG of Pakistan, with the rank of Ambassador, to the Middle East countries of Iraq, Persia, the Lebanon, Syria, Egypt, Arabia and Turkey (*St* 23).

Resigning from the Muslim League, the Maharajkumar of Mahmudabad said in a statement to the press: 'The Muslim League has outlived itself. Let it die its own death.' (*HT* 23).

A number of Muslim policemen reported to have deserted the Indian Union, and escaped into Pakistan with substantial quantities of arms and ammunition (*HT* 23).

Thursday, 23 October 1947

According to Professor Abdul Majid's statement, 'it is no secret that but for the solid support of the Muslim League leaders in provinces such as the UP, Bihar and Bombay, Pakistan would never have come into being. . . . Therefore, important office-bearers like the presidents, treasurers, secretaries of provincial, district and city Muslim League branches in India, in order to ensure immediate dissolution of the League, should forthwith migrate to Pakistan. If they do not do so of their own accord, it is the duty of the government to prevail upon them to quit India. As long as Pakistanis are in this country, ignorant Muslim masses will either again be duped and misled by League leaders or the innocent will continue to suffer for the guilty' (*St* 23).

A special train carrying Hindu and Sikh refugees coming from Jassar was attacked by a huge Muslim mob. Two thousand of the evacuees are said to have been massacred. According to the version of West Punjab Pakistan, 30 evacuees were killed, and about 200 injured. Fifty Muslim attackers are said to have been killed by military firing (*CMG* 25, *Tr* 26).

Friday, 24 October 1947

The Provisional Azad Government set up by some Kashmir Muslims was declared to have been reconstituted with Sardar Muhammad Ibrahim Khan, Bar-at-Law, as its provisional head, with its headquarters removed to Pulandari in Poonch. It declared to have established its rule over a major portion of the state (*CMG* 25).

Captain Lakhanlal Malik stated at Jalandhar how shabbily he was treated by the Pakistan officials at Jhang and how, at Shalimar (Lahore), on his way to India, he was robbed of his pistol and his party, including womenfolk, were searched and robbed of their cash and jewellery worth Rs 3 lakh (*HT* 26).

Saturday, 25 October 1947

Lala Bhimsen Sachar in the course of a statement to the press said that the belated efforts of Ghazanfar Ali Khan and Pandit Sunder Lal to stop further migration of Hindus and Sikhs were bound to fail. 'This was only possible if Ghazanfar Ali Khan can persuade his colleagues in the Pakistan government to restore all abducted Hindu and Sikh girls, hand over all converted Hindus and Sikhs and pay due and proper compensation to the minorities for the huge loss of movable and immovable property sustained by them since March. These constitute the acid tests of the Pakistan government's sincerity. Anything short of this is mere indulgence in platitudes which will take us nowhere' (*CMG* 26).

A resolution urging dissolution of the Muslim League in India and asking the government to declare it an unlawful organization throughout the dominion was passed at a public meeting in the Juma Masjid, Delhi under the presidentship of Mr Aziz Hasan Baqi (*St* 26).

Reported from Peshawar that 'for the first time in Afghanistan's history, non-Muslims, mostly Sikhs, have joined the Afghan Army.' 'They are said to be part of a few thousand Hindus and Sikhs who recently fled from Pakistan and sought refuge in Kabul. Hitherto non-Muslim Afghan nationals were not admitted to the Afghan Army'—*Globe* (*HT* 26). . . .

Monday, 27 October 1947

In response to the request for accession to the Indian Dominion and appeal for help for the safety of Kashmir from an attack by Afridi tribesmen and Muslim National Guards, the Governor-General of India, Lord Mountbatten, accepted the accession of Kashmir to India and sent military help to Kashmir to repel the raiders (*CMG* 28, *St* 28). . . .

Sheikh Abdullah, the Kashmir leader, appealed to his people to realize 'the first duty of every Kashmiri was to defend his motherland against the intruder' (*CMG* 28, *St* 28).

The Majlis-Ittehad-ul-Muslimin of Hyderabad Deccan launched direct action campaign (*Tr* 3).

Wednesday, 29 October 1947

The Frontier Premier, Khan Abdul Qaiyum Khan, in a statement at Peshawar said: 'The news that Indian troops have set foot on the soil of Kashmir is not only a challenge to Pakistan, but to the entire Muslim world. . . . I appeal to every Muslim in Pakistan to get ready' (*CM* 30).

According to Kashmir Premier, Mehar Chand Mahajan, 'there is evidence that a former Political Agent in the tribal areas, a Muslim, had a hand in the organization of the invasion' of Kashmir by the Muslim Frontier tribesmen with the help of Pakistan soldiers (*CM* 30).

Thursday, 30 October 1947

It was revealed that Major-General Kiani and Major-General Habib-ur-Rahman of the INA were commanding the Pakistan forces and irregulars in the invasion of Kashmir. It seems that when Mr Jinnah learnt that Kashmir had acceded to the Indian Union and Indian troops had been despatched to Srinagar, he issued orders by phone to General Gracey, C-in-C of Pakistan Army, to move troops towards Kashmir from Murree. A *Daily Telegraph* (London) report says that General Gracey indicated to Mr Jinnah that moving of troops after Kashmir's accession to the Indian Union would be an act of war. Field Marshal Auchinleck flew to Lahore and threatened his resignation as well as of every British officer from both dominion armies if troops were moved towards Kashmir. Thereupon, Mr Jinnah stayed his hand (*Tr* 31).

Lakha Singh, alias Lakhu, of Patti who taking advantage of the fluid state of political affairs in August 1947, had grabbed several thousand acres of land and had declared himself Raja of Patti, was arrested (*Tr* 31).

A report published of mutiny of troops in Chamba state resulting in the forced resignation of the Diwan, Rai Bahadur

Raghbir Singh, and the superintendent of police, Mr Dina Nath Nayyar (*CMG* 31).

Friday, 31 October 1947

Sheikh Abdullah was sworn in as the Prime Minister of Jammu and Kashmir (*HT* 1 Nov).

According to a Pakistan government press communique, the government has refused to recognize the accession of Kashmir to the Indian Dominion saying: 'In the opinion of the Government of Pakistan, the accession of Kashmir to the Indian Union is based on fraud and violence and as such cannot be recognized' (*HT* 1 Nov).

The working committee of the Panthic Durbar under the presidentship of Maharaja Yadavindar Singh of Patiala decided to give 'all-out support and help to the Indian Dominion in its endeavour to solve the Kashmir crisis' (*CMG* 2 Nov).

The Gilgit province of Kashmir revolted against the Maharaja of Kashmir (*CMG* 2 Nov). . . .

Sunday, 2 November 1947

The East Punjab Premier, Dr Gopi Chand Bhargava, in the course of his address at the Sri Rana Padam Chand Sanatan Dharma College, Simla, announced that the Punjab government proposed to impart military training to every boy and girl in the schools and colleges all over the province. He further declared that within six months Hindi and Gurmukhi will become the court languages of East Punjab (*Tr* 3).

The threatened crisis in West Punjab resulting from the resignation of Mian Iftikhar-ud-Din, Minister for Refugees, Relief and Rehabilitation, on account of his heated controversy with Mian Mumtaz Daultana, Minister for Industries and Civil Supplies, over the allotment of abandoned factories and commercial shops was averted by the intervention of Mr Jinnah, leaving the disputed issue to the department of Mumtaz Daultana (*St* 4).

Twenty-four wagons bound for Pakistan were searched at Lucknow and railway machinery parts, costly saloon cushions, cloth bales, kerosene oil, costly tools and a number of spears were recovered from the luggage booked by Loco and Carriage Wagons Shops of officers of the EIR who had opted for Pakistan (*St* 4).

Thursday, 6 November 1947

Mir Mushtaq Ahmad, organizer, Anti-Pakistan Front, announced that the first batch of 25 Muslim 'satyagrahis' will leave Delhi on November 16 to participate in the Satyagraha movement launched in Hyderabad (Deccan) by the State Congress.

Saturday, 8 November 1947

Baramula recaptured by Indian troops after defeating the raiders in a big fight (*CMG, St, Tr* 9). . . .

Sunday, 9 November 1947

The Kashmir Premier, Mr Mehar Chand Mahajan, revealed that he had seized certain documents which prove that the Pakistan government had been constantly helping the raiders (*Tr* 11).

The Government of India took over the control of Junagadh State on an appeal of the Dewan Sir Shah Nawaz Bhuttoo in view of the unanimous request of the State Council, supported by public opinion (*St* 11).

The West Bengal Muslims Conference, presided over by Dr R. Ahmad, questioned the right of Mr H.S. Suhrawardy to call a conference of the Indian Muslims in view of his past political activities 'which have wrought havoc in Calcutta and elsewhere and in view of the fact that he owes allegiance to Pakistan'. The conference also expressed the opinion that the Muslim League demand for Pakistan based on 'the false and fantastic two-nation theory' had resulted in the division of the country and was solely responsible for the unparalleled calamities and immeasurable sufferings that had befallen the country and its people (*St* 11).

At a conference of the Muslim leaders of India, Mr Suhrawardy said: 'Clearly, unequivocally and without fear, with our hands on our hearts, we can declare that we are loyal citizens of the State and shall remain so, expecting that the state will guarantee our rights' (*St* 11).

Monday, 10 November 1947

Dr C. Rajagopalachari was sworn in as the Acting Governor-General of India in place of Lord Louis Mountbatten who left for England (*Tr* 11).

Kashmir Premier, Sheikh Abdullah, told pressmen at Srinagar that 'after what has taken place at Baramula, Uri, Pattan and Muzaffarabad and other places, the people of Kashmir may not bother about a referendum.' He felt convinced of the complicity of Pakistan in the Muslim tribesmen's raid on Kashmir (*CMG* 12).

In view of the urgent representations made by the Tripura state authorities and the Praja Mandal for assistance in meeting the threatened invasion by 'Muslim sojourners', assembling on the borders of the state, Indian troops entered the state for the protection of the state which acceded to the Indian Union in August last (*Tr* 12).

Tuesday, 11 November 1947

According to a correspondent of the United Press of America, who visited the headquarters of Muslim rebels and raiders at Palandri, the military operations of the raiders in Kashmir were directed by officers of the Pakistan Army (*HT* 11).

Kashmir State authorities arrested Chaudhary Faizulla Khan, the former Deputy Commissioner of Baramula, and some state officials who rendered assistance to the raiders (*Tr* 12).

A band of armed Muslims from West Punjab raided the Mamdot area in the district of Ferozepore and inflicted some casualties (*Tr*12).

Hindu and Sikh evacuees were attacked at Jhelum Railway Station on the tenth and eleventh, and subjected to wholesale loot (*Ajit* 19).

Wednesday, 12 November 1947

The Sind government (Pakistan) banned the migration of Hindu *dhobis* (washermen) and sweepers from the province (*CMG* 13).

This act of the Sind Government, according the *CMG*, 'is a serious interference with personal liberty' (*CMG* 14).

Indian troops captured Mahura Power House of Kashmir, the main source of electric supply to the valley, in their pursuit of the raiders (*CMG* 13).

It was confirmed that the Wali of Swat, a Muslim chieftain of the Pakistan Frontier province, was the main instrument in creating the revolt in Gilgit (*CMG* 13).

Thursday, 13 November 1947

The East Punjab government decided that all schools and colleges would further continue to remain closed until the end of February 1948, to provide shelter during winter to ten lakh refugees arriving from the Pakistan Punjab, in addition to those who have already come (*Tr* 14).

Khan Muhammad Yahiya Jan contradicted the news of the establishment of the Azad Pathanistan government at Kabul (*Tr* 14).

The Government of India officially contradicted the Pakistan government allegation in its statement of 11 November regarding Indian troops helping the Azad Junagadh Fauj (*CMG* 14).

Friday, 14 November 1947

Indian troops captured Uri, 63 miles west of Srinagar, on their way to Kohala (*Tr* 15). . . .

A convention of Indian Muslims held at Delhi passed a resolution advising the 'Indian Mussalmans to wind up the Muslim League and all other communal political organizations and join the Indian National Congress which stands for unity, democracy and progress' (*Tr* 16).

Saturday, 15 November 1947

According to a UPI report, 'following the withdrawal of state forces garrison from Ralcout, in Poonch district, 30,000 civilians were killed by the raiders' (*Tr* 16).

Fifteen prisoners of war and a considerable volume of documents captured by Indians were flown to New Delhi for thorough investigation. Kudrat Shah, belonging to the 48th Animal Transport Co. of the Pakistan Army, revealed that the raiders' primary object was to occupy Kashmir and thereafter to proceed to Hindustan. Another prisoner, Abdul Haq, a Rawalpindi police constable, gave out that intensive propaganda had been carried on by priests in mosques in northern India prior to the invasion of Kashmir. According to him 6,000 persons were recruited in the Rawalpindi camp alone in Pakistan for the Kashmir invasion. Among the officers conducting the operations at Baramula were Capt. Rashid Ahmad (INA), Major Khurshid Anwar, Major Aslam and Capt. Azam (*Tr* 16).

Monday, 17 November 1947

The first meeting of India's sovereign legislature, the Constituent Assembly of India, opened today, with Dr Rajendra Prasad as President. Mr G. G. Mavlankar, president of the old Central Assembly, was elected Speaker (*Tr* 18).

K.B. Sh. Badruddin, a former Muslim League MLA, was arrested for being in possession of unlicensed arms. Mortars, bombs, cartridges and gun-powder were recovered from Muslim houses in Agra (*Tr* 18).

Five armed members of the Pakistan Army raided an Indian village Pakiman under the pretext of recovering abducted Muslim girls and were arrested by Indian police constables (*CMG* 19).

An order of the Maharaja of Faridkot published that Punjabi in Gurmukhi script would the court language of the Faridkot state and that Urdu would cease to be used from 1 January 1948 (*St* 17). . . .

Saturday, 22 November 1947

A refugee train carrying Hindus and Sikhs from Multan, Jalalpur, Shahjahanpur and Ghazipur was attacked by Muslim troops, killing about 300 persons in all. (*HT* 24). . . .

Sunday, 23 November 1947

Contradicting the 'astounding and utterly unwarranted' allegations of Abdul Qaiyum Khan, the Pakistan Frontier Premier, against the Patiala state forces, Sardar Hari Ram Sharma, foreign and political minister, Patiala, in a statement said: 'I definitely assert that no Patiala soldier has associated himself with or has been involved in any killings in any part of East Punjab' (*Tr* 24). . . .

Monday, 24 November 1947

In reply to the enquiry of the Government of India, the Pakistan government replied: 'It was quite impossible for the West Punjab government with its existing resources to make arrangements for the safe passage of Sikh pilgrims to Nankana Sahib from East Punjab' (*CMG* 25).

Tuesday, 25 November 1947

Pandit Jawaharlal Nehru in a statement in the Constituent Assembly said: 'We have sufficient evidence in our possession to demonstrate that the whole business of Kashmir raids both in Jammu province and Kashmir proper was deliberately organised by high officials of the Pakistan government.'

Thursday, 27 November 1947

Referring to the Hyderabad-India Agreement, Pir Ilahi Bux, Sind (Pakistan) Education Minister, said at Karachi in a statement: 'I would, therefore, advise the people of Hyderabad to reject these humiliating terms forthwith and fight for the real freedom of their country' (*CMG* 29).

Friday, 28 November 1947

In a statement referring to the plight of the Harijans in the Hyderabad State, Dr. Ambedkar, Minister for Law, said: 'In Hyderabad also they are being forcibly converted to Islam in order to increase the strength of the Muslim population there. . . . It would be fatal for the scheduled castes, whether in Pakistan or Hyderabad, to put their faith in the Muslims or the Muslim League' (*HT* 28).

Extracts from the statements of Muslim raiders captured in Kashmir reveal that high officials of the Pakistan government were responsible for the plans and mobilization of the Pathan and other Muslim raiders for the invasion of Kashmir and that the Muslims of Kashmir had suffered mostly at the hands of these Muslim raiders (*HT* 29).

The Nizam of Hyderabad signed the Stand-Still Agreement with the Government of India for one year. The agreement means that the Hyderabad state will be under the Indian Union in the spheres of defence, foreign affairs and communications like any other acceding state, without having the right to send representatives to the Indian Constituent Assembly. The Nizam will be able to send agents-general to foreign countries, working under the direction of the Indian ambassadors (*HT* 29).

Saturday, 29 November 1947

Lord Mountbatten, Governor-General of India, signed the agreement with the Hyderabad State. (*HT* 30)

Master Tara Singh declared at Bombay the Akali party's full support to the Congress in all political matters despite certain differences, which, he considered, were 'only of a domestic nature' (*St* 2 Dec). . . .

Tuesday, 2 December 1947

In a statement, published this day, Sardar Kharak Singh called upon the Sikhs to support the national government and appealed to Pandit Jawaharlal Nehru to give special consideration to the Sikhs who were worst affected by the division of India (*HT* 2).

Wednesday, 3 December 1947

Mr Abid Ali Jafferbhoy, labour leader of Bombay, in a statement said: 'The Muslim League and its leaders have already done tremendous harm to the Muslims. Never before were such a large bulk of people in such great peril. . . . Such of the Muslims who want to go to Pakistan can do so but they must not behave as thieves and try to smuggle unauthorised articles into Pakistan' (*Tr* 5).

Master Tara Singh, in the course of a statement to the press at New Delhi, thought that there would be war between India and Pakistan within six months. He added: 'If Pandit Nehru is convinced that Pakistan is behind the Kashmir trouble, and if he had positive proofs to support his allegation, then why does not India change the fronts from Jammu to Lahore?' (*Tr* 5).

Saturday, 6 December 1947

Demanding the official liquidation of the Muslim League in India, the Maharajkumar of Mahmudabad said in a statement that 'loyal Muslims will heave a sigh of relief when this generator of disturbances is buried deep.' Suggesting that members of the Muslim League should migrate to Pakistan or else they should be treated as aliens, he added that 'the authorities should see that they do not go underground' (*HT* 7).

Mahashay Shiv Ram, MLA, was murdered at night (Dec. 6-7) in a military camp at Abbotabad, along with his Muslim servant, Kala, a Hindu shopkeeper of Bannu and a Hindu sub-overseer (*HT* 13).

Sunday, 7 December 1947

Addressing a meeting at Banaras, Pandit Govind Balllabh Pant said: 'Those who were still thinking of themselves as a separate nation had better leave this country and go to Pakistan' (*HT* 9).

Monday, 8 December 1947

Thirty Hindus were killed in a daylight attack by armed Muslims led by a Sub-Inspector at Ahmedpur Lama in Bahawalpur State (*HT*).

Friday, 12 December 1947

A lorry carrying Hindu passengers from Oralai village to Sadiqabad was waylaid and looted by a party of about 300 Muslims (*HT* 9 January 1948).

Saturday, 13 December 1947

A clash took place at Dacca (Eastern Pakistan capital) on account of Bengali-Urdu controversy after some persons had toured the city in a bus advocating Urdu. The clash resulted in five persons being injured. (*CMG* 14)

Monday, 15 December 1947

Sh. Ikramul Haq, ADM [Assistant District Magistrate] Lyallpur, formerly of Amritsar, was suspended by Pakistan for corruption and indulgence in loot (*CMG* 16).

It was revealed by Lal Mir, an Afghan of Ghazni, in a statement before Mr G.C. Bali, DIG, (CID), that while King Zahir Shah had asked the Afghan Maliks not to join the raiders of Jammu and Kashmir, the British Political Officer, North Waziristan, and League leaders and officials of Pakistan, instigated the Afghans to join the raids in the name of Islam. At Wazirabad, a party of Afghans was supplied with arms by Pakistan officials (*HT* 17).

Two Sikh women, Chand Rani and Satwant Kaur, the wife and daughter respectively of Sardar Karam Singh, a retired officer of the CP government's PWD [Public Works Department] were attacked near Bhilsa in the Grand Trunk Express. The daughter was thrown out of the train, resulting into a fractured leg. The mother received injuries. Both were admitted into a Bhopal hospital (*CMG* 18). . . .

Thursday, 18 December 1947

Reports current in Delhi that Kashmiri Hindu women carried away by Muslim raiders were being sold in Pakistan NWF towns and Kabul for four rupees each (*CMG* 19).

Friday, 19 December 1947

Reported that *Maulvis*, with status, pay and privileges of Sub-Inspectors of Police, are being recruited by the Pakistan Government to imbue the Pakistan police with the spirit and outlook of Islam (*CMG* 19). . . .

Monday, 22 December 1947

'Rather than press for a separate homeland, the Sikhs will lend their whole-hearted support to the building of a democratic secular state in India,' declared Giani Kartar Singh in a press statement. He thought that private armies should exist as long as the people felt that the government was not taking effective steps to protect them from foreign aggression (*CMG* 23, *St* 23).

Pandit Nehru, the Indian Premier, handed over to Mr Liaquat Ali Khan, the Pakistan Premier, a formal note stating that the Indian government was satisfied that the invasion of Kashmir had the backing of Pakistan arsenal and trained personnel. The note called on Pakistan to withdraw the tribes and its own personnel immediately, failing which the Indian government would appeal to the United Nations Security Council (*Sunday Times*, New Delhi; *CMG* 30).

Tuesday, 23 December 1947

The Government of India declared Pakistan to be foreign territory for the purpose of levying custom duty on the export of raw jute and jute manufactures from India (*HT* 24).

Radio Pakistan broadcast for the first time the use of aircraft by the raiders of Kashmir (*HT* 24).

Mr Bhim Sen, district magistrate, Poonch, declared on unimpeachable evidence that raiders of Kashmir formed part and parcel of the Pakistan army and that the Pakistan officials were recruiting men and supplying arms and ammunition to them (*HT* 25).

Wednesday, 24 December 1947

'Death or conversion to Islam' was the only alternative allowed to Hindus in some places in Bahawalpur State, according to the statement of the heads of over a dozen converted families who have managed to escape. Wholesale murder of Hindus (except of those who agreed to become Muslims) was carried out in the villages of Allahabad and Moja Talbani. The converted were circumcized and remarried in Islamic ways. They were deprived of their belongings and in some cases their grown-up daughters were taken away (*HT* 27).

About 160 bags of lead shots, 25 of cartridges, and some explosive materials were recovered from the godown of a Muslim merchant of Banaras.

Thursday, 25 December 1947

The Government of India sent a note to the Hyderabad Deccan state saying that it considered the state ordinance banning transactions in Indian rupees in Hyderabad a breach of the Stand-Still Agreement.

Monday, 29 December 1947

Addressing the annual conference of the Ahmadiyas at Lahore, Mirza Bashiruddin Mahmud Ahmad, the head of the community, declared 'that we must return to that holy land (Qadian in East Punjab in the Indian Union) is a matter of faith with us all. That our return will be by peaceful means or by war is for the Indian government to choose. The same power will ordain your entry after banishment into Qadian which ordained the entry of your Prophet into Mecca after exile.'

'Pakistan,' he said, 'is a Muslim state and therefore it must be run on Islamic principles, which comprise a complete code of conduct in the spiritual, moral, political and economic fields.' He said he was prepared to supply a solution of any world problem from the Quran which was the word of God (*CMG* 30). . . .

The Indian Union Muslim Conference at Lucknow passed unanimous resolutions to abjure communal politics and to join the Indian National Congress, a non-communal organization.

Sir Mohammad Zafarullah Khan, Pakistan's Foreign Minister, at a press conference at Karachi 'made it quite clear that the use of force on Pakistan's side to settle the (Junagadh) issue was out of the question' (*CMG* 30).

Addressing a public meeting at Jammu, Sardar Vallabhbhai Patel declared, 'On behalf of the Government of India I can give you this assurance that we will do everything possible to save Kashmir. We will count neither cost nor material and, whatever may happen, we shall not give up Kashmir and we will see this business through' (*CMG* 30).

After saying that to save their honour from the Muslim raiders hundreds of girls of Bhimbar *tehsil* (Kashmir) had poisoned themselves to death and many had themselves killed by their relatives, Smt Shanta Kumari, president of the National Women's Conference, Jammu and Kashmir, said that 'many who were abducted were exhibited in the *bazars* of Peshawar and Bannu, thereby enticing Pathans towards Kashmir. Many were subjected to unmentionable indignities' (*HT* 30).

Tuesday, 30 December 1947

In view of Pakistan, a member of the UNO, being engaged in hostile activities against India, a friendly neighbouring country, by aiding and actively assisting raiders in Kashmir and Jammu State (and pleading inability to prevent the raiders from swarming into India forms a part of the Indian dominion, the Government. of India decided to raise the Kashmir issue before the Security Council of the UNO. The legal councillors of the UNO declared India's decision to be entirely proper and legal (*St* 31, *HT* 31, *Tr* 31).

Sardar Shaukat Hayat Khan, West Punjab Revenue Minister, punished by transfer, dismissal and suspension some officials of the

Lyallpur district for inefficiency and neglect of duty towards the refugees. It came to his notice that 'there had been instances of molestation of young girls by volunteers and of parents having been beaten up when they protested' (*CMG* 31).

The SGPC proposed at a meeting of their executive committee to approach the Government of India to take up with the Pakistan government the matter of the protection of the Sikh shrines in Pakistan, particularly of Nankana Sahib and Kartarpur, suggesting that the latter could be easily included in East Punjab by slight adjustment in the boundary. (*Tr* 3 Jan 1948).

Wednesday, 31 December 1947

The Government of India informed the Pakistan government that as they were helping the invaders of Kashmir, a part of Indian territory, 'it is not possible for India to supply the cash and military stores which may only be used in the war in Kashmir against her' (*HT* 1 Jan 1948).

Commenting on the attitude of the Pakistan High Command towards the Kashmir problem, the special correspondent of the *Hindustan Times* at New Delhi, wrote: 'Large scale massacre of tribesmen and ex-servicemen in a way solves the problem of Pakistan; the liquidation of a part of its turbulent population and the obligation to pay pensions to ex-servicemen' (*HT* 1 January 1948).

Thursday, 1 January 1948

Mr Ali Muhammad Khan, president, Muslim League Branch in Great Britain, who arrived in Lahore last month on a fact-finding mission, on the completion of his three-week tour of West Punjab districts said in an interview with the API: 'What I have seen of the refugees has shattered my nerves and I believe my report to my organization will go a long way in opening their eyes with regard to the utter callousness and demoralisation of the administration in West Punjab which has failed from top to bottom to discharge its official, national and moral obligations towards unfortunate brethren from East Punjab.' The officials, he said were not only unsympathetic, but were positively cruel and heartless (*CMG* 1).

Monday, 5 January 1948

Dr Saifuddin Kitchlew had said at the PPCC meeting: 'Let us unite and see that no outside power in the world cast an evil eye on our country.' The Muslim League, he said, 'under the leadership of Mr Jinnah, had instead of promoting love and brotherhood, spread hatred and rivalry between Hindus and Muslims, and the names of Mr Jinnah and the Muslim League would always be coupled with misery and unhappiness' (*HT* 6).

Tuesday, 6 January 1948

Dr Abdul Ghani Qureshi, a prominent Muslim Leaguer, was sentenced to death for the murder of Dr N. C. Joshi on 8 September 1947 (*CMG* 7).

A mob of some 25,000 (about 8,000 according to Pakistan official figure) Muslims attacked the Sikhs in a gurudwara near Ratan Talao, Karachi, within half a mile of the Pakistan secretariat, followed by a wholesale massacre. The Gurdwara was set on fire and subjected to plunder. Not a single Sikh escaped with his life. The Muslim hooligans later proceeded to the Hindu *mohallas* in the city, subjecting them to murder, loot and arson. The offices of the *Hindu,* the *Hindustan, Sansar Samachar* were attacked repeatedly, and the last named was completely destroyed. The *Sansar Samachar* gives the number of killed as 129, with 73 Sikhs and 56 Hindus, the number of injured being 120 Sikhs and 124 Hindus. According to another report the number of injured was 400. The bodies of the killed were disposed of by the government.

The holocaust, according to some quarters, was pre-planned and well-organized. During the previous weeks local Muslims had been intensely agitated by meetings held in Rambagh maidan and addressed by a Pakistan Minister, Mr Chundrigar, a Sindhi Minister, Pir Ilahi Bakhsh and leading Pakistani Maulanas, Shabir Ahmad Usmania, *Shaikh-ul-Islam,* and Abdul Hamid Budauni. The police and military willfully neglected their duty. According to the *Ajit* (9 Jan.), the gate of the Gurudwara was broken open with the help of the Muslim police and Baluch military.

Wednesday, 7 January 1948

Cases of looting of Hindu and Sikh houses in Karachi continued.

Lawlessness persisted. Over 1,000 persons were rounded up, and over 1,500 arrested by the police for breach of the curfew order.

In a communication to the Government of India, the Pakistan government refused to send their delegation for Sterling Balance negotiations with the UK and India. . . .

Thursday, 8 January 1948

Some Muslims attacked 3 non-Muslim refugees. The Muslim *kotwal*, Mr Agha, abused the refugees when they took the injured persons to the *Kotwali* (*HT* 9).

Friday, 9 January 1948

According to Suhrawardy's interview with API [Associated Press of India], 'What has taken place at Karachi is not merely condemnable but damnable. . . . These incidents bring home forcibly to one that it is little use the government's guaranteeing protection to minorities if the public have not been educated to it. . . . While leaders in high circles talk and tinker, the minorities die in thousands.'

Mirza Bashiruddin Mahmud, head of the Ahmadiya community, in a public speech at Rawalpindi demanded that the Pakistan constitution should be framed in strict accordance with Islamic laws. Regarding the Radcliffe Award, he said that it had been actuated by the desire of the interested parties to cripple the new born Muslim state of Pakistan (*CMG* 11).

Saturday, 10 January 1948

Reported that the Nizam's government had transferred to the Pakistan government, Government of India securities to the value of Rs 20 crore which they were holding (*CMG* 11). . . .

A Sikh deputation including Jathedar Udham Singh met Mahatma Gandhi and other Congress leaders and impressed upon them the necessity of arming the residents of the border districts of East Punjab (*HT* 12).

Sunday, 11 January 1948

Nine persons were killed and 35 injured in stabbing incidents at Ajmer (*CMG* 13).

Monday, 12 January 1948

Muslim tribesmen and others *en route* to Jammu attacked a non-Muslim train of refugees from Bannu in the early hours of this day. According to a West Punjab press communique, the number of casualties is 174 in addition to a large number of injured (*CMG* 13, *HT* 15).

Referring to the activities of the Socialists, Maulana Abdul Sattar Niazi said in the West Punjab Assembly at Lahore that 'the wrong would be undone not by the kind of publicity which was put out by their government but by the well known method, "Quran in one hand and sword in the other" ' (*CMG* 13).

Mr Ghulam Mohammad Bakhshi was sworn in as acting head of the emergency administration in Jammu and Kashmir in place of Sheikh Mohammad Abdullah (*HT* 13).

Tuesday, 13 January 1948

Mahatma Gandhi began a fast to bring about Hindu-Muslim unity.

Condemning the attack on the refugees' train at Gujrat on January 12, Mian Muhammad Mumtaz Daulatana said: 'We bend our heads in shame over what happened at Gujrat' (*CMG* 14).

In a meeting of the Working Committee of the Panthic Darbar at Delhi, it was decided to send a medical mission to Kashmir, and to send Sardar Sant Singh, MLA, as their representative to Kashmir to help sufferers and to keep the Darbar informed of the situation there. The committee also decided to send a *jatha* to look after orphan children in refugee camps (*St* 15).

Wednesday, 14 January 1948

At a representative meeting of the Sikhs it was resolved that 'the Sikhs are greatly perturbed over Mahatmaji's fast. We feel that Mahatmaji is an asset to humanity and his life must be saved at all costs. The object for which he had undertaken it [the fast] is appreciated by every Sikh irrespective of his political affiliations.

'We assure Mahatmaji that the Sikhs will make a supreme effort to preserve peace and promote harmony among the various communities' (*CMG* 15).

Thursday, 15 January 1948

As a gesture of goodwill to Pakistan, in response to the non-violent and noble effort made by Mahatma Gandhi by undertaking a fast for communal unity, the Government of India decided to make immediate payment of 55 crores of rupees held by the Reserve Bank of India as part of the cash balance due to that country (*HT* 16).

Discussions started at Lake Success in the USA on the Kashmir question at the UNO (*HT* 16).

Friday, 16 January 1948

A deputy superintendent of police, 1 inspector, 17 sub-inspectors, 18 assistant sub-inspectors, 19 head constables, and 115 foot constables have been found guilty by the West Punjab Government of being in possession of looted property (*CMG* 16).

Love is Stronger than Hate
KHUSHDEVA SINGH

At a time when people were busy killing each other, some people somewhere provided the healing touch and shared their love and compassion with the hapless victims of the communal riots. Major Khushdeva Singh, a medical doctor, was one of them. 'I love Muslims as I love my own kith and kin,' he wrote in September 1947. Everyone living in Dharampore had faith and confidence in his humanity and generosity. Notice, that Muhammad Umar wrote to him: 'With great humility I beg to state that I do not feel myself safe except under your protection. Therefore, in all kindness, be good enough to grant me a seat in your hospital.' Or, the distress call from Abrar Ahmad: 'With folded hands we request you to be kind to us for God's sake and for the sake of Guru Nanak protect our lives.'

Khushdeva Singh's vivid account of what happened in and around Dharampore was published in 1973 at the behest of Justice Harbans Singh, Chief Justice of the Punjab and Haryana High Court, and Professor Ganda Singh of the University of Patiala, whose diary is reproduced in this collection with some editorial changes. The letters he received from Pakistan are not included.

Khushdeva Singh received 317 letters from those Muslims whose lives he had saved during the dark days of partition or from their family members. One of them wrote: 'No words can express the innermost feelings of gratitude and thankfulness which sprout from my grateful heart every moment, when I cast a look upon my children and wife who have escaped from the very brink of the other world; you are doubtlessly an angel doing humanitarian work which befits a true doctor.' Likewise, Riasat Husain was relieved to know that her sister was staying with Khushdeva. 'I have got no words to express my thanks to you for your noble act and I am extremely happy to see that even in these days when most of the people of all communities have become

Love is Stronger than Hate: A Remembrance of 1947 (Patiala: Guru Nanak Mission, December 1973), pp. 11-41.

mad, there are noble persons like you who are still sticking to the golden principles of humanity and are above communal feelings.'

All that is narrated in the following pages is not of my deliberate doing. It was the will of God which He in His extreme benevolence and grace exercised at a time when the storm of hatred and violence among different communities was at its highest in many parts of the country. I only happened to be a humble witness to what He chose to do at Dharampore at that time. The memory of events which occurred more than twenty-five years ago is still as fresh in my mind as if they occurred only yesterday. Often as I sit alone, the whole sequence passes before my eyes like a silent movie. All the letters and other documents connected with these events had been treasured by me as sacred relics. Never in my mind had I the slightest intention to share this information with, or show the letters and documents connected with it to anyone. It appears, however, that God willed it otherwise.

A few weeks ago, I went to see a friend of mine in the Punjabi University. The talk ranged over several topics. One of these was the partition of the country. While on this subject, I happened to mention that I had with me letters of some Muslim friends whom I had been able to help during those troubled days. He asked me if there were any Muslims living at that time in my street. He did not know that I was not then at Patiala but at Dharampore.

A few days later I took some of the letters to him. I do not really know what prompted me to do so. However, he showed keen interest in those papers and I left them with him. When I met him again after a few days, he told me that he had gone through them with great care. He had a suggestion. He urged me strongly to write of those events.

Another good friend joined him and gave the same advice. It was under their friendly pressure that I started writing this brief account.

I was posted at Dharampore in 1947 and was working as the Medical Superintendent of the Hardinge Sanatorium, and as Tuberculosis Adviser to the Government of Patiala, I was also Honorary Secretary of the Tuberculosis Association of Patiala. Other offices included the honorary magistrate, the president of the Small

Town Committee, and the rationing officer for the area. My main interest was tuberculosis work in the state, and I wished to devote all my time to my professional duty. I, therefore, submitted my resignation from all the nonprofessional assignments. But the resignation was not accepted and I had to carry on with these diverse duties.

The position provided me with a greater chance to come into close contact with the people of the area. It helped me deal with many difficult situations that came up in the year 1947.

DHARAMPORE

Dharampore is a small town in the Simla Hills, situated at a distance of about 16 miles from Kalka on the Kalka-Simla road. It enjoys a central position as the roads from Kalka to Simla, Dagshai and Subathu pass through this town. The road from Kalka to Kasauli passes near the police station at Dharampore. The town was well-known all over the country on account of its sanatoria for the treatment of tuberculosis. There were three sanatoria in Dharampore itself. One out of these, the Hardinge Sanatorium, was run by the Patiala government, and the other two, the King Edward Sanatorium and the Arcadia, were run by private societies. There were three other sanatoria situated near it on the Dharampore-Kasauli road. One of these, the Nenavati Sanatorium, was about two miles, and the other, the Lady Irwin Sanatorium at Sanawar, was about six miles from Dharampore. The third one, Lady Linlithgow Tuberculosis Sanatorium, was in Kasauli itself. Dharampore is surrounded by three cantonments, namely Dagshai, Subathu and Kasauli, which are situated in different directions and at a distance of four and eight miles, respectively, from it.

The population of the town fluctuated according to the season of the year. In winter it consisted mainly of the permanent residents who belonged to the two major communities, Hindu and Muslim. There were a few Sikhs also. In summer, however, its population increased owing to the influx of patients, their attendants, ex-patients, and some visitors who came to the hill station for reasons of health. There was always quiet and peace in the atmosphere. Complete communal harmony prevailed among the people.

DIVISION OF THE COUNTRY

With the announcement of the Partition plan, the non-Muslim refugees began pouring into the Indian Punjab in tens of thousands. The Government of India was caught unawares. They never expected forcible eviction of Hindus and Sikhs from Western Punjab. They had, therefore, made no plans to receive and rehabilitate them, much less to feed them for months and provide them with other necessities of life.

These people, who were now called refugees, were a few weeks earlier respected as law-abiding citizens of the country. They had their secure homes, their vocations and business, their relatives and friends, close associations with the people and places of their residence. Their only crime was that they were non-Muslims and happened to be living in that part of the country which fell to the share of Pakistan. They were made to leave their hearths and homes and all their worldly belongings. Many of them lost their kith and kin, mercilessly killed before their very eyes. Their womenfolk were snatched away from them and retained in what had become Pakistan. They passed through an indescribable ordeal of terror and torture.

The homeless refugees, when they reached India, had no shelter. The future was uncertain. Their world was dark without a ray of hope. It was at this time that Maharaja Yadavindar Singh of Patiala made the historic announcement welcoming the refugees to Patiala, and offering to rehabilitate them to the best of his resources. This came as a godsend to the bewildered refugees, who started coming to Patiala in the second week of March 1947. A camp was set up in the grounds behind Gurudwara Dukhnivaran Sahib and the number of immigrants soon approached twenty-five thousand. The figure rose much higher subsequently.

Additional camps were opened at Bhatinda, Dhuri, Barnala, Sunam, Pinjore, Mansa, Raman, Lehragaga and Narwana. The officials and the public of Patiala State, including a large number of business associations and industrialists, generously responded to the call for donations which went a long way in alleviating the sufferings of the refugees. The organization set up by the Maharaja of Patiala for the relief and rehabilitation of the uprooted Punjabis was not only a source of hope and encouragement to the homeless and the afflicted, but it also gave time and inspiration to the government of the Punjab, and to the Government of India, to plan and organize the evacuation of Hindus and Sikhs from the dangerous areas in Pakistan and to set up machinery for their resettlement in India.

There was overwhelming sympathy for the refugees from all quarters, and people had a great desire to serve and help them in their time of need. We at Dharampore also wished to contribute our humble share in this humanitarian work. The beginning was made with a sum of Rs 2,500 which we collected from amongst the people of Dharampore and sent to Sardar Mohan Singh, managing director of the Bank of Patiala, who was in charge of one of the refugee camps at Patiala. A few days later, I collected another sum of Rs 500 from amongst my friends and sent it to the Indian Red Cross Society, Delhi, for the purchase of blankets for the refugees residing there.

A little later, we learnt that a refugee camp had been started at Ambala, and there was a great need for food. I convened a meeting of a few friends to consider the question of collection of rations for the Ambala camp. Some of the members, however, felt that it would be much better if, in place of rations, we could take cooked food to the camp so that it could be used immediately. This plan was approved, and the necessary rations were collected. The next step was to prepare the food. Cooking food in such a huge quantity was beyond the resources of a small town like Dharampore. The main problem was to make of *chapatis* on this large scale. We had to set up six centres, for making *chapatis* alone. Two centres were started for the cooking of *dal*, *subzi*, and some *halva*. The cooking began at 3.00 a.m. and it took a full twelve hours before all the food was ready. A truck had already been engaged and the baskets full of *chapatis*, big *degchis* full of *dal* and *sabzi* and a large part of *halva* were loaded into it. I, along with four others from Dharampore, proceeded towards Ambala, and reached the refugee camp there by 5.30 p.m. I approached the officer in charge of the camp and told him that we had brought a truckload of cooked food which we wanted to hand over to him for distribution among the inmates of the camp. He, however, suggested that it would be better if we could distribute the food ourselves. He promised that he would send word to the inmates about the arrival of the food.

We agreed to his proposal and took our position in the rear of the truck. In a few minutes the refugees began coming and we started the distribution of the food. I, along with one helper, took up the distribution of chapatis, and the other two friends were to handle the *dal, sabzi* and *halva*. All went well for some time, but soon there was a great rush and the truck was besieged. We found it extremely difficult to distribute the food when every one wanted to be the first to get it. However, we managed to finish the distribution of food in about three hours. When it was over and the refugees had gone back into the camp, we felt completely exhausted. My hands bore marks of scratches, caused by the fingernails of the refugees, some of whom had actually snatched *chapatis* out of my hands. These people were neither beggars nor paupers but had been reduced to this state of helplessness by the cruel turn of circumstances.

The unending stream of refugees, and their harrowing tales of woe had an unpleasant reaction. A spirit of retaliation arose. Thousands of people, who had been living for centuries as neighbours in homes and in professions, flew at one another's throat. Incidents of stabbing became a regular feature in many parts of the country. This had its effects on the public of Dharampore and the surrounding area as well. I thought something should be done to cool tempers in Dharampore. With this end in view, I called a meeting of the citizens of Dharampore on 1 July 1947. It was held in the spacious ground in front of the sanatorium and was attended by all sections of people in large numbers. I said a few words and stressed the importance of maintaining peace and sticking to the old traditions of communal harmony and brotherhood. Handbills emphasizing the same ideas were also distributed at that time. Everyone listened with care, but from their faces I could see that they were not convinced or converted. Later I learnt that the Muslims were feeling that it was not right for them to depend upon the government which could let them down at any time. On the other hand, the Hindu population were of the view that when their non-Muslim brethren had been forcibly evicted from across the border, they could not allow the local Muslims to keep on staying here.

After a few days a person called Shri Gopi Chand came to me and said that he had come from Rawalpindi with his wife and children. His wife Kunti Devi was suffering from pulmonary tuberculosis, and he wanted me to admit her in my sanatorium. He also wanted his three children to stay with their mother, while he wished to go back to Rawalpindi to bring some of his belongings, if he could. He promised that he would be back in two weeks, and added that if by any chance he failed to come, I was to look after his wife as my daughter. It was very difficult to accept such a responsibility under those conditions. Yet I could not help saying 'yes'. Fortunately, he came back after two weeks with some of his belongings. His wife got cured of her disease and was discharged from the hospital after about a year. Then the whole family shifted to Delhi to start their business of dry fruits. Shri Gopi Chand and his family never forgot what little I had done for them in their hour of need. Kunti Devi never failed to send me *rakhi* and *tika* every year regularly like a good daughter.

Shri Gopi Chand's visit, and his day's stay at Dharampore, during which he met the people and narrated stories about what was happening at Rawalpindi and other places in that part of the country, added to the existing tension and greatly enraged the non-Muslim population of the town.

A few days later, I learnt that a shopkeeper at Dharampore had started manufacturing small daggers and was selling them for Rs 3 to Rs 4 each. These daggers were in great demand and were purchased by many young men of both communities.

The sale of unlicensed firearms flourished. These firearms were primarily those which belonged to the British military officers in the cantonments near Dharampore. They had collected these at different fronts during World War II and had kept them as souvenirs. Since these officers were to leave India for good in the near future, they thought it best to sell the arms and make some money. These arms were mostly rifles of Japanese make and their bore was different from those used by the Indian Army. These were being sold for Rs 700 to Rs 1000 through a broker living at Sanawar. Many well-to-do people who had never handled a rifle in their lives purchased these weapons. All these developments created more and more tension and mistrust.

After a few days a batch of refugees arrived at Dharampore. They came to me and narrated the indescribable and inhuman cruelties they had suffered. Their plight was really pitiable. Some of them had nothing more than the clothes they were wearing. I listened to them with great patience and sympathy, and entered their names in a register so that I could have some idea about their numbers, the places from where they had come and the vocations they had been following there. They had many problems which required immediate attention. The first problem was of providing them with some shelter which I somehow managed satisfactorily. There was a mosque at Dharampore which was under construction. It had four rooms which had been given on rent by the management to some ex-patients and visitors. At that time seven women and five men lived there. Of them, two ladies, Miss Abbasi and Miss Abida, and their brother were sent to Aligarh. I arranged to accommodate the remaining five women in my sanatorium, and four men in the Arcadia. In this way I got all those rooms vacated in the mosque and allotted them to the refugees. In addition to this, I tried to meet their other requirements, as much as was possible, with the help of my friends and the general public. I was informed that more refugees would be coming to Dharampore in a few days. I requisitioned all the available accommodation in and around the town. Small groups of refugees started arriving at Dharampore every day, and by the end of August 1947 the number of refugees, as entered in my register, was more than the total population of the permanent Muslim residents of the town.

On 1 September 1947, a batch of refugees arrived and came to me. They were seventy in number. Six among them looked different from the rest as each one of them was wearing a long flowing yellow shirt, a *kirpan*, and a yellow turban. They called themselves *Sevadars*. I somehow learnt that they were Bhatras who had left their families at Patiala and were now out to try their hands at loot and arson, so that they could collect some booty and take it to Patiala.

They put on a miserable appearance and had sorrowful tales to tell. I listened to them patiently. Then I told them that I had not the least objection to their staying at Dharampore, but there was no roof available in or around the town, as all the available accommodation had been given to those who had come earlier, I further told them that if they still wanted to stay there, I could hire some tents and get them pitched up in the spacious ground in front of the sanatorium. I, however, made it clear to them that the number of refugees who had already arrived and whose names had been recorded in my register was more than the total Muslim population of the town and that there was no chance of their being rehabilitated there permanently. I further advised them that it would be better for them if they visited the surrounding towns like Kasauli, Subathu, Dagshai, etc., to find out what accommodation was available there. In that way, they could decide among themselves how best to divide themselves into three groups, for those three places. My advice seemed to have appealed to them, and after some consultation with the refugees then staying at Dharampore, they left the place.

They came back on September 3, and reported that they had visited all those places, and that there was no accommodation for them anywhere, nor was there any industry or project at any of those places where they could work and earn their living. They had suffered terribly at the hands of the Muslims in West Punjab. Their patience had been exhausted. They had wandered from place to place. The winter season was fast approaching and they wanted some accommodation and means of living as soon as possible. They urged that unless I made the Muslim population at Dharampore move out from there, nothing could be done for them. While this talk was going on, a few of them, who looked very bitter and revengeful, said that if I did not move them out immediately, they would finish them all in a day.

I said that if such were their designs, they should not have come to me. I told them that they could go and try to kill the Muslims. But this was something I must resist with whatever resources I had. I further said that I would have nothing to do with them and that they need not come to me again. The saner element among them intervened. They snubbed the more zealous among them. We resumed our talks. I told them that I would do my maximum to help them if they promised not to indulge in violence. At first, they did not seem prepared to give such an assurance. After some discussion among themselves, they, however, assured me that they would not indulge in violence within the boundary of Dharampore town. In turn, I told them that I would soon do something to help them. After this, they all left.

The Muslim population at Dharampore, and in the nearby villages, was heterogeneous. It consisted of permanent residents of the town, ex-patients and visitors who had come to Dharampore from various parts of the country for health reasons and were now accommodated in the Hardinge Sanatorium and Arcadia, in addition to the patients suffering from pulmonary tuberculosis getting treatment in one sanatorium or the other. There were also a few government servants. These groups, in turn, posed different problems which were to be understood and faced with courage and tact. The permanent residents of the town were engaged in various vocations like general merchants, grocers, hospital and military contractors, fruit-sellers, *tonga-wallas*, coolies, and those engaged in agriculture. All of them had, however, one thing in common: they all owned some immovable property. These people were in the greatest danger of being killed and looted.

The ex-patients and visitors who were staying at Dharampore for reasons of health belonged to different parts of the country. Those who wanted to go to Pakistan had to be sent to transit camps, while others, who wanted to go to their homes in India, had to be retained and protected till their safe conduct to their homes could be arranged.

The patients who were suffering from pulmonary tuberculosis were getting treatment as indoor patients either in the Hardinge Sanatorium, the King Edward Sanatorium or Arcadia, while others who had been staying in rented rooms had already been removed from there and accommodated in Arcadia. The patients had come from all parts of the country. This group was divided into two subgroups, i.e. those whose relatives were in Pakistan, or were in some transit camp from where they had to be sent to Pakistan, and those whose relatives were staying in India and had chosen to remain there. Their problem was that some of them had to be sent to a transit camp from where they could proceed to Pakistan, while the rest had to be kept at Dharampore till they got better or decided to go home.

There were two government employees from the sanitation department who wanted to go to Pakistan and had to be provided with safe transport from Dharampore to Kalka.

The cantonments at Dagshai, Subathu and Kasauli had sizeable Muslim populations. Some of them were permanent residents of the town, some were serving in the military in different departments, like the MES Stores, and the like. Some were contractors, while others were engaged in one vocation or another as bearers, butlers, butchers, bakers, barbers, etc. These people were in a slightly better position than those living at Dharampore, as they enjoyed protection from the military, which was however relative and temporary. It was relative in the sense that the military could not directly interfere in the law and order situation of the town without being asked by the Government, and temporary as all the regiments posted in these cantonments had received orders of transfer and they had to leave these places within a few weeks. The safest course for the Muslim population living in those places was to evacuate before the military had left for good.

The problem had been caused by the political leaders. The Muslims had to leave whether they were evicted by the refugees through arson, loot and killing, or were persuaded to evacuate peacefully without any loss of life or honour. I called the leaders of the Muslim community and informed them that, with the arrival of the refugees there, the situation had completely changed. The best thing for them was to leave the place as early as possible, or they would meet the same fate as those of the refugees who had been forcibly evicted from their hearths and homes in Pakistan. They felt naturally reluctant, and, after some thought, proposed that they could leave if they were allowed to sell their property or exchange it with some of the refugees now at Dharampore. The sale of property was not admissible under law, and the question of exchange did not arise because the properties of the refugees which had been left behind were now with the government of Pakistan. It was with great difficulty that I made them understand this point. After a long discussion, they promised to talk the matter over with the people of their community and let me know their final decision the next day.

The following day they came and informed me that they had decided to leave their property, but that they should be allowed to carry their luggage and belongings with them. I told them that, as far as I was concerned, I had not the least objection to their doing so, but they should know that the luggage they tried to take with them would expose them to the danger of attack either at Dharampore itself or later during the course of their journey. Moreover, it would be very difficult for the government to provide transport. About this they felt perturbed and, without replying they left. The tension was increasing every day. Sardar Chitwant Singh, who was posted at Dharampore as sub-inspector of police, was an obedient, reliable and resourceful young man. Personally he had affection and regard for me. I had been controlling the situation with his help but, at this stage I felt that it would be impossible for me to control any eruption with the help of only a dozen constables then posted at the police station at Dharampore.

On the morning of 6 September 1947, therefore, I sent a telegram to the Nazim of Kohistan at Kandaghat requesting him to send a military guard immediately.

That very afternoon I received a letter from Dr. F. Master, medical superintendent, King Edward Sanatorium, Dharampore, which read as follows:

At 3.30 p.m. a batch of two persons, a Sikh and a beardless man, chased one Pir Bux residing near Hafiz Fazal Ahmed's house in Dharampore up the sanatorium road, near the entrance, and killed their victim who is lying in a drain near the Lady Reading Ward and the motor garage.

The victim's four children are without their parents, and are stranded here. Will you please arrange for the disposal of the dead body and safe refugee for the orphan children?

This was shocking news. I reached the spot immediately and found that a crowd of people had already gathered there. I examined the dead body and found a number of sharp-edged wounds on it. I arranged for the burial of the dead body and took the orphan children to my sanatorium. The news about this murder spread like wildfire. For me, it was a warning signal to evacuate the Muslim population of Dharampore to safety as quickly as possible.

In the evening, a guard of five people arrived. The officer-in-charge had brought this letter with him:

Your wire to the Nazim. A guard of five military people is being sent for help. Please see that arrangements are made for their board and lodging. As soon as sufficient police guard reaches you, then send this military guard back to Kandaghat.

The arrival of the military guard at that time had a very salutary effect.

On the morning of 7 September I received the following letter from Dr. F. Master:

Since yesterday afternoon's occurrence, the Muslim inmates are begging for their safe transit up to Kalka. Thereafter, they will mind their own onward journeys. I am aware that both the routes, the cart road and the railway are very uncertain, but could it be arranged to send them along with any passing military convoy?

I would very much appreciate your guidance in the matter as their departure would ease considerably the present tense local atmosphere, and the sanatorium inmates will find ease and peace of mind.

I immediately sent a message to the commandant at Dagshai requesting that he might kindly send me a military truck to evacuate the Muslim inmates of the King Edward Sanatorium, Dharampore, who felt they were in danger. The commandant not only sent the truck but also came himself with an armoured guard. I explained the whole situation to him and sent him to the sanatorium. He evacuated all the Muslim inmates of the sanatorium and took them to Dagshai, from where he transported them to the transit camp at Kalka.

After the evacuation of the patients, Dr. F. Master sent me a letter which said:

> Many thanks for your note earlier in the day, and immense thanks and appreciation for such prompt and satisfactory action taken so kindly by you. The commandant from Dagshai with an armoured guard reached the sanatorium entrance with a military truck for removal of all the Muslim inmates from the sanatorium. With the single exception of one Mr. Naziruddin Ahmad who is bedridden with advanced disease, every other patient, their relations, the two sanatorium Muslim employees, their wives and children have left for Dagshai at 6.45 p.m.

I gave a sigh of relief at least for the time being, for, after the evacuation of the Muslim patients from the King Edward Sanatorium, Dharampore, and their safe passage to the transit camp at Kalka, the problem of Dr. F. Master was solved.

But the bigger problem still remained and it required urgent attention and immediate solution. The killing of Pir Bux by two refugees was not meant to harass the Muslim patients of the King Edward Sanatorium: it was a warning about the disaster that lay ahead. The Muslim residents of Dharampore had to be evacuated in the shortest possible time, or the refugees would start their campaign of mass killing and looting.

I called a meeting of the leaders of the refugees and assured them that I would try my level best to rehabilitate them as early as possible provided they promised that they would not indulge in violence for two days. I also promised them that I would evacuate all the Muslim residents of Dharampore the next day. They gave me the assurance that they would not resort to violence in Dharampore at least.

I then called a meeting of the leaders of the Muslim community and apprised them of the situation. They too had sensed the danger and said that they were willing to leave the next day, 8 September 1947, if I could arrange for two trucks to take them to a transit camp and provide them protection for their safety on the way. I agreed to their proposal, after which they all left. The date for their evacuation was set, but I was not sure yet as to whether these people were to be sent to Kalka where the government had started a regular camp for Muslim evacuees of the hill area, or to Subathu where the Muslim population of that place and the surrounding area had collected and started a camp of their own. After giving a serious thought to this problem, I decided in favour of Subathu, as the distance between Dharampore and Subathu was half that between Dharampore and Kalka and the Muslims at Subathu had some sort of protection from the military regiment stationed there. I informed the leaders of the Muslim community about it. They also welcomed my decision and promised that they would be ready for the journey the following day by noon.

The next day two trucks arrived at about 10.00 a.m. The Muslims were getting ready to leave. It appeared as if all would go well. But it was not to be. I got the disturbing information that some of the refugees and miscreants had blocked the road from Dharampore to Subathu at four different places with tree trunks and coaltar drums. Some refugees were also seen moving about near those blockades. I was further informed that the truck-drivers had been bribed.

My entire plan was upset. I went home in great distress. I wept and prayed to God to show me the way so that I could help to save the lives and honour of these people. For a time it all looked dark, and then a thought flashed which gave me a ray of hope. Why not send them to Dagshai which was only four miles from Dharampore? It was situated in a different direction. There was a direct road between Dharampore and Dagshai, and there was no Muslim camp there. Nobody was thus likely to forestall the move. The other advantage was that Dagshai was a cantonment where their protection was more or less guaranteed.

The truck-drivers were also to be changed. I sent one of my trusted men to Dagshai, with a message to a friend that he might kindly send to me two truck-drivers in plain clothes immediately. The scheduled time for departure arrived. All were ready. The refugees pressed me to ask the Muslims to get into the trucks. The Muslims were also getting a little suspicious as to why I was delaying their departure. But I was waiting for the new pair of truck-drivers. It was about 3.00 p.m. when the truck-drivers from Dagshai arrived. I sent the original truck-drivers to my hospital on some pretext. As soon as they were gone, I asked the Muslim residents to get into the trucks. And they all, men, women and children, got in within a few minutes. I then called the truck-drivers, who had come from Dagshai, and quietly told them to take the trucks to Dagshai. As the trucks moved in that direction, everyone, including the Muslims in the trucks, were surprised as to what had happened. In this way, all the Muslim residents of Dharampore were transported to Dagshai without the loss of a single life.

Some of the refugees, however, felt embittered and angry about this. After the departure of the Muslims, I went to my house. The Police Sub-Inspector Sardar Chitwant Singh returned to the police station. Hardly had we moved away from the place, when the refugees, and even some of the local residents, fell like hungry wolves on the shops of the Muslim evacuees. They broke open the locks and laid their hands on whatever was left there. If one was running away with a bag of rice, the other was removing a case of medicine, while still another was carrying a tin of *ghee* on his head. Chitwant Singh and I reached the bazaar again. We got all the shops locked and sealed and put the police on duty.

The road was littered with all sorts of articles, sacks, empty cases, vegetables, and so on. It presented the picture of a recent loot. We got the bazaar swept and tried to make things look orderly once again.

After that I called a meeting of refugees and told them that I had already promised them the fullest help and support. I renewed that promise. My sole concern was that there should be no violence. Everyone realized the most painful experience they had passed through and their suffering and losses. I assured them that everything possible would be done to resettle and rehabilitate them. This had a reassuring effect on the refugees and they reposed their full confidence in me.

On 9 September 1947, I took stock of the situation and found that all the Muslim inmates, the patients, their relatives and the sanatorium employees of the King Edward Sanatorium, and all the Muslim residents of Dharampore had been evacuated. There were, however, some Muslim patients left who were getting treatment in the Hardinge Sanatorium, and some in Arcadia. Some of these patients had their relatives with them. Besides, there were five ex-patients and visitors, and two government employees. All these had to be safely evacuated. I had them all, patients and others, brought to Hardinge Sanatorium, as it was easier for me to provide them with medical help and safety there and it was also comparatively easier to evacuate them from one place.

I then made enquiries and found that 21 persons—patients and their relatives—wanted to go to Pakistan. I made the necessary arrangements and evacuated twelve of them to the transit camp at Kalka. The two government servants also wanted to go to Kalka, but they wanted to leave only when the Muslim residents now at Dagshai were evacuated from there to Kalka. These, along with nine remaining patients, were handed over to the military commandant on 27 September 1947, when he passed through Dharampore and were evacuated to Kalka.

Now I was left with five women who were staying in Hardinge Sanatorium. These were ex-patients and had come there for health reasons. Three of them were related to some of my close friends. Mrs. Maimoona Begum was closely related to Syed Jamil Husain, an advocate of Sunam, who with his family was in the Samana Muslim Evacuee Camp. She wanted to be sent to Samana. Shamshad was related to Mohammad Ismail Khan, who was then staying at the Bahadurgarh Muslim evacuee camp. So, she wanted to go there. Miss Sayeeda, who was related to Dr. Abdul Majid Khan, wanted to go to Aligarh, and the remaining two, Fatima and Chhoti, wanted to go to Kanpur. None of them was willing to leave the place unless my wife or I accompanied them. For a time we all stayed there. Then I took Maimoona and Shamshad to Patiala, and from there I took Maimoona to Samana and left her with her family. I left Shamshad with my friend Mohammad Ismail Khan at Bahadurgarh camp. The remaining three stayed at Hardinge Sanatorium, Dharampore, for a few weeks, as they were afraid to travel alone in those days of disturbances. I too could not guarantee any protection during their journey to Delhi. However, when conditions became slightly better, I wrote to their relatives to come to Dharampore. Nobody came. Then I decided to escort the ladies to Delhi myself. I informed their relatives of my plan and asked them to meet me at the train by which we were travelling. I felt greatly relieved to see them all at the railway station and entrust my charge to them. It is not possible to describe in words how happy they all felt at this reunion. With this, the drama, which had suddenly erupted at Dharampore more than two months ago, came to a—in that situation not an altogether unhappy—close.

On 9 September 1947, some refugees and miscreants started looting Muslim shops at Kasauli. The situation was soon brought under control. But after this incident, the Muslim community at Kasauli realized that it was time for them also to leave.

On the tenth, I got information that the Muslim population at Kasauli had decided to leave bag and baggage by truck for Kalka. I learnt that they were doing so on the assurance from some quarter of protection being provided to them for this journey. I considered this an ill-advised plan.

I sent one of my compounders to the leader of the party at Kasauli to tell him that it would be dangerous if the party travelled with their belongings. For safety's sake they should leave all their things in their homes. I also suggested that they should avoid travelling by road and should take instead the bridle-path from Kasauli to Kalka without letting anybody have the slightest notion about their plans.

The sense of possession is far stronger in man than the sense of reason. In spite of the warning, those migrating from Kásauli were not prepared to leave their belongings behind. However, they made a slight modification in their programme. They loaded the trucks with all they wanted to carry. These trucks were left under the charge of four elderly persons. The rest of them left Kasauli on foot by the bridle-path. They all reached Kalka safely.

The trucks moved soon after the Muslims had left Kasauli by the only road connecting the place with Kalka. Some of the refugees took up positions at strategic points in the Bhagat State area, midway between Kasauli and Dharampore, and were eagerly waiting for their prey. These trucks were headed by a military truck. As the trucks reached the place where the refugees and some miscreants lay in wait, they started firing and made an attack. The military truck did not stop. It did not even care to find out what had happened and continued its onward journey. The truck drivers left their trucks and ran away to hide themselves in the bushes to save their lives. All the four Muslims in charge of the trucks were injured and the goods looted. I heard the firing and reached the spot. A transmitter was found in the goods. I brought this to Dharampore and made it over to Sardar Bir Devinder Singh, superintendent of police, who came to Dharampore the next day. I removed the injured persons from there and sent them to Dagshai Military Hospital for treatment.

I had some friends in the Muslim evacuee camp at Subathu. On 12 September, I got a message that the entire Muslim population living in the camp at Subathu had decided to leave for Kalka on the fifteenth. They had planned to leave by trucks with their goods during the night and wanted me to provide protection during their passage through Dharampore. I expressed my inability to guarantee any safety or protection in that unfavourable situation. I also told the messenger that they should not insist on taking their belongings with them and thus expose themselves to the risk of attack. The safest course for them would be to leave Subathu late in the evening on foot, and, after travelling for about four miles by road, they might take the footpath which diverted from the main road and reached Kalka directly. The path undoubtedly was narrow and difficult, but that was the only safe course. I also conveyed to them that their safety lay in keeping this plan of action a guarded secret.

Rumours, however, spread that the Muslims at Subathu were going to Kalka on 15 September. This became the talk of the town. Some conjecture that they would be going by trucks, others thought that they would be going on foot. Some others thought that they might stay at Dharampore for the night and from there proceed to Kalka.

These rumours had different effects on the various sections of the public. While the local residents of Dharampore felt panicky, fearing that the outgoing Muslims might cause some mischief passing through the town, some of the refugees felt that it was a good chance for them to waylay and loot them at some point outside Dharampore area.

On the fifteenth morning, a deputation of the residents of the town came to me and wanted me to make arrangements and take precautions so that no mischief was caused by any member of the caravan. I promised that I would not only make all possible arrangements but would also stay with them till the caravan had passed. I requested them that they, on their part, should keep their shops closed that evening. To this they all agreed.

However, some of the refugees went to a place two miles beyond Dharampore and took up positions at a curve near Cheel Chakar, and waited for the caravan there.

Sardar Chitwant Singh and I reached the *bazar* by 6.00 p.m. and found that there was a great excitement and fear among the people. At about 7.30 p.m., information came that the caravan had started. We had waited for over an hour when news came that the caravan had left the main road. Everyone was wondering what had happened. The caravan had taken the direct footpath to Kalka. This change in plans saved the lives and honour of the evacuees from Subathu.

On 27 September, the Dagshai cantonment had to be vacated by the regiment stationed there. I got a message from the commandant on the twenty-sixth to this effect. He had requested that the bazaars at Kumar Hatti and Dharampore might be kept closed from 10.00 a.m. to 12.00 noon on that day so that the military convoy along with the Muslim residents of Dharampore and Dagshai could pass peacefully without any untoward incident. This was a reasonable request. I sent a message to the bazar *chaudharis*, both at Dharampore and Kumar Hatti, to keep the shops closed on the twenty-seventh from 10.00. a.m. to 12 noon. Everyone complied with my instructions except one person named Jai Parkash, who chose to keep his shop open. The convoy started from Dagshai exactly at 10.00 a.m. and when the first jeep heading the convoy reached Kumar Hatti *bazar*, they found that a shop was open. On this an officer got out of the jeep, kicked Jai Parkash, pushed him into his shop, and bolted the shop from outside. The convoy passed on peacefully and reached Dharampore. I met the Commandant and thanked him for his full cooperation and help in those difficult days. I also handed over to him two government servants and nine patients who were still with me and who wanted to go to Pakistan. I then heaved a sigh of relief.

Soon after, Jai Parkash along with a few other shopkeepers came to me. He was very annoyed and angry because of his having been manhandled by a military officer. I listened to him with great patience and tried to pacify him as much as possible. He, however, would not listen to any of my arguments, and in great indignation sent a telegram to the Prime Minister of India. He also sent a lengthy letter to the same quarters in which he complained that a British officer had kicked and insulted him, and that when he approached the local authorities, nobody had listened to him.

His petition after passing through various departments reached me after a few months, and I was asked to enquire into this matter and submit my report. I called Shri Jai Parkash and told him that I had received his complaint, and that I had been asked to enquire into the matter. I asked him if he could give me the name of the

British officer who had manhandled him or give me his address, so that I could conduct an enquiry against him. His reply was: 'He was a monkey, and all monkeys look alike, so how could I distinguish one monkey from another, but I was sure that he was a monkey.' We all laughed at this. By then he had also cooled down and he joined in our laughter. I recorded his statement as given above and sent it back to the office from where his complaint had come. After this nothing was heard about it.

Two Muslims, Abdul Hakim, a PWD overseer posted at Chail, and Nur Mohammad Khan, a railway gang-*jamadar*, became Sikhs. Abdul Hakim wanted his children to be sent to Lahore while he would stay on in India. The evacuation of his children was duly arranged. Some months later he felt lonely and frustrated and left for Pakistan. At the request of Nur Mohammad Khan, his children were sent to Pakistan. He himself continued to stay in India.

After the departure of the Muslims from Dharampore, I was asked to work as officer in charge of the Muslim evacuee property, till the government appointed another person for the job. As such, I, with the help of the revenue officer, got a complete and detailed list prepared of the Muslim property like shops, stalls, houses, agricultural land, etc., at Dharampore and the surrounding area.

A list of the names of the refugees who were staying at Dharampore was already with me as entered in the register at the time of their arrival. They were pressing for an early allotment of houses and shops, and had submitted their applications for this purpose.

On 20 September, I wrote a letter to Sardar Durga Dhar Jayal, Nazim Kohistan, informing him that I had got prepared a complete list of the evacuee property, and requested him to visit Dharampore at an early date so that the seals on houses and shops might be broken in his presence, the goods contained therein auctioned and the work of allotment started. In response to my request, the Nazim visited Dharampore on the afternoon of the 27 September.

I gave him the list of the evacuee property, the register containing the names of the refugees and the applications they had submitted for allotment of houses, shops, lands, etc. The seals on the shops and houses were broken, and all the goods that had been left were taken out and auctioned in his presence.

I strongly urged him to have refugees rehabilitated as early as possible to save them from further hardship. We discussed this matter and he explained that the real difficulty was that he was not authorized to make permanent allotment. He, however, offered to make allotments on a temporary basis to which the refugees agreed. The work of allotment was started in the Nazim's office at Kandaghat. All formalities of temporary allotment were completed in two or three weeks and the refugees were resettled as best as could be done in that situation. They were happy and grateful to have some place which they could call their own.

I feel it my honest duty to say that all this was possible with the ungrudging cooperation of friends who were prompted by the same ideology and thinking which lay behind my own actions.

At the time the country attained independence, Punjab had to write its history with the blood and tears of lakhs of Punjabis who had to leave their homes and hearths and all that they possessed in West Punjab that had fallen to the lot of Pakistan. Many of them had to sacrifice their kith and kin at the altar of freedom.

About eight million people were displaced from what became Pakistan. They kept pouring into Indian territory for months, a ceaseless stream of human misery. About twenty-four lakhs of them settled in the Punjab. This was about one-fifth of the total population. The absorption of such a vast number into the strained and limited economy of the state was no small matter. Apart from the expenditure involved, it put the administrative machinery to severe test. Nobody knew how the state would recover from the shock.

The government made plans and provided budgets for them, but these could never have been implemented successfully had not the people in general, and the refugees in particular, displayed a spirit of cooperation and courage. The displaced persons had lost their homes, but not their hearts. They were hard-working, enterprising and business-minded people. They mixed freely with the older population and began to plan their future without brooding over the past. There were fresh lands to conquer and fresh heights to scale. New farms, villages and townships sprang up. Industries, large, medium and small, and small crafts began to take shape. In brief, the displaced persons gave ample proof of their native Punjabi resilience and hardiness. The Punjab, which presented a scene of utter desolation in 1947, is now a progressive state, with the highest growth rate and highest per capita income in the nation. To this all-round development the displaced persons, have made an invaluable contribution. The Punjab has not only recovered from the devastating effects of the partition but has also marched ahead. It would be no exaggeration to say that like a phoenix a new Punjab has arisen out of its ashes.

This brief account will, perhaps, be incomplete if I do not mention what I received from my friends and well-wishers in lieu of the humble efforts I made to discharge my duty as a human being towards fellow human beings. I have paid two visits to Pakistan. The first one was in 1949 when I visited Karachi on my way to London, and the other in 1968 when I visited Panja Sahib (Hasan Abdal), Nankana Sahib and Baoli Sahib at Lahore as the leader of a party of Sikhs from India who had gone there on a pilgrimage.

Here I will confine myself to my first visit as it was soon after partition and it was in my private capacity. In 1949, I was awarded a fellowship, under the Norwegian Help to Europe Programme, to undergo a course in tuberculosis at Oslo, and to particularly study the antituberculosis programme as conducted in the Scandinavian countries. I decided I would first go to London, stay there a week, and then go on to Oslo.

I planned to go through Karachi so that I could meet some of my friends there. I informed them about my programme and of the date and time of my arrival. I had to enplane from Palam and reached there well in time. About fifteen minutes before the takeoff, I heard an announcement over the public address system saying that Dr. Khushdeva Singh should visit the police office at the airport. I was a bit surprised. However, I went. There a gentleman asked me why I was going through Karachi. My reply was: 'Is it forbidden to go through Karachi?' He said it was not that, but all the same it was better if I could reconsider my decision and go through Bombay. I in turn told him that I had already informed my friends at Karachi, and it would not be proper to disappoint them by changing my route. I left the office and proceeded to board my plane. It was a Dakota and there were only a few passengers. All of them were Europeans.

The first halt was Jodhpur where one passenger, a Muslim, boarded the plane, and occupied a seat near me. He was a complete stranger to me, and, without any introduction, began to say: '*Sardarji, gharan wadhoo hi ho jo Karachi noon ja rahe ho?*' (Sardarji, you must be an unwanted member of your family that you are going to Karachi.) I was taken aback by this remark. Yet I gathered myself and said, 'Yes, sir, I am an unwanted member of my family, but you need not bother about me.' I then sat quietly, but it set me thinking. Then the plane reached Karachi.

There I saw a crowd of people, men and women, some in *burqa* waving their handkerchiefs at me. As I stepped out, the first man to greet me was Mr. Abdul Wakil Khan, superintendent of police, who was posted at the airport. He touched my feet and greeted me: 'How are you, uncle?' I embraced him. In the meantime, the Muslim passenger, who had enplaned at Jodhpur, came out. The police constables pounced upon him. I did not know what was happening. Abdul Wakil Khan told me: 'Uncle, he is a smuggler and we are tired of him. Today, we will teach him a lesson.'

My friends took me to a room at the airport where we all sat down and talked. Then we all had lunch together. I had to travel from Karachi to London by the KLM airlines which was scheduled to arrive at 2.30 a.m. I had, therefore, to stay there for about twelve hours. We had tea at about 5.00 p.m. and I told my friends that they had given me so generously of their time, I thought it would be too much for them to wait the whole night and suggested that they must spare themselves the trouble. But nobody left until it was dinner time. We ate dinner together. Then they said that they were leaving and that I must have a little rest before enplaning. I closed the door and went to sleep, but all of them, as I learnt later, had not gone anywhere. They only moved to the adjoining room and stayed there. I got up at about 1.45 a.m. and, when I opened the door, I saw that all of them were still there. They had retired only to allow me to get some sleep. They all accompanied me to the plane, and, before parting, presented me with a small basket of grapes. I had no words to express my gratitude for the overwhelming affection with which I was treated and happiness this stopover had given me.

For my return journey, I again chose the same route, and informed my friends at Karachi about my schedule. It was a bright sunny day—something unusual in the month of December in this part of the world—as I reached the Oslo airport to catch my flight. The departure of the plane was announced and all the passengers hurried forward. Strangely, a cat appeared from somewhere and passed across the runway in front of the plane. We went up the gangway and occupied our seats. I was tying my seat-belt when a gentleman sitting next to me looked behind and said in a low voice, 'Oh God, help us!' I was rather surprised to hear this, and enquired as to what was the matter. He said, 'Don't you see the cat crossing our path. And here are two clergymen travelling with us. Could there be anything more ominous than this?' I felt as if I were in the eastern hemisphere.

The plane took off. The first scheduled landing was at Amsterdam. As the plane reached there, we found that the weather was very bad. Dense clouds and fog had reduced visibility to almost nil. The plane circled over the airport twice, but got word from the ground authorities that the weather was too bad for it to land. The pilot directed the plane towards Brussels. There the fog was even denser than at Amsterdam. The plane could not land there either. By now the passengers were becoming anxious. However, the pilot took the plane into the interior of the country and landed safely at a military airport. The moment the plane landed, it was surrounded by military police. After a few minutes an officer arrived. According to the rules, the baggage of all the passengers was searched, and certain documents were signed by the pilot. After this we were all free, and we moved on to a lounge, where drinks and snacks were served. The passengers were now in a mood of gay abandon. They sang, danced and laughed. I was wondering to myself how those people who were the very picture of panic and misery barely an hour previously had forgotten those tense moments of anxiety and given themselves up to gaiety. But that is how we human beings are built, I thought.

After some time two buses arrived, and all the passengers were loaded into these. We were provided with packages of food for the journey and the buses moved. For a time the occupants continued to be mirthful, but slowly all became quiet. Some of them started dozing in their seats. Others looked on blankly while some were snoring heavily. The journey continued till we arrived in Amsterdam, where we were accommodated in the American Hotel for the night. The next day we all got up rather late. We had our breakfast in the hotel, and from there we were taken to the airport. There too we had to wait for a few hours before resuming the journey, and the plane reached Karachi at 11.30 p.m. There was no friend to meet me as they had come the previous day and returned disappointed.

Hardly had I stepped out of the plane when a group of journalists surrounded me. They started off like this: 'Sardarji, where are you coming from?' I replied that I was a doctor and was coming from Oslo after attending a course there. Then they asked if I had come to Karachi on some mission? I replied, 'Yes, I have come on a goodwill mission.' Then they wondered if I represented any society. My reply was that I was a member of the largest society in the world, the Society of Mankind. On this they all laughed, and became more inquisitive. They asked many questions which I answered as best as I could and kept me engaged for about half an hour, after which they left with a handshake and *khuda hafiz.*

From there I moved on to the customs counter to collect my baggage. There was a young man on duty. He asked me, 'Sardarji, how have you come to Karachi?' 'Dear son,' I said, 'I have come from Oslo, and am on my way to Delhi.' The next question he asked me was what I was carrying in my suitcase. My reply was: 'Here are the keys; you may open it and search it.' He said it was none of his business to open boxes, and I, in turn, politely said: 'Dear son, I am an old man and I am tired. Can't you do even that much for me?' He took the keys, opened my suitcase, and closed it without making any search. He directed me to proceed to my room on the first floor where I had to spend the night, for my plane was to leave the next morning.

Emboldened by this change in his demeanour, I asked the officer if he could do me a little favour and send word to Mr. Abdul Wahid Khan informing him of my stopover. 'Who is this Abdul Wahid Khan?' he asked. I told him that he was the father of the superintendent of police posted at the airport. 'You mean the father of Wakil Sahib,' he said, and asked me how I knew him. I told him that he was one of my dear friends. He gave me a porter to take the baggage to my room. I locked the room from inside and was just going to bed when there was a knock at the door. As I opened the door, I found Abdul Wahid Khan standing there. I cannot describe my happiness. We settled down to a long chat about the good old days we had spent together and continued till three in the morning. He then left insisting that I must get some sleep.

I was up again at 7.30 a.m. and was getting ready when again I heard a knock at the door. Wahid had come now with a breakfast basket. We had our breakfast and then came down to the lounge. We had hardly been there a few moments when a police constable came, saluted me and offered me a betel. He asked me if I remembered him. Before I could speak, he told me that once he had accompanied me from Samana to Patran for a postmortem examination. He was still there when another constable came, and after saluting me offered me a betel. I recognized him, for he had been at Sunam during my posting there. In this way, one after another, six constables came to me and I gratefully accepted betels from each one of them.

It was now time for the takeoff. I embraced Wahid and proceeded towards the plane. The constables accompanied me right up to the plane, and, when I was about to enter the aircraft, all of them stood in a line and saluted me. I acknowledged it with folded hands and tears in my eyes. I quietly went up the gangway and occupied my seat. As I was involuntarily fastening the seat belt my thought ran to those simple constables and their most charming gesture. 'Love is stronger than hatred, love is far stronger than hatred, love is far stronger than hatred, love is far stronger than hatred, love is far stronger than hatred at any time and anywhere. It was a thousand times better to love and die, than to live and hate,' I kept repeating to myself.

Oranges and Apples

This is adapted from an interview of Kamlabehn Patel by Ritu Menon and Kamla Bhasin.

The loss of lives and property, and the widespread violence that accompanied partition have been well documented by historians and scholars of Independence. Less well-known is the incidence of the large-scale abduction of women of all three communities, Hindu, Muslim and Sikh, during that period. No official estimates exist of the exact number of such abductions, but it is safe to assume that there would have been well over 10,00,000 or more. In the aftermath of partition, the governments of India and Pakistan were swamped with complaints by the relatives of 'missing' women, seeking to recover them either through government, military or voluntary efforts. Recognizing the enormity of the problem, the two governments entered into an Inter-Dominion Agreement in November 1947, to recover as many women as possible, as speedily as possible, from each country and restore them to their families.

In all, approximately 30,000 women—12,000 Muslim and 18,000 non-Muslim—were recovered by the police and social workers of both countries, primarily between 1947 and 1952. Kamlabehn Patel, an Indian social worker, was stationed in Lahore for a few years and was actively involved in recovering Hindu and Sikh women from Pakistan. Recovery work had been entrusted to the Women's Section, Ministry of Relief and Rehabilitation, under the direction of two principal honorary advisers, Rameshwari Nehru and Mridula Sarabhai. Kamlabehn Patel, a Gandhian, was Mridula Sarabhai's right-hand woman in Lahore till 1952, and represented both India and Pakistan on the Special Tribunals set up by both governments, to resolve disputed cases.

How I got involved in recovery work was by accident. Actually, I was supposed to go and work with Bapu at Sabarmati Ashram but I didn't really want to go there. Mridulabehn came to my rescue.

She told Bapu there are other things she can do as her health is fragile. I will find something else for her. So she asked me to work with her. I said, but what can I do? She said, you be my personal secretary. But I can't type, I said, I don't speak English, how can I be your secretary? She said, look all these skills can be bought, I don't need those from you—I'll give you a typist, you don't worry about all that. What I want from you is that you should be able to take decisions on important matters if I'm not around, so that I know, Kamla is there, I don't need to worry.

I thought about it for a while and then she said I would go on six months' probation! I first went to Pakistan in November 1947. Mridulabehn sent me a telegram asking me to come to Delhi. When I reached there, she wasn't around, but I was handed a ticket to go to Lahore. I didn't know why I was being sent there, I was just told, you have to reach there immediately.

Shiv Prakashji, our first High Commissioner, was already there. He was quite adamant that proper arrangements should be made before we went—he thought Bimlabehn was crazy not to have insisted on it. However, we went. We had to establish a camp in Lahore, meet government officials and start a dialogue. We had not attended any conclave regarding this work and so at times were quite at sea about it, and yet went ahead.

Gradually, we learnt how to handle the work and situations as they arose. We made mistakes, small as well as big ones. For instance, one day a peon came and said to me that Kapur Saheb (an ICS officer) sends his *salaams*. I did not understand the meaning of this '*salaam*', so I said please give him my *salaams* too! At night, when all gathered, I mentioned this episode to everyone. Then I understood that this was his way of calling for me and that I should have gone to see him. The next day I went to see Kapur Saheb and apologized for not understanding his message!

There were approximately 22,000 women who were in my charge. Thousands of women who came from various districts of Pakistan and so many others from several places in India, all had to be rescued. Now when I look back at all that I was able to accomplish, I myself marvel at my own courage and the circumstances that pushed me into this work.

There was an ICS officer, Mr. K. L. Punjabi, who felt that we had not recovered enough women in proportion to the money spent on this work. But I said to him: 'When you see a family reunited, you see a father meet his daughter and the joy on their faces, you don't remember the lakhs that have been spent. When you see their happiness, you realize it is worth it.'

Let me tell you about Sialkot. I went to Sialkot which was a closed district. I had no intention of going there because of the whole Azad Kashmir business. It was an anxious time since there was no agreement on Kashmir. I was instructed to go with the SP, wearing a *shalwar-kameez*. No sari, under any circumstances. This SP was a complete rogue. He used to worm out all the information from us by being on his best behaviour. Often I told Mridulabehn that I was afraid of dealing directly with him and because he was waiting to catch me out, I would make a mistake. And my mistake would be India's mistake. She said, don't worry, only you can do this work, and I'm as capable of making a mistake as you are.

You can imagine how I felt, an Indian woman entering a closed district at that time. . . . We were fighting about Kashmir. . . . But they were so excited that an Indian woman was coming! People came to see me, cried while asking about their relatives on this side. They asked about the situation obtaining on the other side. In their anxiety they asked questions which seemed foolish, like: 'My mother's relative went that side, would you know where he went? Did you ever meet him?' They were very hospitable towards me— a woman had come from Hindustan to see them—in spite of the fact that we were within five miles of the fighting.

I was still afraid because I was an Indian. Suppose a crowd had gathered to throw stones, attack? But the opposite happened. On the way nothing happened because the SP was in his uniform, but I was afraid that he himself might start something.

You see, the Hindus never did accept the Muslims because if they had, these things would have been avoided. If they had looked upon them as one does on a younger or older brother, then they would not have developed this complex. Even the common people treated them like untouchables, never let them get close. Look, I am a Gujarati. Among us, there was not much warmth for them. In Gujarat, there were no Muslim *zamindars* or highly educated people, only farmers or artisans. They could not equal either the money or education of the Muslims of the Punjab or UP. At the time of partition, when I went to Punjab for the first time, I realized that there was a lot of socializing and warmth among the two communities. They used to embrace each other and when they were forced to separate, they longed to see each other again. If they were together alone, they would embrace, but in public they would shout slogans against each other!

When the recovery work started progressing, this antagonism became much sharper. Of course, it became an issue between two countries then. There was this young Pathan girl—she must have been about 15 or 16, whose family used to go to Kashmir every year for the summer. They were from Rawalpindi. There she used to meet a young boy from Amritsar, a Hindu, whose family also used to go to Srinagar.

When the trouble after partition began, and she saw all the camps being set up around Rawalpindi she realized something was going on and that she wouldn't be able to meet young Jeetu any more. Her name was Kismet. So what did she do? She ran away to Amritsar. She had no idea where Jeetu's house was, but all she knew was that he lived there. How she got there is a story by itself.

She arrived at the Hindu refugee camp in Rawalpindi—she had taken a few belongings with her in a small bag—went to the camp commander (the Indian Army was in charge of this camp) and said, 'I am a Hindu girl separated from my parents—please help me reach India.' Because she was so young, he took her himself in his jeep to an Amritsar-bound train and saw her off.

When Kismet got down at Amritsar—she was not at all anxious because she had succeeded in running away—she waited patiently in one corner of the platform. A volunteer saw her—those days Bhimsen Sachar (later Chief Minister of Punjab) sometimes used to be at the station to receive incoming trains. He was there that day, and the volunteer took Kismet to him. She told him her story—that she was from a village in Rawalpindi, had been with her maternal aunt when the riots broke out. After some days, when she finally reached the safety of a camp, she was told that her parents had already started out for India. Now she was quite alone. Bhimsen Sachar instructed one of the local workers to take special care of her and she managed to find Jeetu's parents' address from this worker, in the course of conversation. She then sent him a message to come and fetch her from the camp! No one doubted her story or the fact that she was a Hindu refugee! But because she was a minor she wasn't allowed to leave the camp with Jeetu. Somehow, he and his parents managed to get permission from the deputy commissioner to take her away from the camp, and before anyone knew anything, they had got married in the Golden Temple.

Now this case became a prestige issue between India and Pakistan. Her parents reported her missing, the Pakistan Rehabilitation Minister requested Gopalaswamy Iyengar to look for Kismet and send her back to Rawalpindi. Gopalaswamy Iyengar called Mridulabehn and me and asked us to make a special effort to find her.

Now, Jeetu knew that something was going on. So when I next came to Amritsar from Lahore, he rushed to my office and told me the whole story. It had been discussed in the Search Service Bureau at Amritsar and was registered as a case of abduction, so he knew about it. He pleaded with me, saying it was not an abduction at all, that Kismet had come on her own, that they had been properly married. But by now it was an inter-dominion issue: K. L. Punjabi and another senior officer, Nagpal, and myself, discussed the case. I was not at all inclined to hand her back to Pakistan. How could we consider it an abduction when the girl had travelled all the way from Rawalpindi herself, taking such a risk? And how could the Government of India force her to return against her will? But Punjabi did not agree with me. He said, 'If we don't honour the agreement, how can we expect Pakistan to enforce it— we have to consider the wider interests of the country.'

Well, we managed to persuade Jeetu and Kismet to meet Mridulabehn at Hotel Amritsar—that was where she camped when she came there—but it was a difficult meeting. Mridulabehn offered to accompany Kismet up to Wagah to meet her parents, but she refused. She told me afterwards, 'If God himself came with me, I wouldn't go! My parents will kill me as soon as they see me.'

Now, Jeetu was very worried because he thought the police might come and take her away forcibly. So both of them ran away to Calcutta! Nobody knew where they were, and the Pakistan government was putting great pressure on India to recover her.

It's a long story, but ultimately Jeetu and Kismet returned to Amritsar and a message was sent to Kismet's uncle, in the External Affairs Ministry of Pakistan, to come to Delhi to discuss the case. We arranged for him to meet Kismet, in our presence, and it took almost five days to persuade her to return to Lahore and meet her parents. She was told she would stay with the IG of Police there,

Khan Qurban Ali. She needn't go to Rawalpindi, and after a week she should decide what she wanted to do.

Jeetu, Kismet, her uncle and the Pakistan SP Rizvi, arrived in Lahore by plane—Kismet was loaded with gold jewellery. We went to the Secretariat where we were supposed to hand Kismet over to the IG, but she refused to get out of the car without Jeetu. After a lot of arguing finally Jeetu persuaded her to go in, saying he would come and get her in seven days' time.

From Khan Qurban Ali's place her parents took her home— Khan Saheb should not have allowed it, but he did. We were very upset but what could we do? Mridulabehn and I went to her *Abba's* place where we were made to wait for a long time. Finally Kismet came out from the *zenana* and we got a real shock. She was completely transformed. Her walk, her dress, her behaviour—we thought it must be her sister, not her. Then she turned on us and with an accusing finger pointed at Mridulabehn, said: 'There she is! That woman with short hair is the one who prevented me from coming back! I asked her so many times but she wouldn't listen. And let that Jeetu come near me—I'll tear him to bits and feed him to the dogs!'

We couldn't believe our ears. Could this be the same Kismet who had refused to come? But there was no point in staying there any longer, so we left. I was both shocked and dismayed: what would I say to Jeetu? How could I explain this turn of events to him? When he came to see me in Amritsar, he was very angry and very sad, and he said I had betrayed him. 'You should have taken me with you,' he shouted. 'Why didn't you take me? She would never have stayed back if I had been with you.' He never recovered from Kismet's action, and tried many times to find her in Lahore. I tried to dissuade him, but he wouldn't listen. He was like a man possessed. He never did find her, of course.

Even today, I tremble a little when I remember this incident. We were hundred per cent sure she would come back. Kismet said all those things to rehabilitate herself in her parents' eyes, out of fear, that is why she changed. I met her mother, father and sister— they were so happy that their daughter had come back. Jeetu's family were *banias*—he was the only son and they were all very happy with Kismet—what was special was that she was a friend's daughter. And Kismet argued with us for almost an hour. Rizvi, her uncle, Jeetu and I were there. She said to me, I will not leave Jeetu behind, I will take him with me. I understand that she was only a 14-year-old girl and that after the thrill of eloping passed, she was afraid that her parents would kill her, would not keep her. She was very young, if she had been older, it may have been different. Now, Sudarshan was older, about 23 years old, very strong-willed, but she melted when she saw her brother and father crying. So, she went with them, but then she thought it was wrong to do so and she came back.

It was such a difficult time, so many people leaving their homes, so much violence.

But I think there were economic reasons, too. The number of Hindus in the Punjab was greater than the number of Muslims in India. Another reason could be that wherever the Hindus went, they exploited the Muslims. There were quite a few *bania* moneylenders who lent money at such exorbitant rates of interest that they were like bloodsuckers. When an opportunity offered itself, they took their revenge. So many factors were involved, it was not only one factor that brought about partition. One cannot only blame the Muslims for subjecting Hindu women to violence, the Hindus also did it. In the Golden Temple 200 women were made to dance naked for the whole night.

Yes, in 1947, not in the Durbar Sahib, but in its compound. And so many people enjoyed this unholy show. If I tell this to anyone, they don't like it, but these are facts. I will talk on behalf of women. I was not a politician. If I had been one, I would have said that the Muslims did everything, but we never did anything. But we were no less—how many we kept back, how many women we sold in the same way that baskets of oranges or grapes are sold or gifted. Women were distributed in the same way. You may ask why we uprooted these women again, but in my view, they were never ever secure, had never put down roots.

The Muslim women we recovered in India were mostly sent back; there were approximately 12,000 women. Ours were about 9,000. Most of the Muslim women were recovered from the Punjab, from the villages and towns.

But more from the villages. That is because economic factors played a great part. Those nine or ten thousand women who were brought back from Pakistan were accepted by the Hindus. Why? Because of economic factors. People had come from there as refugees and so they did not have money. They did not have a woman to do the housework—a housewife. But here, there was a woman available. So forgetting everything, they took her. They accepted them out of helplessness, not out of broad-mindedness. It was not so important for the Muslims because they did not think of the women as impure, and they hesitated much less when taking them back. But not the Hindus.

This was my experience. A Hindu woman felt that she had been rendered impure, had become sullied, was no longer *pativrata*. A Muslim woman did not feel like this. It was not in her blood; it is in ours. We feel we have been polluted, we are no longer worthy of showing our faces in public. How can we face our family when we go back? We reassured the women saying, 'See how many times your father has come to fetch you.' Even then they would feel ashamed of themselves, because this tradition is so deeply ingrained in us. And Muslims were not stigmatized by society. While Hindus say that since they (the women) have lived for so long with a Muslim. . . . Their parents would say that they had left their daughters with one or other of their aunts—they could not say openly that their daughters had been abducted.

This is our psychology. In the upper and middle classes this difficulty was there, but not in the lower classes. A middle class woman might commit suicide. There were some cases like this, of course, but not too many. I have written about a case where the parents thought it was all right to sacrifice the life of a young girl in order to save a whole family. And when we were arguing about her recovery the father said, this is our girl, and the girl denied it because she was terribly hurt by their behaviour. She said, 'I don't want to go back. I have married of my own free will. I don't want anything from my parents.' When she refused to return, it became very awkward. She was in the home of a police inspector. We felt that if we had found an abducted woman in the house of a police inspector, then how could we expect the police to do any recovering? That is why we had to bring her back. Our social worker went to Multan and met her. She said, 'I will not go.' Then we requested the Pakistan authorities to leave her in our camp in the Ganga Ram Hospital (Lahore) for a couple of days. Then if she said that she didn't want to return it was fine, but she would have to report at the camp and confirm that she didn't want to. So, she was brought by force. Her husband said, 'I will take her back at night.' I said, 'She will not return at night, she will stay the night with me.' He said, 'Why should my wife stay with you, what right have you to keep her?' Then I said, 'She is after all, our daughter. When a daughter comes to her mother's place, she stays for a few days. She has no parents.' That girl kept saying that she didn't want to go to her parents, she wouldn't budge an inch. After two or three days, she broke down, she told us that her parents had been told by the police inspector, 'If you leave your daughter, gold and land with me, I will escort you all to the cantonment in India.' That man was already married and had children. He didn't need to marry her. He told her father, 'You give me this girl in exchange for escorting you all to an Indian cantonment.' Then her father give him his daughter, 30 *tolas* of gold and his house. One night I called the girl to my bedside and said, 'If you want to go back (to the inspector), then I will send you. If you don't want to go back to your parents, don't go, but please tell me why.' Then she became tearful and said, '*Behenji*, what can I tell you? I am not happy at this inspector's place. As long as he is in the house, I am all right, but as soon as he leaves on duty, his wife harasses me, calls me the daughter of a *kafir* and so on. She makes me do all the work as if I were her maid. The man loves me, but he is under pressure from his family. But those parents who sacrificed me—I will never go back to them.' I said, 'All right, don't go back to them, stay with us.' We couldn't let her return to Pakistan. This was a prestige case. If we let it go, we would have to eat humble pie in front of Pakistan. We had to bring her before the Tribunal when it met. Just before that I had thought that I would get her married to a nice boy in India, specially because she was not happy with this man. If she had been happy, I would not have thought this way, but she was unhappy and would have had to spend the rest of her life in this fashion. There was an officer whose private assistant was a very good man. I let the boy and the girl meet once, in secrecy, because it was against our policy. For this Mridulabehn got very angry with me, but I was quite obstinate. I insisted that we had no right to keep a woman in this manner. When everything was settled, I decided that this young woman could now face the Tribunal without flinching. During the cross-examination, the Pakistan SP called for the Inspector (her abductor) as a witness. Imagine that! But we were forced to agree because we were told that as a police inspector he could make trouble for us in our recovery work, later. So he came. Meera (the girl in question) was also called in and asked,

'Where do you want to go?' She said that she wanted to go to India. The man glared at her and shouted, 'So you want to go to India, eh?' She said, 'Yes, I want to go to India.' Then he yelled, 'What do you think you are saying? I saved your parents, I have spent so much money on you. Even the bangles you are wearing are mine.' I intervened and told them (the escorting police) that she should be taken in to change into her own clothes. Then I gave him back the clothes, gold and other things he had given her, saying she could do without.

She got married later, but not in Pakistan obviously. We had the marriage in Amritsar afterwards, with the proper arrangements. The boy got a posting to Shimla after a transfer from Pakistan. Her parents also came to the wedding. Five or six of us friends, got together and arranged a tea party for her. Now this fact, after being exaggerated, got to Mridulaji's ears and, of course, she put me on the mat because these kinds of cases were outside our jurisdiction and we should not have been involved in them—they were really Mrs. Thapar's responsibility, because they had to do with rehabilitation, not recovery. Mridulabehn said, you were my representative when you did this, you exceeded your brief. I said well, if you like, I will put in my resignation and go back to Bombay. I felt deep inside me that I had carried out my responsibility faithfully. If, because of me, their policy had been harmed, then I would go back. At that she cooled down. Then, after a year when I was in Amritsar, this girl came to see me with her child. She came to see me specially, all the way from Shimla. They were both very happy, she said. But I can't forget her anger at being sacrificed by her parents.

One of the best things about our recovery work was the fact that all parties—Communist, Socialist and Congress, etc.—sank their differences and worked together. Our social workers used to accompany the police party—their women never did, they didn't have the motivation to go with the police. The police used to bring the women and leave them in the camp. We had several members of the Congress, Socialists and even Communists among our social workers. One day, Begum Fatima of Lahore said to us, 'I have heard that you have kept a Muslim girl as a prisoner and hidden her in the camp.'

'What are you saying Begum Fatima,' I replied, 'we have hidden four crore people, if you wish you can take them all.' And, in truth,

I *had* hidden her! She was a disputed case. But one had to do these things because the circumstances demanded it. I said that for one thing, our girls have gone to sleep and for another, you're talking about one girl, when I have four crores here! We were always being accused of keeping Muslim women. I was especially prone to this charge because I had to meet the Collector for sorting out problems relating to the camp—its site, rations and allotment of houses. Urdu newspapers published reports that India had sent out very inexperienced young girls to do recovery work!

We Are Still Theirs

This is adapted from an interview of Amrik Singh of Doberan village by Sudesh Vaid and Urvashi Butalia.

Amrik Singh, a retired schoolteacher belonged to Doberan village, in Rawalpindi district. This village was seriously affected by the Rawalpindi riots of March 1947, though not perhaps as badly as Thamali, where the gurudwara was burnt down and several people were killed, or Thoa Khalsi where over a hundred women jumped into a well to escape threatened conversion. Amrik Singh tells us that about 70 persons were killed—he says 'martyred'—in the gurudwara by their own families and several homes were looted and destroyed. He is also, however, convinced that the attackers were not from their village but were outsiders.

This interview was part of a larger project that studied the experiences of ordinary men and women during and after partition. They are still so real that the time interval does not seem to matter.

From what I understand, partition is all politics. The Muslims from there (i.e., Doberan) did not want at all to send us away. Nor did they want to kill us. In fact, the truth is that those people who came and attacked our village, those who burnt down the village, did not belong to our village and were not from nearby. They had been brought in from far away. They did not even know us. In fact, some Muslims even rescued our daughters. Such a girl was Krishan Kaur. On 9 March 1947—I'm speaking of the time when the riots took place in Rawalpindi district—this was not partition, it was before partition. The children's exams were finished. In fact, it was at the time of Holi. The wheat harvest was not quite ready; it had not ripened; it was only half-ripe and this took place in March; the rains had not yet come. The harvest was standing, though not ready to be cut. On 9 March my son arrived, my mother had come earlier. All my other relatives—my *mamis*, *masis*, nephews, nieces, brothers-in-law, *nani*—they were all in the village. There is a *thana* about

10 miles from my village, and also a post office. My son used to study there. On Saturday he took a bus and came home. . . .

Our village is Doberan; he took a bus from Kallar. He said he had come to know that there would be an attack on the village. The people were surprised. As it happened, in our gardens—we had two gardens—a man called, Santji, used to live there. This boy left the *haveli*, untied the horse and went to our garden and said: 'Santji there's some trouble in the village, some noise. Come along with me.' This place is some way, about a mile from our village. We had two gardens by the river, one on its right and one on its left. The river flows throughout the year, the water is very pure. Our village was about a mile from there. But Santji did not come, saying, 'I'm a *sadhu*, what do I have to do with this?' So the boy returned. He tethered the horse. Suddenly, lots of people descended, they even brought camels and they started looting the shops. Thousands of people—in our village there were 595 persons on 9 March, that included old men, old women, children, young boys, young girls, married and unmarried. One or two had some arms, some a little ammunition. These people started collecting at one place. . . . We have two *gurudwaras*. It was mostly in the Nirmala Sant Gurudwara that people collected because there was a lot of space there.

These people began to loot, then they began setting fire to one side of the village. There was an old man, a good man and they said to him, 'Go to Inam Khor *Zaildar*, to *Zaildar* Sejawal Khan. . . .' Sardar Jagat Singh went to him, and said, 'Do something.' Sejawal Khan answered: 'What can I do? I don't know these people.' Nevertheless, there were some from among them who joined them and took part in the looting. They snatched jewels from us, money also, they looted houses, shops, jewels, wood. . . . These people were in the gurudwara, three days, from 9 March to 11 March. There was a reservist from the army named Thera Singh. He used to get on top of the roofs of houses and throw stones at them, at the Mirzas. In my village there were 6 or 7 Mirzas whose houses stood together at a slightly elevated place. From there a Mirza shot at him and he fell and died instantly.

The Mirzas were local, but the invaders who came were from outside. My village is Doberan. The next one is called Thamali. Further there is Kallar or Thoa or Choa. . . . They were not from these villages, they were from much farther away . . . somehow there was the feeling that these people [Sikhs] should be eliminated.

As far as I can understand, this was a game played by the British. Even if Attlee wanted to give us independence, there were many others who were against it. In Rawalpindi, the commissioner, a man called King, said (these were his very words): 'You've seen nothing here, this is nothing, wait till you see it there. This is nothing, wait till you see what will happen in East Punjab.' This meant these people had some knowledge of what was going on. The Rawalpindi people appealed to the senior officers and asked for help. They said our villages are being burnt, please help us. But nothing was done, if help had been sent . . . on the twelfth when the army truck went, all those people who left could have been rescued. This could have happened earlier, couldn't it?

On the twelfth, the military trucks reached all the villages, one truck in each village, they could have done this earlier, this was all a game. It did not help the *angrez* (the British) to stay, but it did a great deal of harm to us. Some of the Mirzas' sons were among those who killed our people.

Otherwise, we had a very good equation with those people. For example, my *mamaji*, his was the second death in his family; he was on top of the gurudwara; he was not a military man and he did not know how to stand on the roof. A shot was fired, and he fell. The question now is, if on 9 March the fighting took place, if even on 10 March, there had been something from the government, if there had been a truck, even one truck with one or two soldiers in it, none of this would have happened. This was their plan, the plan of the British government. They felt these Hindus and Sikhs are Congress people. They are the ones who want us out, let's kill them. It did not help them at all. On the ninth, the village was set on fire. Our people were gathered in the gurudwara. Little by little the fire spread to the gurudwara too . . . . All our people, some five or six hundred people gathered in one place. . . . They needed bathrooms, latrines, food. . . . Those people were standing outside. . . . Our area is very rocky, there are round stones there. They would throw a stone from far away and it would come and hit the gurudwara.

These poor people could not even get out. In that gurudwara there was only one well, in which there was very little water. . . . This was actually some distance from the gurudwara, and people had great difficulty even to get there, those three nights, on the ninth, tenth and eleventh. They said, 'Come on, come out, we will free you.' What choice did they have? They went. In the fields stood

Sardar Barkat Singh's *haveli*. They were locked up there. Once they were locked up . . . some of the Mirzas from our village . . . and there were many outsiders, they took up sticks and axes and started killing them, even as they just sat there.

At first in the gurudwara they were throwing stones. Our people understood that nothing could be done unless there was help from outside. And there was no sign of such help. . . . So they thought, what about the young girls, the women? What can we do about them? The girls said, 'They'll take us away, they'll treat us badly, they'll do all kinds of things, they'll make us change our religion. Why don't you finish us off with your own hands?' So there were about 70-80 girls whom their brothers, their husbands, their fathers killed. They just lay down on the ground . . . and they killed them, they slit their throats.

There's a girl, Krishan Kaur (I mentioned her earlier). She was taken away by a Muslim by force. She kept crying and shouting. He took her some two kilometers away from our village. He had an old father. It was winter, not so warm, the month of March. The father kept the girl inside. The son wanted to do all kinds of things to her, but the father was sitting outside. He said, 'Son, don't do these things, she is my daughter. If you do anything to her, you will be doing it to my daughter; you can take it as that. Take her back to where you brought her from, leave her there. I will not sleep while she is here, I will mount guard over her.' So the father protected her honour. When the son went to sleep, the old man said to the girl: 'Daughter, now leave.' The girl then ran, she came back to our village. . . . There she saw (this was on the eleventh) the village was burnt down, it was still burning, the gurudwara was also burnt. . . . She saw the bodies in the gurudwara. So what did she do? She had met another girl, Prem, from the same village. They thought and then decided to burn themselves. They collected pieces of wood and other stuff. . . . There was a *kolu*, oil-press, used to make (*sarson ka tel*) mustard oil. There was oil in the *kolu*, they collected lots of wood, put it is close to the *kolu* and set fire to it and then sat down on it. But life is precious. When the flames licked them, they could not bear it. They did get burnt, but they couldn't bear it. This was on the twelfth.

Suddenly there was the sound of a lorry . . . there was a commotion and a military truck arrived. They put them in the truck and took them away, all burnt, to Rawalpindi. They were saved.

That girl came to Amritsar and died. She was beautiful, really, but became so ugly that it was impossible to look at her. These people who were locked up in a *haveli* were attacked with *lathis* and axes and kept falling. They were grabbed by their legs, dragged out and piled on top of each other. Some 40 to 50 bodies were piled up. . . . These people were helpless, hadn't eaten, not even had water for days. . . . In one sense they were like *ghulams*, they had left their strength behind, they no longer had any. They did not think, we are going to die now, let us fight them—they had become weak, demoralized. There was Sardar Lochan Singh, an ex-major, deputy director of Telegraphs, who was in Delhi. He had a sister, Raj Rani, who was also there. Her husband and children were killed. She was also hurt in this . . . she was dragged out and thrown in with all the other dead bodies. But she still had some life in her. At night, the jackals came to devour the bodies, and she was crying out from underneath. . . . In the morning the lorry arrived and removed the bodies and managed to extricate her. She's still alive and lives in Delhi now.

They did so much . . . our *mama*, he's a good *sahukar*. A Muslim from a village was my *mama*'s—Bala Singh was his name—friend. The man said, 'Bala Singh, whatever you want to give me, give. These are troubled times. When the trouble abates, you can take your things back.' My *mama* pulled out his books and his stamps (*bai khata* and stamps) and wanted to give them to him. He said, 'Throw these things into the fire, I have not come to take this. If you have any money to give, give it. I'll return it to you. Surely you must trust me.' Whatever he had—he had a big iron almirah full of things—there were other things, all these people looted and took away. So, this is what happened from the ninth to the twelfth. Some of our village people also had a hand in the looting. A few miles from our village, there is a Hiran ka moda. . . . Moda Hiran, it's a village. All the Muslims of that area had good relations with us.

Once in our village plague broke out, and we had all gone and stayed in Moda Hiran then, in a man's house there . . . he had never even lived in it. We lived there for some two or three months. There was a retired *Subedar*, Karam Ilahi, from the village and on seeing my son, he enquired: 'Is there any man of Shani's here?' Shani was my mother's name. The others asked, 'Where are you taking this *kafir* (meaning my son)?' He said, 'I'm going to make him my

servant, he will graze my cows. . . .' For two days he kept him at
Hiran ka moda. He said to him, 'Look son, it's like this, you won't
eat our food. We'll give you milk, we'll give you eggs. You eat these,
drink the milk. And at the crack of dawn, in the dark, we'll take
you to the well. You fill your jug with water and keep it inside with
you. But you are not to get out. If you get out and people see you
it will rebound on us.' Two days they kept him. When the military
came, they told him to go. What I mean is, there were good people.

The attack was on the ninth, they took him on the eleventh—
tenth or eleventh. Now the question is: The locals out of the people
there felt this should not happen—the majority, I could say that
95 per cent of them. But the mob that came was a very large one.
The local people were no match for them. Then, they also came
somewhat under the mob's influence. Kill them, they are *kafirs* (*sic*).
But normally they were not like that.

I told you about Subedar Sultan who came to meet us when
we returned in January 1984. I had also gone in 1976. Bhutto was
the Prime Minister then. I was just walking down, my leg was
hurting. My wife was with me. A Muslim boy came up to me and
asked, '*Chachajaan*, why are you walking like this? *Chachajaan*,
what is wrong with *Chachajaan*? Why is he walking like this?' My
wife said, 'He has a pain in his legs.' He said, 'I see.' Then there
was a shop. He asked the shopkeeper for two chairs and made us
sit there. He said, 'I'll just be back.' He went across the road; there
was a *halwai* called Jalandhar Sweet Shop, in Anarkali Bazar. From
there he bought some kind of medicine. He said, there's this
medicine. When you take it, the pain will go away. I said but who
has given you this? He said, 'There's a *halvai* who gives it.' I got
up and went to the *halvai*, I asked about this medicine. . . . He
said, 'This has certain properties. You eat it, you will get all right.
I said, 'But with this little medicine?' He said, 'Yes, you try it first,
if it suits you, write to me and I'll send you more. I said, 'But
sending takes money.' He said, 'What does money matter, if this
medicine brings you some relief?' Then, as I was leaving, he gave
me a box of *mithai*. I tried to pay, but he would not let me. I mean,
these people, they still feel that we are theirs. But it is politics and
dirty politicians that have killed us all.

That shop where we were sitting at that time—this is of 1976
that I am speaking—I said to them, now you must be happy. They
said, 'What do you mean?' I said, 'Earlier the *angrez* were rulers,

now you have your own rulers. Bhutto *Saheb* is Prime Minister.'
He said, 'So what? After all, what was there earlier, the same thing.'
So I asked him what he wanted. He said, 'We want many things,
but we won't get them. What we want is to become again what we
once were, that we should be together again. But that will not
happen . . . these are battles to win power, these people want their
kursis [literally : chair but used to denote power] here, your people
want their *kursis* there, and we're just caught in between. We really
feel that it is best as it once was. If we can become like that again,
we'll really be happy, we'll celebrate. . . .'

They told us, he went on, that our lane was still empty. The village
is full of people, but we have not let that lane be settled. You people
are still there . . . and we keep hoping that one day you will come.
We will help you with your work. . . . Mirza Sultan, he is the son of
the *zaildar*, the same *zaildar*, he has now also been to *Haj*. We met
him and I asked him how he was. He said, it's all right. With you
people we had some respect, you've gone away, you've been
uprooted, we can't see you now. . . . That is not nice; we don't like
that. And the people we do see, we don't like them . . . we don't
even know who they are, someone is from Ferozepur, someone from
Jalandhar, they're not from our village, we have nothing to do with
them.

But he said, 'Surely you can come back some time? That is why
we have kept your place for you.' There was so much love in their
hearts for us. Then I said, 'You have come to see us, you know
me, but these three or four men with you, who are they?' they said.
'Your gardens—two of us have been allotted one.' The other man
added that others have been allotted to other people. 'So we have
come to see those people to whom the gardens belonged.'

I had written to them and then I reached Punja Sahib. (Amrik
Singh now travels back in thought). I told you that there was an
announcement that such and such a man and some people have
come from the village. We went outside, and the Muslims were
there. My wife is a lady and they were men, but even then they
embraced her, saying sister, now you are old and we can do this.
We met and talked and I asked, 'Is there any fruit in my gardens?'
They said there were mangoes and guavas. One of them said to
me, the kind of guavas we have, you won't have in the whole of
Hindustan. I said how come? 'These *amroods* have no seeds in
them,' they said. I said, that they have to have seeds. They asked,

'How do you know?' Subedar Sultan, (he said) this is the man who planted them, after all he should know. So I asked how are there no seeds? These *amroods*, I had got them from the government nursery in Lahore. They were so heavy, and I looked after them with such care. . . . We had gardens on this side of the river and on the other side were vegetable plots. They used to be ploughed and irrigated. The nourishment from them would reach to the fruit also and because of this the amroods were so large. So the number of seeds is the same they've just got more place in which to spread.

They said, we've brought our car. Come along with us. We'll spend the night there and we'll bring you back in the morning. I refused saying, 'I don't want to be guilty of going without orders, especially in a foreign country. I don't want to be guilty of breaking the law.' They had brought a lot of dry fruit from Punja Sahib. This, they gave me.

I knew people from my village would come, so I had taken ten *pagris*, some coconuts, some bananas, some pineapples—they don't have coconuts, bananas or pineapples there, not even the *pagris*. At that time they did not even have so many textiles. This is in 1984. I gave them *pagris*, and some plastic baskets that we had taken.

In Lahore I met a young man. There I went to Dera Sahib Gurudwara and then I thought, let's go to Anarkali. We took a *tonga*. A boy was sitting there. He asked, Chachajaan, where do you want to go? I said we want to go to see your city. He said, 'Come let's go.' When we got to Anarkali, he said, 'Come on, come to my house'. We were surprised. We didn't know him, we thought he's a Muslim, but he said, come to the shop, we make *gota* at home. His brother is a member of the municipal corporation in Delhi. Anyway he took us to the shop, and he took us home. Not me, he took my wife home, saying '*Ammi*, you come. My *Ammi* remembers you'. I was taken aback.

I've come here with my wife, I thought, and here I am in the shop while he's taking my wife away. What will happen now? Will I see her again? She went . . . His mother was reading the *namaz.*. She picked up the *misal* and put it away. She greeted my wife warmly, saying, 'Have you come from Amritsar ?' My wife said, yes. 'Did you stay in the Durbar Sahib? Yes. Did you listen to the *kirtan*? You are lucky at least you can listen to the *kirtan*.' My wife asked why. She said, 'We too are from there. We used to go to the Durbar Sahib, used to listen to the *kirtan*. Now Allah has taken this away from us.' And then, when my wife was coming away, they gave her cloth for a suit. And that young boy Latif, he gave me four or five bundles of gota, we still have those. We still write to each other. So I want to say that those people are not against us. The public is against our government and their own government. They say that the fight is over seats of power. There are no Muslims, Hindus or Sikhs, there's no difference in the love they have for each other. In Lahore we were walking around, we saw a kulfi shop. 'Sardarji, come and eat *kulfi*'. She said. '*Kulfi*.' I said, 'yes, let's eat.' We ate. What do you mean, how can we accept money from you? You are our guests. There's not one person there. Once when we were at Lahori Gate, a Muslim came. *Khuda* himself is veiled, he said, he doesn't come out from behind the veil, he is not seen. Women ought to wear the veil, they should not be seen. But on the whole, the public has a great deal of love for us.

When I revisited in 1976 and 1984, I went around Muslim homes. There was a little girl and I asked her if she was going to school. 'Which class?' I asked. 'Class 10,' she replied. I observed that she answered monosyllabically and as if reluctant to do so. Pressed, she said that her government did not want girls to study, and women there had difficulty studying. So I went out and bought her bangles, instead of books. Muslims like bangles, I thought. The bangles were of all colours and the women were very beautiful. They asked me if I had come from Hindustan, and I said yes. Then I asked the little girl to give him her hands so that he might put the bangles on. 'Don't you want money for them?' she said. Money! No indeed, no money! These are for love.

Thinking of the lost village, mine had a Sikh majority, the whole *biradari* was ours. I'm a *Mahajan*. You may have heard the name of Sardar Teja Singh—he was the Chief Justice of PEPSU. He is my brother's *sala*. His sister is my *bhavaj*. His son, Gurdev Singh, retired as a Sessions Judge and as a Justice of the Punjab High Court. Gurdev Singh was my class fellow in Rawalpindi. So, our villages were mostly of one community—there were Sikhs or Hindus. Most of them were Sikh villages, therefore five or ten Hindu houses and five or ten Muslim houses, a *lambardar*, and a *zaildar*.

But relations were such that they used to attend our weddings. The women would gather together and sing, come from two or three miles away. We used to give them *shakkar*, *gur* and other things.

Our people used to have very good and very strong relations with them. We couldn't live without them. On the whole it is like this, that the people of Pakistan love us. They like us. . . .

I told you about Moda Hiran where there was once a plague and we had gone to stay there. There were about 20 houses or so; it was a larger village. The farmers lived close to their fields. Their houses stood at the top of our gardens. When I married for the second time, after my first wife died, a woman from there plucked *moti* buds at night and in the morning when my wife was still asleep, the woman came and put a garland of these buds round her neck. My father died when I was five years old. It was my mother who did all the work. There was no mother like my mother. She was a great horse-rider. She was brave and had no fear of guns or bullets and she rode a horse that galloped like the wind. Our Doberan was the last village in Punjab. After that there was the State of Jammu and Kashmir, and then the river Jhelum. But there are lots of little villages. There's Pina, there's Nalla . . . and there the whole population was Muslim. But you see those were small villages, some of them mere households. About two kilometers from Doberan is Thamali, a village of Sikhs and Hindus. It was smaller than our village. About five kilometers away was my wife's village of Nara which Hindus and Sikhs called Mauze, that is, a village that does not have a *thana* or *tehsil*. About four kilometers from here is the village where the well-jumping incident took place. If you climbed a roof in my village you could see Rawalpindi from Gajjar Khan—they were at a height, it was a hilly area and we used to be able to see the lights of Murree at night at a distance, But of 592 people, only 85 were left and 507 were killed.

One of the reasons for the disturbance that took place earlier was this *nafrat* (hatred) that had been instilled in these people's hearts by the British government. The British government did not want this . . . actually as a whole, to become independent. Attlee had wanted to give us freedom, but the rulers, the British rulers, did not want this.

The Sikhs (in the village) had their own shops, they had lands, they used to get some things from the land. Mostly they were shopkeepers . . . they (the Muslims) would eat with us, but we never· dined with them . . . never. The reason for this was that if there was a pot of water lying with a cup on top, someone would come, drink from the cup and put the same cup back there. We did not do this. . . . If they cooked beef, they would not do so in our presence. We would not cook pig's meat in their presence. So no one's feelings would be hurt, not theirs, not ours. . . . The wells were quite broad, and from one side our *lotas* would be suspended and from the other side theirs. The wells were shared. At the river it was the same. If a Muslim was bathing at the top of the river, I was there at the bottom. There were no Muslim villages as large as ours in the area. I told you about Moda Hiran; that was a good *qasba*, there were about 20 to 22 houses there. There were villages that also had Sikhs, one or two shopkeepers, they used to supply things. You know Mator village, that was close to ours. There was a Muslim there, he was the one who helped and protected everyone, including the Sikhs. It was Colonel Shah Nawaz, a Congressman, who was in the INA. He was a minister there—he refused to allow any Muslims to attack Sikhs. Later, in Nehru's time he came to India.

In Nara, people fought back quite hard, even the invaders suffered some damages—my wife's father, my father, brother, his wife, their children, they were all killed in Nara. On 9 March all those places, Nara, Thoa, Thamali, Bewal were affected. Bewal was also small. In fact, Doberan was the largest of the lot. In Bewal there were about 350 people or so; of these nearly 325 were killed. The people of Nara faced the enemy. Our people gave up, they lost courage. . . . There was Sarwan Singh, a shopkeeper from our village. His mother and sister were also there—his own family. He was in the gurudwara with everyone else. He came out, went about half a mile in to the fields and then suddenly thought what about my family? What about my mother? My sister? So he came back and that is how he was saved.

He now lives in Lajpat Nagar. He was saved and came away, my mother was also saved. A Muslim friend saved them—they stayed in his house . . . The Muslims also came to fetch my elder brother, they came with a horse. My brother said, 'I don't want to go.' They insisted, but he said, 'No, you can take my things, but I won't come.' You see, there was no trust. Who knew what they would do?

We came from there some time in the month of March. It was on 12 March that the attacks stopped. Then after that our *gaddis* went, we sent one person . . . our brother used to live in Mator,

he was a government doctor, the person in whose house we were
hiding. They asked, do you have anyone there because we've heard
that vehicles have come from there. We had written to his nephew.
We then wrote to our brother and he sent us two vehicles and then
we could leave.

There was a *lalari*; at first they kept taking us from place to place,
but then when the riots started, and when even the houses in our
street, right below us, caught fire, then . . . from there bullets were
flying so the eight or ten of us who were in the *rasoi*, we lined up
and took *thalis*, to use as shields. Bullets were coming through the
door. Then Sardarji said, 'This is becoming very difficult. The
downstairs is on fire; around us people have begun killing their
daughters.' So he went outside. Quite far away there was a Muslim
who signalled him, like this. Then Sardarji beckoned us to come
outside. So many of us jumped down from the roof. The *thana*
was quite far away and there were so many people around [pointing
to floor chips] as many people, crowded like this. So then he came
and took us away. He helped us to cross the road, he said, 'Give us
anything you have, and we'll let you go.' Some of the people who
were with us managed to survive, but others got killed. One person,
I remember, was killed. The man who saved us, he then left and
went away. . . .

We kept sitting and waiting. His elder sister's husband was with
us. He said, 'What should we do now? I have a friend, who lives in
a small village about a mile and a half from here. So we went to his
house. We were small, 17 or 18 years old, we had no one grown
up like him, so we thought we must follow him and do what he
says. When we got there, we found his friend's attitude had changed.
He did not want to give us a room, and not even a decent place to
stay. There were no *kundis*, no way to close the windows, and the
whole night we were unable to sleep, we were scared of shadows.
What could we do? And then it was morning. At night they kept
watching us, we kept sitting, it was quite cold, no one slept. In the
morning we heard that some people had come from outside and
had said, 'Don't say anything to anyone'. Then some people arrived
and told us to collect all our people and come out on this road, all
those who are left. So all three of us went and collected people who
where hiding in different places. Even then we felt their intentions
were not good. The man who kept us at his place, the *lalari*, kept
warning them after all. Whenever we went out, he stopped us,

saying, 'Don't go out, things will be worse there.' So we sat there for three days. We didn't know what happened outside. Then the vehicles came, for three days there was a lot of damage. Then we went to Rawalpindi where my *jeth* and another one of our neighbours asked us where their families were. We said, 'They were here till last night, but now we don't know, perhaps they have been killed.' Now they were too frightened to go further, so they came back with us. The vehicles then left us at Rawantan. There, we settled down in the stables. We were told to wash and look after the children and that arrangements would be made to take us to Rawalpindi in the morning. In the morning we came to Gujjar Khan, and a few days later went further on. Some people came with blankets and other things, and so we came here.

Only One Junoon

This is adapted from an interview with of Simret Singh of Thamali
village by Urvashi Butalia and Sudesh Vaid.

Thamali in Rawalpindi district was attacked during the week 6-13
March 1947. Several of the mainly Sikh villages in the area were under
attack and in some almost the entire population was wiped out. It was
in the village of Thamali that young women in some families drowned
themselves or were drowned by their relatives to save them from the
'dishonour' of forcible conversion to the 'other religion,' i.e., Islam.
It was here in this village that 500 people, mostly women and children,
took shelter in the gurudwara, but were later killed or 'martyred' or
burnt to death when the gurudwara was set on fire.
   Simret Singh of Thamali village is now in business and lives in Delhi,
in the Bhogal area, with his family. Several of the survivors of the
Rawalpindi riots were relocated in this area after 1947. Among those
still left, the memory of those who became *shaheed* in March 1947 is
kept alive through a memorial service that is held on 13 March every
year in the local gurudwara.

Our village and all the other neighbouring villages had a mixed
population; it was only our village that had two-thirds Sikhs, one-
third Hindus and only four or five Muslim houses. They did mostly
gharelu work. There were no Muslim landowners in our villages, the
Sikhs owned all the lands; the Sikhs and the Hindus . . . the Muslims
were so few, only five or six families and they used to go along with
us. In fact, there was one Khan or somebody. When the riots took
place, he sent warning messages to the Hindus and Sikhs to save
themselves because they were being surrounded.
   Yes, he helped us. Gujjar Khan *tehsil* was about 12 miles away.
We sent someone there to ask for help, to say that we're surrounded.
Someone was sent to Rawalpindi as well. . . . There were many
villages, some ten or so that were wiped out in these riots. . . . On

13 March 1947 the rioters totally finished, spoiled, looted and burnt our villages.

You see news used to appear in the papers about what was happening outside . . . we didn't have much interest in this. The papers were in Urdu; people used to read that Pakistan and Hindustan would be made, but for the common people it didn't seem to matter much. What difference would it make for us if Pakistan and Hindustan were made? If the English went away and we had Muslim rulers instead, what difference did it make to us? What happened? No one ever thought there would be this kind of killing, this kind of looting. We were still young, still children. It was on the fifth or sixth that it started in Rawalpindi. . . .

Then on the eighth it happened in Kallar, and after Kallar it reached us. For four or five days we were surrounded, and on the night of the twelfth they came in force. Because the whole village was almost totally purely . . . there were only a few lanes that had their houses. Close by, there were a few other villages: Doberan, Choa Khalsa, Thoa Khalsa, Mator, Nara, Basali—there were several like these—all of them had already been finished and ours was the last, on 13 March. They had told them that by 13 March you should destroy as many villages as you can because on this day the military will arrive. The same thing happened there as happened in 1984! Nobody did anything for three days, and then the army moved in. There the Muslims had been given a week . . . the *angrezis* had told them that they could do anything till 12 March, and then the military would move in. . . . It was in the time of the *angrez*, it was under their rule, who else could have done it? Until August 1947 it was the *angrez* who were ruling; these people only came in later, but it began in Noakhali. They took revenge for Noakhali in Bihar, from Bihar it moved to Peshawar and from Peshawar they moved gradually towards our area.

As I told you we were children and were studying. We didn't know anything. But we used to hear from others, particularly our elders who read newspapers, that there would be partition, that Hindustan and Pakistan would be made, but we used to think what difference would it make to us? Earlier we had *angrez* rulers, now we would have Muslims. Nobody thought they would have to leave, certainly not the common people.

The twelfth deadline . . . It was like this. If we sent a message, they would say they couldn't do anything. We had a police-station close to us, even if we told them, they would not do anything. And on the twelfth, the military arrived, as if by itself.

On the morning of the thirteenth, when all the villages had been finished, they were there. Even at that time, the *angrez* had this feeling that they should make us fight, that they should create divisions between us. . . . And the divisions were created. In our village some 5,000 to 6,000 people were killed. . . .

The killers were all from outside. Yes, the local Muslim families may have joined in the looting, but the killers were all from outside. After all, the locals are known to one another, there are some kinds of relationships, links . . . no, they might have joined in the looting, but they were not killers. Whatever they found they looted and even burnt, but killing, no—you know it happens even here. What do the leaders do? They breed *goondas*, and when they need them, they get people from outside, they use these *goondas*, and then the locals join in. The same style.

On the night of the twelfth, we left at 4.00 a.m., in the early hours of the morning. Our own family, all the people, we collected them in the gurudwara and got some men to guard them. We gave them orders to kill all the young girls, and as for the gurudwara, to pour oil on it and set it on fire.

We decided [this] among ourselves. We felt totally helpless . . . so many people had collected, we were totally surrounded. If you looked around, all you could see was a sea of people in all four directions . . . wherever the eye could reach, there were men. After all, you get frightened. At that time, around 4.00 p.m. in the afternoon on the twelfth, some families went away, the Muslims called them and said, come we'll save you. The others then collected in the gurudwara. They collected together to comfort one another. But then we found that we were helpless . . . we had no weapons, whatever little we had they had taken. . . . Then they took a decision in the gurudwara about all the young girls and women; two or three persons were assigned the duty of finishing them off. Those in the gurudwara were asked to set the gurudwara on fire with those inside it. Some of them (after all, people are scared to die) ran away . . . all those who were in the gurudwara were killed. Of those who came away, some got killed, some were wounded; we also came away.

I was 16 years old, my brother was 9. Our father was with us, but he was killed on the way. In the morning, we reached another village. There were some 40 of us left, and of the 40, 12 got there. The others were all killed. Then close by, there was Kallar camp, we were taken there, and then from there to Gujjar Khan camp. . . .

First, we killed all the young girls with our own hands; kerosene was poured over them inside the gurudwara and the place was set on fire. . . . Women and children, where could they go? There was another village, Thoa Khalsa, there they pulled everyone out and said we will convert you to Islam, either you agree or . . . but they had not started to kill them, and close by there was a well and the women jumped into it. I think some 150 women jumped into the well and took their lives.

We came away around four o'clock . . . [but] there were survivors. Some were killed, some survived. The next day we reached Kallar, the military took us. They asked about our families. . . . There were some women who got frightened, some whose husbands were killed, so they hid and came away. . . . The harvest, the wheat was ripe, so they hid in the wheat fields and came. Then in the morning the military arrived and took their children out. There was killing and arson. This history about the Congress and the Muslim League we don't know. That, only the older leaders can tell you about. We can only tell you the reality of what we saw, that's all.

At that time I had only three articles of clothing on my body, and the boots I was wearing. We came running. There's a sort of *nala* on the way; it's difficult for a man to cross that. But out of fear, my boots got left behind, so I had only my three articles of clothing. . . . Our *phupaji* lived in Delhi from 1934 onwards. His wife, our *bua*, had gone to our village to see our grandfather who was ill. She was also killed there. In April 1947 we came here, by train. . . . Yes, there were trains, and after this time we went twice to our village by train. . . . Our area was called Potohar. Here the majority of the population was Muslim. To one village of ours, there were five to seven of theirs. They wanted to get rid of us, so all the villages of Potohar, all the *dehat* area, was wiped out before August 1947. Yes, we went back, twice. The military used to go with us. The people who had died there, all that was left of them were their bones. We used to go and collect them, to perform the last rites, we used to collect the ashes (*phul*), fill *boris* with them, and then cast them into the Jhelum. We were small, but our elders used to go with us. We went twice . . . on foot. By train up to Rawalpindi, then by bus, then the military vehicle or something. Yes, the Muslims used to come, the ones we knew. But they were also very scared that the military would take them away. Some did come and meet us, they gave us money and things also. They feared that the military would catch them and take them away. Whenever the military went there all of them would leave their houses and run away. After all, the Muslims had done the killings, whether or not anyone's name was included, so they were afraid. . . .

The people from the police station were also in league with them. At the *thana*, on the night of the twelfth, the report stated that most of the villages had been destroyed, and only two were left, and that if they tried, they could save these two. Even then, when one of our vehicles went with help, it was stopped halfway and sent back. On the twelfth, the police sent two vehicles. Our village was the last one left—the others had been wiped out earlier. Some people surrounded the vehicles and told them to go in another direction, to villages that were already safe. There was only one *junoon*, obsession, at the time and all the other relationships, the equation with each other, all that was over. There was only one obsession—to loot, to kill.

Where people live and eat together, there have to be such relationships. But at that time there was, as I said, only one obsession: loot, kill, throw them out and everything would become ours. All the lands, all the houses, would become ours. Because in our area the Muslims were very poor, they felt that once they had killed and thrown us out, everything would be theirs.

Till the 5th Standard our school was in our village and then we studied at Kallar—Kallar High School. We studied at Kallar, and then there were these riots . . . we only found out later, at the time we didn't know. Later, we found out that they had secret meetings in *masjids* on Fridays, at which decisions were taken. People used to come from outside, and weapons were distributed.

At that time there were only axes and *talwars*. But the meetings were held in such secrecy that the common people did not even notice them . . . things were not discussed at home—we used to get the papers, *Milap* and others. Yes, we did get some news from there. When partition was declared, we heard about it. But mostly people used to think that the *angrez* would go and the Muslims would come. What difference does it make to us? The common people believed this. No one expected they would have to leave their homes or that their homes would be destroyed. This is all the manipulation of those who hold seats of power, and who want to protect them. . .

At home we had my grandmother, grandfather, father, mother, three brothers and three sisters. Our *bua* lived in Delhi, she had come to see us with her daughter, they were killed there. In fact, our entire family was killed. The two brothers were the only ones who survived.

Some were killed in the gurudwara and some elsewhere. Our grandmother and grandfather were killed in the house, they were killed by Pathans. The others . . . my mother, and younger brother were killed in the gurudwara. Our father managed to escape, but was killed somewhere along the way. . . . Only a few left, and only some survived. About 40 men, left those who were young and my father. Only some 12 or 13 survived. . . . After about a couple of miles, some got left behind; some lagged. And the villages were quite far away. It was only later that we found out that some had been killed . . . it was afterwards that they attacked and they tried to get the people who were outside the gurudwara, who were leaving, when they saw that those in the gurudwara had become *shaheed*. When the gurudwara was set on fire, a number of people left, jumped out. Outside, some of them were killed, some were saved and some hid. Those who didn't leave the gurudwara were killed in there . . . with *talwars*, with *kirpans*, some with kerosene, as they set themselves on fire.

My *phupaji* was in Delhi at the time. After coming here, we stayed with him for some seven years. We did different kinds of work, whatever fate had in store for us. Our father . . . my *phupaji* had lived here since 1934. He had often asked us to come but we had not done so. The first time we came to Delhi was in January 1947.

It took us two to four years to figure out exactly what had happened to us, to our lives. At that time we had no elders left, so we got very little. There were people who filed false claims and they managed to get land. . . . But people like us, our claim was rejected because we got an allotment of land in Punjab, close to Ambala, near Ropar. And here too, because we had no elders, we could not look after it. Those people who had taken it over, were living on it, kept it. So we got nothing. We people, we who were once well-known zamindars in our area, after coming here became zero. Farming is a seasonal business. A few months in the year and then you're more or less free. Our occupation was finance, what people call financiers. We did *sahukari* but this had ended a couple of years

before partition. In the time of the *angrez*, there was Sir Chhotu
Ram. He made a law that whatever the *angrez* had taken need not
be returned. And there couldn't be any legal proceedings brought
against him/them. The Second World War was on. And all those
who were in the war . . . several Muslims of all kinds joined the army,
earlier. Some of them had not even seen the face of money, and now
they made some money. They too began to change. In our relations,
in the giving and taking. Only some people would give them loans
etc., only to those who really needed them. Otherwise on the whole,
the business had more or less stopped. . . . A lot [joined the war]—
all kinds, *lulas*, *langdas*, and they made money from the war. And
of course, the law said that whatever they had taken on loan need
not be paid back and we couldn't bring proceedings against them
. . . for three generations our family had been there, our father, our
grandfather, his grandfather. . . .

Almost the whole population of Bhogal, apart from the *banias*,
is from that area. We came in April, but the majority of people came
in August. We had a link here, that is why we came. On the way
some people stopped in Rangpura, some in Ambala, some in
Amritsar, some stopped in Rawalpindi, thinking that things might
change and they could return, go back. Or they went to Wah camp
near Rawalpindi. That was the main camp, a big one.

They went to the camp thinking that perhaps they could go back
after 15 August. But once it came, the killing and looting started
again. They killed mercilessly everywhere. You must have seen the
serial *Tamas,* on TV—it was exactly the same scene. No one from
that area survived. Some were affected earlier, others later. In 1947
we suffered some six months earlier, perhaps they thought they
could teach us a lesson, and others would learn from it.

In our villages the population was mixed, there were more
Muslims in some villages. In my wife's village there was not much
loss, except in terms of property. Lives were not lost. In Thoa Khalsa
they pulled the women out of the village and said either you become
Muslims or we will kill you. At that time people felt very strongly
about their religion. Today all this has changed. Those days it meant
something, so when they saw that they had pulled the women out,
the older women said it was better to jump into the well and some
150 women jumped in. All the men of the village had left and these
people were ready to die. Everyone had said let's go to Thamali. . . :
The Muslims said let's go to Thamali and take care of them first, we

can always come back here and sort these people out. So 150 women and children jumped into the well and died. And apart from that the few people they could find in their houses were beaten up thoroughly and even killed.

No, we have not been back, but people do go . . . others have been, they have been back to our village and told us about it. When 13 March occurred, we came away, to Delhi. From Delhi we went in May . . . but not after that. Often we plan to go and we say let's get a passport made, let's go to our village; we want to. We keep telling ourselves that to make ourselves happy. Many people have been. . . . One family was left in our village . . . they're still living there. They became Muslims. You see, Sikhs couldn't have stayed at all and even the Hindus who did became Muslims. Earlier these people used to stay among Muslims in Muslim villages, so they had been influenced by them and later they were converted. They were Sikhs, but they must have thought God knows what will happen there, let's just convert and stay on in our homes.

Those who remained in Punjab continued to farm but those who came further on, stopped. They could not continue. And in families where there were no elders left, only children, how could they resume farming? Those who had some male survivors could have started afresh, but when there was no one left, just women and children, how could they restart? . . . We tell our children these stories but they do not believe us.

Humiliated and Harassed
They Left
SHORISH KASHMIRI

The ancestors of Shorish Kashmiri (b. 1917) belonged to Kashmir but were settled in Amritsar. His early public life was inspired by Zafar Ali Khan, editor of *Zamindar* and other Ahrar leaders—Mazhar Ali Azhar, Habibur Rahman Ludhianvi and Syed Ataullah Shah Bukhari—who burst on the political scene in Punjab and Kashmir. Shorish was drawn into active politics in 1935-36 when the Muslim-Sikh dispute over the Shahidganj mosque-*gurudwara* caused great excitement and led to widespread violence. He was jailed for his activities, especially during the Second World War. By that time, he had emerged as a prominent figure in the Ahrar movement. Shorish was a front-rank journalist. He edited the popular weekly *Chattan* for over three decades. He wrote a number of books, including *Pas-i Deewar-i Zindan* and *Tehrik-i Khatm-i Nabuwat*.

Fourteenth August was certainly the Independence Day of Pakistan—it was actually the day the country gained freedom. But what a strange revolution; the common people were dying while the gentry was lost in revelry. From Ras Kumari to Amritsar, from Sialkot to Dhaka or from Calcutta to Delhi and Lahore to Khyber, the entire subcontinent was drenched in blood. In a word it had become one big slaughter house.

Fifteenth August, the proclamation of India's Independence was read at five past midnight. Along with Jawaharlal Nehru, Choudhry Khaliquzzaman saluted the tricolor and took the pledge of loyalty. But Abul Kalam Azad, who had once secured the proposal of independence from the Cabinet Mission, lay quietly in the retiring room of his residence. His heart was sinking as he thought: 'Was this the day we looked forward to all these years?'

From *Boo-i-gul Naala-i-dil Dood-i Chiragh-i Mehfil*, (Lahore: Chattan Ltd., 1972), pp. 509-13, 517-20, 521-3, 526-9, 530-4.

His lips were sealed. Abul Kalam Azad was not his own self. He had become someone else. His heart was pounding. In his subconscious mind, his eloquence had conceded defeat. His joys seemed contrived. His cheerful countenance was tinged with sorrow. He was overcome by depression. Outside Parliament, thousands of *sadhus* were blowing their conch shells. But Abul Kalam Azad wept in solitude. Lakhs of Hindus in the country were rejoicing. With them was a throng of Nationalist Muslims, indulging in hollow laughter. But crores of Muslims were seized with fear at the approaching morrow about to dawn.

Those who got the worst of it, both in India and Pakistan, were the honest, sincere Nationalist Muslims who, in the eyes of the Hindus, were Muslims, and *vice versa*. Their sacrifices were reduced to ashes. Their personal integrity and loyalty were derided. Their morale was shattered like a disintegrating shooting star; their lives lost meaning. Like the crumbling pillars of a mosque, they could neither be saved nor used. India, for whose independence they had fought the British, refused to offer them refuge. So much so that they incurred the wrath of their own community. They were like that distant sound which rises in the desert and then descends and disappears into the sand dunes. To them Pakistan was a political orphanage, where ordinary people looked at them with hatred and suspicion. The joy of winning freedom had not even touched them remotely. For them the special day of independence was unusual, spent in the seclusion of the four walls of their homes. The League had made them untouchables to their fellow-Indians; they were reduced to the state of political *harijans* in India.

Conches were blown in India. Drums were beaten in Pakistan. All India Radio proclaimed Independence by broadcasting *Bande Mataram* and Pakistan Radio did so with recitation from the Quran. But as day dawned, both sides began to butcher their minorities in the name of religion. The clashes that had ensued sporadically for the last eighteen months became one-sided and fierce on August 14 and 15. In India the Muslims were butchered: in Pakistan the Sikhs and Hindus. Now the riots had ceased to be communal. On the contrary, the minorities were simply being butchered by the majorities.

The upper classes were running away while the poor were dying. Girls were stripped of their clothes just as bananas are peeled. The skulls of the young ones were broken like almonds. The old were thrown into the fire like dry wood: the middle-aged were made to smoulder like cowdung cakes. But even so, in the deep caves of that dark night, the light emitted by some *jugnus*, fireflies, persisted.

There were still some people in Pakistan who protected Hindu and Sikh families like their own. In India, too, there were people determined to save the lives of Muslims. In the Frontier Province, the Red Shirts did a wonderful job by saving the lives of thousands of Hindus. If, in India, Patel and Kripalani behaved like Maharana Pratap and Rana Sanga, then Gandhi and Nehru became the shield of Muslims. Pandit Nehru went to meet the Hindu refugees at Haridwar. They were the people who had lost their children and parents in Pakistan. Some young people, whose parents were butchered and whose sisters and daughters had been left in Pakistan, surrounded Panditji. He said to them: 'The argument over the excesses committed by Hindus or Muslims is futile. Just think that so many human beings were butchered in Pakistan and so many in India.' One young man lost his temper and slapped Panditji; a slap on the face of the Prime Minister of India. But Panditji said nothing to him. He just placed his hand on the young man's shoulder. The young man shouted: 'Give my mother back to me! Bring my sisters to me!' Panditji's eyes were filled with tears. He said: 'Your anger is justified, but, be it Pakistan or India, the calamity that has overtaken us is the same. We have to pass through it.'

I had a vivid memory of those girls who were gang-raped. I knew that these Sitas had been passed around by those Muslim scoundrels like dry dates distributed at Muslim marriages. But whenever I looked at them, I shuddered. I saved a Hindu girl who was gang-raped by a whole caravan of Muslim fanatics and delivered her to her people at Lajpat Rai Bhavan. As I handed her over, the sadness in her otherwise enchanting eyes deepened. She looked at me from their depths. It seemed she doubted my being a Muslim and thought that, had I been a real Muslim, I too would have had a taste of her.

In some cities, towns and villages of India, hundreds of Muslim girls jumped into wells and ended their lives. In the Hall Bazar of Amritsar, they took out a procession of naked Muslim girls. After taking them around, they were brought to the Khairuddin mosque where flames leaped out of a fire kindled in the dry water tank. They were told: 'This is the way to Pakistan.' The girls jumped into the fire. This happened in a city where the blood of Hindus and

Muslims once flowed together in the Jallianwala Bagh, and where together they crept on their bellies at the orders of General Dyer. In Tarimoo Head, a town in Punjab, the local Muslims assured the Hindus that anyone who came to harm them would have to pass over their dead bodies. But when the humiliated and impoverished Muslims started pouring into Punjab and both sides began stopping trains and butchering each other, the elders of the town changed their minds. It was then that the Hindus of the town gathered in a *haveli*. They collected hundreds of maunds of wood. Maunds of grain were added to it. Hundreds of tins of *ghee* were poured and a fire lit. And then the young daughters were thrown into the inferno. One of them extricated herself from the father's grip and ran away. Her father ran in pursuit. The girl jumped into the river Chenab. That is how another *Sohni* (*Savitri*) was swallowed by its waves. The gold and silver jewellery, along with the silk garments, were thrown into the fire. When the fire began to burn fiercely, these people challenged the *rustams* of the majority community to come and kill them. The hoodlums, who had already arrived beating their drums and cymbals, raised their swords and severed their heads, and then started looking for gold in this extraordinary funeral pyre, cutting off fingers, chopping off ears and snatching the necklaces from human bodies. Sati was being reenacted with the difference that this time those who jumped into the fire were not widows but virgins.

On both sides, the hoodlums were busy looting. Decent people were robbed and plundered with impunity. On page 1083 of his autobiography, *Shahrah-e-Pakistan* (Pathway to Pakistan), Choudhry Khaliquzzaman writes: 'The stability that the Muslims desired had been destroyed. . . .' Shahid Suhrawardy's opinion was absolutely right that the two-nation theory had assumed a monstrous shape for the Muslim minority, and the future of the Muslims in India had become bleak. During the months of August and September, their fate all over India hung in the balance. Calcutta refused to offer respite or refuge to Muslims even for a minute. In Delhi people chanted 'blood for blood'. In the vicinity of Delhi, the entire Muslim population was exterminated. A few who survived were converted to Hinduism. Muslims were forced to cremate their dead. They were compelled to give away their daughters in marriage to low-caste Hindus. A delegation of Muslims from Alwar and Bharatpur came to Maulana Hifzur Rahman Seoharwi and complained: 'We do not mind being killed. But we cannot do two things. First, we are completely averse to cremating the corpses of our kin and, second, with what heart can we give away our daughters in marriage to Hindus? If the earth opens up we are ready to disappear into it!'

Those Muslims who were left in India or wanted to stay on, or those who had no way of escaping, were in a quandary. India and its capital Delhi had no place for them. Circumstances were such that big and small leaders of the Muslim League had left them in the lurch and gone away. No one was left in the League to give them a helping hand. The entire class of the Muslim nobility was in the process of emigrating. Many had already left; the rest were preparing to do so.

Apart from a man like Mian Azim Husain, who had inherited a special temperament from his late father, Fazl-i-Husain, almost all the Muslim bureaucrats had fled to Pakistan. No one was left to take care of the masses.

The Quaid-i-Azam told Choudhry Khaliquzzaman to lead the Muslims in the Indian Parliament. Khaliquzzaman voiced his preference for Nawab Ismail Khan of Meerut. The Quaid-i-Azam vetoed his suggestion. The next day Mr. Chundrigar said that the Quaid-i-Azam asked him to become the leader. Choudhry Khaliquzzaman maintained that he had already confirmed Nawab Ismail Khan's appointment. But when the time for selection arrived, Khaliquzzaman himself became the leader. Choudhry pledged loyalty to India and saluted the Indian flag. But on 2 October 1947 he accompanied Lord Ismay to Karachi, where he met the Quaid-i-Azam and decided not to return. Chundrigar too shifted his position. The children of Nawab Ismail Khan migrated to Pakistan, but he stayed back. But cut off from his own people and unable to bear the loneliness, he died. His pseudonym was Zabih, which meant the one to be sacrificed. He died on the day of *Id-ul-Zuha*, the day Ibrahim sacrificed his son. . . .

All the funds at the League's disposal, i.e., Rs 75 lakh of the Bihar Fund and Rs 83 lakh of the League Fund, were transferred to Pakistan. President Ayub Khan seized the money at the height of his power.

A large part of the gentry known for its prudence and foresight came to Pakistan after selling off property or selling it at a bargain in Pakistan. In both the countries the poor remained miserable.

Whereas some of the *nawabzadas*, members of the Muslim nobility, brought their concubines and dogs, the poor people found it impossible to bring their daughters and sisters with them.

The Indian Muslims were on their own. No one was left who would take their responsibility. Some senior workers of the Jamiyat al-ulama tried to provide succour. At some places, the Nationalist Muslims tried to boost their morale, but such was the malady that no one had any cure. Muslims were bluntly told to leave. When they did not, the local Hindus robbed, killed or burnt them. And the caravans which made it to Pakistan arrived after being plundered and decimated on the way. The Muslims of Delhi were completely uprooted from their homes. After Gandhiji campaigned for their safety, a curfew of 72 hours was clamped on the city, but it was of no use. Families belonging to the gentry fled from their homes and took shelter in Humayun's tomb and other Mughal ruins. Gandhiji's son, Ram Das, wrote to him saying, 'At the time of the Kohat riots when Maulana Shaukat Ali wrote you a letter, you dropped out of politics and detached yourself from the whole thing. Now when the time has come to teach the Muslims a lesson, you are threatening to undertake a fast unto death. The very existence of a man like you is extremely harmful to the Hindu community.' This was a letter from a son to his father. How other Hindus felt can well be imagined!

Choudhry Khaliquzzaman maintained that Gandhiji had told him: 'On this issue I will stake my life, but I will never allow the Muslims to creep on the roads of India. They too should be given the confidence to walk on the roads of India with dignity.'

Gandhiji called General Shah Nawaz by telegram from his home. He was given the task of cleaning up the mosques of Delhi which had been turned into toilets, and restoring them to their former glory.

Apart from that he was told to assist the Muslims of Delhi and stop them from running away from their homes. Gandhiji said: 'Shah Nawaz! If the Muslims are uprooted from Delhi, they won't be able to stay anywhere in India.'

Gandhiji wrote letter after letter to Sardar Patel that, as Home Minister, it was his duty to save the lives, property and honour of the Muslims. But they had no effect on him. Twenty crore rupees, which was to go to Pakistan according to an agreement, was stopped by Patel. Gandhi condemned it at an open meeting and had the money delivered to Pakistan.

General Shah Nawaz took some of his Hindu and Muslim comrades and began cleaning some of the historic mosques. The grandest of all mosques had become a vast dump of dirt and filth. Shah Nawaz told me that there was so much excrement and filth that it took them quite a few days to clean it. Lifting the baskets on their own heads, they completed the task of restoring it. When some noble Hindus and Sikhs living in the vicinity of the mosque came to know that General Shah Nawaz was sweeping the floor of the mosque with his own hands, they too joined him.

Gandhiji took Shah Nawaz with him and went to attend Khwaja Bakhtiyar Kaki's *Urs*. There was a camp with thousands of Muslim refugees in it. Those who once occupied the position of spiritual heads at his tomb had fled to Pakistan saying that they had been told by the Hazrat Khwaja Saheb himself that he was going to Pakistan, so they too should come there. After inquiring about the ceremonies to be performed on the occasion, Gandhiji washed and cleaned the Khwaja's tomb, repeated the *fateha* and then prayed: 'O pious man of Allah! I have come to you to seek your forgiveness for the barbarities inflicted by my community on yours. Forgive. . . .'

From there Gandhiji went to Humayun's tomb. Hundreds of Muslims fell at his feet. Many began to weep and wail. Gandhi consoled them and said: 'You are Muslims. And a Muslim does not bow his head before anyone except Allah. By bowing like that (before me) you are committing a sin. Keep your spirits up. Allah will help you.'

After returning from there, Gandhiji said to Shah Nawaz: 'The condition of Muslims is really bad. Tell me about their general condition within the walled city.'

Shah Nawaz replied, 'Mahatmaji, the plight of Muslims is pitiable. The Sikhs from the Punjab climb on their roofs stand stark-naked before their women, who live in seclusion, and say: 'Vacate the houses, otherwise (pointing to their penis) we will thrust these into your . . .'

'Are you telling the truth, Shah Nawaz?'

'It is absolutely true, Mahatmaji.'

Gandhiji said: 'If that is true, then it would be better for Gandhi to be under the earth than to walk on it. . . . It is better to die.'

Gandhiji immediately announced his fast unto death.

Sardar Patel was so upset that he left for Bombay. The Congress was panic-stricken. The Congress leaders took recourse to lying in a big way and said that they would be responsible for establishing peace. But Gandhiji did not agree. He said it was not a question of assuming responsibility but of establishing peace.

Gandhiji looked at Shah Nawaz and said: 'Shah Nawaz! These people are politicians. . . . And politicians avoid telling the truth on such occasions. You are a soldier. Tell me, are they speaking the truth? Have the Muslims really regained their confidence?'

Shah Nawaz denied this was so. Some members of the High Command were furious with him, but Gandhiji refused to break his fast. As a result, the Muslims won respite. There was much less panic now than ever before. Now they could leave or stay in peace. . . .

What is the true definition of a human being? This question has remained a puzzle. It is very difficult to discover the limit of either his goodness or his villainy. The partition of the country was undoubtedly a revolution, but it was also a tragedy. Every revolution is a tragedy; its excesses, manifestations and consequences are not just for the revolutionaries but also for large sections of the population. But a revolution is the collective death of a system. It is equivalent to destroying the old order. . . .

The bloodshed that took place for the establishment of Pakistan and the price that Muslims had to pay was not unexpected. The lives of nations are moulded by such incidents. The blood of one glows on the other's face. The bones of one are transformed into flowers that embellish a groom's garland. It is only by pruning a plant that its flowers bloom and its branches look beautiful. Pakistan was undoubtedly the name of sacrifices offered by the Muslims of India.

Slogans are always exciting, demonstrations are always dangerous, and revolutions are always tragic. If the masses thought that the journey to Pakistan would be like having a stroll in a garden, this was an illusion, something, which people begin to nurse because of emotionally-surcharged slogans raised in communal politics. If the sacrifice of seven or eight lakhs of Muslims had brought about the renaissance of Islam in Pakistan, this would not have been too high a price to pay.

But the truth is that the promises made by the leaders were like the promises of a girl who makes and breaks them day after day. I had written in *Daily Azad* that the result of partition would be that Muslims would disappear from India and Islam from Pakistan.

The Hindu mentality would strive to create a situation in which the Muslims become apostates, were killed or made to leave the country. The people with whom the Muslims would gradually come into contact in Pakistan would try to shirk the duties imposed upon them by Islam. They would conduct a new experiment on Islam in Pakistan. Inwardly, their endeavour would be to turn Pakistan into a secular state and to play into the hands of the nobility. But they would never want Pakistan to become an Islamic state or a democratic one. Pakistan was actually an expression of a historic need, but if its results did not come up to the expectation of its people or if conditions deteriorated, this was for good reasons. For example:

1. In such a movement the masses cannot keep pace with the tempo of a movement. They either run (ahead of it) or drop out of it.

2. Whenever a movement is monopolized by the intellectual elites, most people close their minds and cease to think for themselves.

3. When the people cease thinking and surrender, their enthusiasm becomes uncontrollable. The results are then negative.

4. The movement for Pakistan was more of an all out protest of the Muslim minority against the domination of a determined Hindu majority rather than a fight against (British) despotism. Their real target were the people who were already engaged in a struggle against the Englishmen, whose political struggle had passed through immensely difficult stages and whose temperament was politically more mature than theirs.

5. Nobody other than the Quaid-i-Azam was considered to be trustworthy. All the people with him were his subordinates. Without him, their personalities were reduced to a cipher. Those who were not with him were nonentities.

6. The people who helped the movement for Pakistan to reach such an emotional upsurge, when every Muslim was ready to sacrifice and suffer for it, had no idea about the unfortunate results.

The late Mian Bashir Ahmad (ex-Ambassador to Turkey) wrote in an article that when the League decided to join the Interim Government, the Quaid-i-Azam was told that he too should join it because all the big guns of the Congress were already in it. To this, the Quaid-i-Azam replied: 'To whom shall I hand over the League?' I told him that he had many faithful followers. The Quaid-i-Azam said: 'The community does not trust anyone except me!' This sentence will bear scrutiny.

But the question is: what sort of opinion can the masses have about a public body, about which the Quaid-i-Azam himself thought as he did? When the Muslim masses adore a person they worship him like God. When they hate, then like the Jews, they don't stop short of killing their own Prophets.

Anyway, whatever happened was unavoidable. Both communities had pushed their differences to such an extent in British India that their coming together in one united nation in the near future was impossible. In the contemporary period, the foundation of the political movements was not based on ethical values, and religion was used to inflame the sentiments of the masses. Consequently, whatever happened or was happening was against the true spirit of religion. The hoodlums used religion to suit their own designs. Those people had committed such barbarous acts in the name of Hinduism, Sikhism and Islam that decent people felt ashamed to utter the name of religion. Exalting themselves above a Hindu, Sikh or a Muslim, they talked of humanity, but, morality, religion and humanity within them was already dead.

People had acquired a taste for plundered wealth and abducted women. Even big people tainted their hands. Magnificent carpets, one better than the other, found their way into the houses of officers. All the paraphernalia of the big mansions reached their residences. Girls were distributed like alms are distributed outside shrines. The locks of the big cloth shops were broken and the expensive materials were stolen by the wives of those in authority. Many officers married off their children with the help of plundered items. The stock lying in the furniture shops was taken away to furnish government bungalows.

The police inspectors of some rich neighbourhoods acquired immense wealth. They collected maunds of gold. Some of the *mujahids* kept exploiting the *kafir* girls for months. They formed gangs and plundered shops and homes. When night fell, they retired to the brothels and sought their pleasure with that money. Some of the political bigwigs deserted their wives and began living with prostitutes, to pander to their newly-acquired addiction. He who has tasted blood once gets hooked on it for life.

The denizens of the 'flesh *bazar*' started patrolling the Lahore railway station. Many girls and, more frequently, the women who escaped from East Punjab fell into the hands of these Muslims. In the name of sympathy, the denizens of the *bazar* did atrocious things. The madams of the 'flesh *bazar*' offered help to these hopeless victims and took them away to lead a life of humiliation and indignity. Hundreds of such incidents took place in the camp of the Walton Training School. There, in the camp, was a huge flock of underage girls whose parents had been mowed down on the way, or who had been swallowed up by the waters of the Sutlej and Beas, or those who were taken off trains and killed. Their children were sold like the cheapest commodity in the market. I have published interviews of these girls in my book *Oos Bazar Mein (Tarikh-e-Fahashi)* or *In That Bazar (A History of Debauchery)*. The story of Neelam is about one such miserable girl, her helpless sisters and their blind father. They came from Patiala as refugees. When they reached Lahore, they were called 'asylum seekers', and were sold in the *bazar*. The famous musician and playback singer, the unfortunate Nasim Begum was one such girl, who was bought from her unfortunate father by her so-called mother for a few rupees. At the time she was barely five or six years old. She was brought up by the famous courtesans of Amritsar (Shamshad, Imtiaz, Mumtaz and Shahnaz), learned music and became a famous singer.

But with this spate of evil blew the breeze of good and noble deeds. Man was not dead. Humanity was not only alive but aware that a river of blood and fire cannot destroy our morale. Nobility has been conferred on us by Nature. We cannot turn away from it. We can turn these flames into flowers. Determination can steer our ship with our arms as oars.

Before partition, the office of *Chattan* was located in a hotel. During that period we opened its gates to the uprooted people. It was *Shab-i-Barat*. I had just come out of the room of General Shah Nawaz and Makhdoom Shah Binori and was going home when my attention was drawn to a woman reciting the Holy Quran. The recitation was enchanting. The door was closed from within and the woman was reading the sacred word of God with the utmost tenderness. I realized that she was also crying. She had a six-or-seven-year-old daughter who was exceptionally beautiful. Finding a great resemblance between her and my daughter Shaista, I often picked her up and showered her with my affection. These people had come from some town in U.P. and were cultured, educated, decent. One day that little girl told me that her mother wanted to see me. I went and stood by her door. From behind the door, she said to me: 'The father of this girl has deserted me. Before going away, he handed me over to a person and told me to live with him for some time and pay the bill and go anywhere I could live. That person spent two nights with me and went away without paying anything. Now I have nothing.' And she burst into tears.

'Where has her father gone?'

'He eloped with a woman living in the opposite room, and took away all the jewellery given to me by my parents.'

She was sobbing uncontrollably. I consoled her and told her not to worry about the bill. In future no stranger would come to her. Whatever she needed would be arranged. 'God-willing, everything will be alright in a day or two,' I said.

I related the story to Shah Nawaz and Makhdoom Shah. They were flabbergasted. But it so happened that her husband came back the next day. We found out that the wretch with whom he had eloped had taken the jewellery and disappeared.

Shah Nawaz summoned her husband. He confessed that his wife stated the truth. Shah Nawaz was a soldier. He was so infuriated that he tied the man's hands and feet and gave him such a whipping that cries could be heard at a distance. In the meantime, the woman who was really as beautiful and delicate as a rose, became restless and came out. Her face was covered with a veil. She said: 'Please forgive him. After all, he is my husband.'

Shah Nawaz asked her husband: 'Is she your wedded wife?'

'Yes Sir!'

'Is the child yours?'

'Yes Sir.'

'Where are her parents?'

'They have been killed.'

'All right, prostrate yourself before her, kiss her feet and swear by the Holy Quran that in future you will never do such a thing.'

The woman said: 'My husband was not like that. He has made a mistake. I ask him and you people to forgive me. This won't happen again. My heart says so.'

Shah Nawaz was not a man to be convinced so easily. He actually made the man prostrate at her feet, made him swear on the Quran that he would not repeat such a thing in future. Within a week I met the DRC of Lahore and arranged for a furnished house to be allotted to them. Later they went to Karachi. I hear they did well and led a good life.

The night of 13 August was coming to an end and this was the beginning of 14 August. At one minute past midnight, the radio announced the establishment of Pakistan. The Quran was recited and a hymn of Zafar Ali Khan was sung: 'Quaid-i-Azam, we are indebted to you.'

We people, who had spent years in jails and whose motto was that the British had no right to rule over this country, were trying to hide ourselves from people's eyes like a widow. . . .

The day had yet to dawn when the voice of a *muezzin*, proclaimed: 'Allah is great!' I said my prayers and went to sleep. 'When I woke up, the radio was on: 'This is Radio Pakistan.' Someone was broadcasting the translation of the Holy Quran: 'Do not call them dead who sacrificed their lives on the path to Allah. They are alive, but you do not have the intellect to realize it.'

Shorish Kashmiri   Karachi Civil Hospital
(In Prison)   21 August 1968
                                    4.00 p.m.

Translated from Urdu by A.S. Judge

In the Shadow of Freedom
BEGUM ANIS KIDWAI

Begum Anis Kidwai (1902-80) a social worker, came from a family of staunch nationalist Muslims. In 1947, Anis Kidwai's husband, Shafi Ahmed Kidwai (his brother was Rafi Ahmad Kidwai), a government servant, was killed in communal violence in Mussoorie because he refused to abandon his post and flee. Devastated by his death Anis Kidwai took Gandhi's advice and gave herself to social work, working with partition victims at the Muslim camps in Delhi at Purana Qila and Humayun's Tomb. Alongside, she kept a diary in which she recorded her experiences and thoughts. This record published in full only after many years, appeared in Urdu and Hindi under the title *Azadi Ki Chaon Mein*. In the words of the novelist Mukul Kesavan: 'Anis Kidwai's account of her husband's courage, . . . his murder and her grief-stricken search for direction in a country aflame with anti-Muslim feeling, reminds those of us who did not experience partition, of the stoicism and fortitude with which millions of people endured tragedies. In these memories, the reader finds nobility, matter of fact goodness, self-justification, polemic, accusation—everything that violent tragedy calls into being'. [Editor]

We have lived through the times. An epoch has come to a close and my generation has either retired to their corners or are preparing to leave this world. Through this piece of writing, I can only say this to the younger generation:

> *Dekho mujhe jo didai ibrat nigah ho*
> *Meri suno jo gush haqiqat nyosh hai.*
> Look at me if your eyes can take a warning
> Listen to me if your ears can bear the truth.
> Builders of tomorrow, keep away from that chalice of poison

'Azadi ki Chaon Mein' from *Andhi* (Delhi: National Book Trust, 1980), pp. 5-21.

which we drank and committed suicide. And if you build anew on the foundations of morality, strength, dignity, and steadfastness, you will be esteemed.

I am grateful to the National Book Trust for having brought out this book a second time and published its translations into several languages of this country. I hope, by this act, my cry will not be a cry in the wilderness but reach every corner of this country. Once more I thank them.

Sipurdam ba tu mujai khwaish ra
Tu dani hisab-e-kamo besh ra.
I entrust what is mine to thee
You know best whether it is much or little.

Begum Anis Kidwai
7 January 1978

Karta hoon jama phir jigare lakht lakht ko
I piece together the threads of my broken heart.

September 1947 began, and brought with it many anxieties. In fact from the beginning of the year, news of Hindu-Muslim riots had been pouring in—from direct action in Calcutta to Noakhali. The heartbreaking events in Bihar, Rawalpindi, Multan and Garhmukhteshwar were still fresh in public memory. Thousands had fled from Pakistan and already come to India and a several mile long caravan of people whose homes had been wrecked was creeping towards the India-Pakistan frontier.

At that time I also recall the glee with which votaries of both religions reacted to the news of the riots. One person gleefully remarked, 'We may have missed out on Calcutta but we taught them a good lesson in Noakhali.' I looked at him in shocked surprise and wondered what would become of this country which has produced such brave warriors (by proxy). I said to him, 'Sir, do not gloat so much over the destruction and ruin of others. After two days of glee, you had to cry over Calcutta. Who knows, we may have to shed tears of blood over Multan and Rawalpindi.'

There was wholesale slaughter of Hindus in Rawalpindi. A Pakistani friend told me about his misfortune. He said, 'When I· arrived in Rawalpindi from London, I saw hundreds of corpses hanging by their hair from trees. Bewildered I ran away to Mussoorie where I witnessed the same bloody scenes. For a month, I was stuck in a refugee camp where my wife had her first child. If Shafi Ahmad Kidwai had not taken care of me, I do not know what would have happened. Finally, I regained my freedom with Rafi Ahmad Kidwai's help.

'I still remember the wells of Garhmukhteshwar glutted with corpses, and the children of Bihar being burnt alive. How can you forget them?'

In the same vein another gentleman, expressing his pleasure remarked, 'In Noakhali only three or four hundred were killed. But I hear, four thousand women were converted to Islam. Four thousand!' And so saying, his face flushed with pride.

And then I also recall a journalist who, accusing the government of weakness, declared in anger: 'If I had my way, I would not leave even one Muslim alive. If we do not take revenge for what has happened to us in Pakistan, we would have done nothing. We must make it difficult for them to live here.' Not only that, he had surreptitiously begun supporting and helping the Rashtriya Swayam-sevak Sangh.

What beastliness was rampant those days! Chickenhearted individuals were celebrating the plight of other human beings and well-educated persons were helping to spread the fires of hate and revenge. I kept thinking what would be the state of those mothers whose infants were seized from their breasts and hurled into the blazing fire, those young girls seized from their parents and women snatched from their husbands who were forced to change their religion. What kind of neo-Hindus and neo-Muslims would these mothers and sisters make, whose hearts have been pierced through and through. A curse on these hideous proselytizers. Hindu or Muslim!

Watching this, I thought with nostalgia of the peace and order of the old regime. I thought of those gentle people who lived under the heel of British rule, who seemed decent and who could be trusted to respect daughters and wives.

Only some time ago, in June 1947, cinemas, theatres and other places of entertainment in Mussoorie used to remain open till 2 a.m. in the morning, and there was liveliness all around. Once out of cussedness, I stayed for the night with a friend. Both of us walked up to Charleville Gate. There was no fear or apprehension.

On the Mall Road of Mussoorie, below the library, thousands of people would gather to listen to the band of the Indian National Army, among them *burqa*-clad women and burly Sikhs. People would entrust their infants to Pahari errand boys without fear, they would take them round and deposit them safely in their homes in two or three hours. A ten-year-old girl could be seen walking fearlessly with her four-year-old brother from Charleville to Collectory Bazar. India had been partitioned and sometimes fear of impending dangers gripped our hearts. People were saying, 'You will see that the newcomers (from Pakistan) would not desist from causing disturbances here too.' Hindu-Muslim relations were beginning to get strained. Nevertheless, life flowed on its even course.

In the Bhangi Colony in June, my sister who was excitable, got restless and decided that she would catch Bapu at the prayer meeting and ask him what he had done. 'India belongs to all of us, and we have to live and die here. But why this partition and exchange of population? How can we who have been dreaming of a huge united country console ourselves?'

As soon as the prayers ended, she darted forward and started elbowing her way through the crowd towards Gandhiji. But she was prevented by her husband. 'This is not the occasion for it,' he told her. 'We will see sometime later.' By the time he let go of her, Gandhiji had left. She still regrets that she could not pour her heart before to Gandhiji.

In fact, everybody was fearful that the British policy would succeed in bringing about partition, and that the migration of population from here might bring about a catastrophe. One felt angry with the leaders.

INDEPENDENCE DAY

Now I recall our first Independence Day. From Calcutta to Eastern and Western Punjab, the country was in a fog rent with sighs and shrieks. We had freedom drenched in blood and gore. The corpse of independence was being trampled upon. Women were being robbed of their virtue and Government House echoed with the victims' cries. Nevertheless we strove to be happy. Despite everything, the yoke of slavery had been cast off. Later, perhaps, the ghost of communalism would also depart. No doubt the country had been divided, but perhaps, both communities would be happy in their own parts of the country.

But no. Disappointment and hopelessness overwhelmed us, we felt alienated. Even on such a happy occasion, our hopes were turned to dust. I covered most of the city on foot, rickshaw and car but I came back in the same mood. There was no happiness anywhere.

My heart sank, as if someone was strangling my happiness. The tricolor did not tug at the heart. The cries of *Inqilab Zindabad* had no emotional impact. Our blood was no longer hot. The signboards, slogans and posters inscribed in Hindi looked as though they were mocking us.

At that moment India was going back to the past, with people donning *tilaks* on their foreheads. And I wondered why they had sent for Brahmins from Banaras. Why were they looking for a *Qazi* (reciter of the Quran)? What will *bhikshus* do in Government House? I felt suffocated. Lost in these thoughts I reached Government House. Momentarily I experienced a sense of pride. The national flag flew on the stately entrance which provided free passage to the common folk. Now, everything here was ours and our comrades in the national struggle lived in it.

But soon my heart sank again. A language was being spoken there which was stranger to us than English, a language in the words of Josh Malihabadi:

Jis ko dewon ke siva koi samajh na sake
Zayr mashq hai woh andaze bayan ay saqi.
What cannot be understood except by giants,
O Saqi, that is the current style of expression.

The *chowkis* on the right side of the dias were adorned with Buddhist priests. Many languages were spoken. English, Sanskrit, Arabic, chaste Hindi. But not a word in our precious language [Urdu], each expression of which 'sends a hundred flowers in bloom'.

So much was said. But we could make nothing of it. Like me, there were many others who had witnessed the scene with dry throats and bewildered eyes. They returned feeling that their backs were broken. Even the first Governor of free India, Mrs. Sarojini Naidu, could not read the oath [in Hindi] correctly.

Had we waited for this kind of future all these years? Who wanted to dig up the dead culture from the past? Who wanted the government to take on the contract of religions in place of its responsibility for democracy?

This scene was painful—heartbreaking. Our hair stood on end, watching this spectacle of Brahmanism. We saw a glimpse of the future. Those who had been mere spectators of our struggle for twenty years were pleased and taunted us. 'See, were we not saying that as soon as we get power, there will be Hindu Raj in India? That is why it has become essential for us to create Pakistan.' In fact, it is this mentality which has created Pakistan.

Another gentleman remarked, 'I have already written an article showing that Brahmanism has always dominated India. Buddhism spread and reached its zenith, but Brahmanism suppressed it so well that there's hardly a trace left in this country. How well Islam shone in this land! But it also got caught in the coils of Brahmanism and lost its individuality. Christianity too bowed to Brahmanism in the shape of the Theosophical Society. Brahmanism will dominate this country. Gandhiji may knock his head against it, or you people may wail against it, but India cannot be rid of it.'

It needed enormous patience. We were numbed. There was no glimpse of hope, no light ahead. And we were wondering how workers, peasants and the poor would get out of this morass. We would have to look for a way out. We had seen through the veil of the Congress and would have to raise the curtain drawn over reality. Prognosticators could see in which direction the wind was blowing. The Muslim Leaguers were pleased that they were not alone in being shorn; others were too. The progressives (of the left) were wondering whether those tried soldiers who had won the battle against the British would serve the country's new objectives and whether they should bolster their strength or try to weaken them. Young men thought of a new battle front in which they would have to face their own people instead of aliens. A handful of them would have to wade through blood to build a new India. But who knew that the biggest price would have to be paid by the Father of the Nation himself.

September came again (in 1947). Hardly 15 days had gone by since Indian freedom, that beating and killing began in Delhi. The tricolors on houses and shops had hardly become grimy when they began to be streaked with blood. A flood of confusion and disorder from Punjab swamped Delhi, Mussoorie and Dehradun. One day in a gathering (around Gandhiji), someone remarked that the Ganga of communal riots was flowing throughout the whole country. Gandhiji laughed and said: 'But its Gangotri in the Punjab.'

The telephones were dead. The mail stopped. Trains stopped. Bridges were demolished. Human beings crawled like insects in lanes and fields, dying, trampled upon and robbed. There was such a stampede. God's invisible stick was driving them here and there. Probably, India had never witnessed such a storm of murder and mayhem in her history. Carthage used to enslave the inhabitants of the country it conquered and set them to bake bricks. India too had witnessed the great battle of *Mahabharata*. Nadir Shah had sacked Delhi for three days. But these were of days, when even a province and district had the status of a country. Not more than twenty thousand people died in these large massacres. But what we saw with our own eyes might not have happened since the beginning of civilization.

In Lucknow, men, women and children, weeping bitterly would beg me to telephone Delhi and get news of their relations. 'For God's sake, arrange for our family members to get out of Mussoorie. If any of them has been left alive in Dehradun, find out their whereabouts.' I used to pester my brother-in-law in Delhi.

Every morning I used to take a walk for a mile or two along La Montessori Road after prayers, alone. Who could accompany me so early in the morning? But at that time, there was no menace. However, as September began, the atmosphere began to weigh me down. I would pass by groups of four or five taking their morning walk, and having heated discussions on the politics of Punjab and India.

One day, seeing them carrying sticks and clubs, noticing the expression on their faces and overhearing their angry voices, I felt that peace in Lucknow was also going to be disturbed. People at home had been warning me not to go out on such lonely strolls, but I never paid them any heed. Sensing this change in the atmosphere, I had to stop my morning walk.

In the city, peace committees had been formed in various quarters to try and prevent the breakdown of peace. Thank God they succeeded in these efforts, and Lucknow was able to preserve

---

'Anis Kidwai's husband Shafi Ahmad Kidwai was administrator of the Mussoorie Municipal Board at that time.

its reputation for civilized living. But news of disturbances exploding elsewhere were enough to destroy our peace of mind. We were less worried about our relations in Delhi as they were living under some protective arrangements. But anxieties about Mussoorie had robbed us of sleep at night. We believed that Shafi* with his characteristic obstinacy would not leave Mussoorie. In fact, if prevailed upon to leave, he would become even firmer in his resolve.

At this time, as one gathered from his letter, he was headlong into providing relief and succour to those uprooted by the riots. In this situation, he was not prepared to come away. His brothers were worried.

He was expected on 21 September in Lucknow on some official business but soon he informed them to postpone this date. And the date kept on being extended. Earlier he was worried about the safety of some of his relations, friends and employees in Dehradun. But when the riots caught up with Mussoorie, he was calm.

Mushkilain mujh par pari itni
Ki asaan ho gayen.
I suffered so many hardships
that I became immune to them.

He would never write to me about his condition and would instead enquire about the safety of a whole lot of people. Once he wrote to me: 'I am missing my eldest daughter very much, send me her address so that I may write to her.' He enquired about me and the children, as if all of us were in peril while he was safe.

But one day a letter came from him in which he related the whole story of Mussoorie. He said, 'While I am writing to you, I hear the din of the populace down below, the sounds of firing and the shrieks and wails of the victims. Houses and shops are on fire, shops are being looted and the police is watching the spectacle. This is happening in broad daylight.'

In the next letter, he wrote that he had closed his office and was confined to the house for the last three days. 'It is raining hard. The workers who ply horses and mules could not escape the bestiality of the attackers. The *jamadars* have covered their corpses with grass and straw.'

The next letter was at the peak of the disturbances. Those happenings broke his heart. He wrote: 'Since 1921, I have seen several phases of the country, witnessed the soul-stirring period of

Hindu-Muslim unity and also seen British atrocities during various Congress movements. I have seen the tumultuous period of 1942 with its upsurge of passion for achieving freedom, and the frenzy of the Muslim League during the elections. And now I am watching the madness of the majority community. Those days have passed. These will pass too. But I will remember the partiality and the insensitivity of government officials.'

In his letter of 27 September, he wrote: 'The telegraph lines have been cut. A telegram from the government dispatched on 12 September reached Mussoorie only on the 22nd September. One cannot get through to Delhi on the telephone. Four or five days ago, I thought of talking to Pantji [Pandit Govind Ballabh Pant] about the state of affairs here but I could not get the telephone line to Lucknow. Both telephone and telegraph are useless.'

On his way to the office in Mussoorie, he would see corpses on the road. But who was there to bury them? He was the only Muslim walking the streets of Mussoorie. There were only some *jamadars* available to drag the corpses off the roads or throw them into ditches, covering them with earth or stones so that they were secure from vultures and kites, and to keep the city air clean. Probably, no municipal administrator had faced such a gruesome responsibility.

When I thought of all this I felt like committing suicide. He was facing alone the responsibility which belonged to both of us. And here I was sitting secure in Lucknow. Greatly agitated, one day I started from home with the intention of going to Mussoorie. I had gone up to Nazarbagh when my younger brother caught up with me and asked me not to go as no train could reach Mussoorie safely, 'Don't go now. You can go sometime later.' He was anxious about my safety. But I wish I had gone on that day.

Shafi would write to me, 'You should not worry about me. Despite the rain, I am attending the office except for one day a week.' His Muslim employees had been sent to refugee camps. The Hindus did not feel obliged to come to the office. But as soon as the riots subsided, he felt it essential to keep his office open for the sake of riot relief activities. On 28 September, he wrote a long letter to his brother (Rafi Ahmad Kidwai) and another to a friend. The contents of both letters were the same. That detailed letter was lost. After Shafi's murder, when someone asked him about it, he said he had sent the letter to the district magistrate of Dehradun. We did not see that letter again and one does not know why the district magistrate even postponed the enquiry over his murder after seeing that letter. Why? Only the district magistrate could throw light on it. But we have seen the letter he wrote to the friend. In it he said: 'I go to office every day. People consider this a rash step. But had I let fear overcome me, some accident would have befallen me by now'.

In the next letter he wrote: 'All my Muslim clerks are in refugee camps. I have to get their salaries to them and arrange for money to keep them alive. I have ordered that they should be treated as if on leave so long as arrangements are not made for their safe transportation to office and back. To relieve their distress, they should be advanced money from their provident fund. The Education Superintendent is a Congressman, who is hard working and helpful. So long as I have life in me, I will serve them. I am deeply anguished by the cruelty they have suffered.'

For five days after 1 October, no train could reach Dehradun, nor could the buses and motor lorries which had left Dehradun return from those trips. He was worried. He wrote, 'I used to listen to the news on radio. But for three days, the radio has also stopped. I do not know why I cannot telephone Pantji nor talk to my brother on the phone.' And in a letter to my brother and to a friend he wrote: 'These are the moments for sensing God's presence and pervasiveness. Pray for me that I may not weaken. Every man's day is appointed. Death is inevitable but pray for me that God may give me strength and the fear of death may not goad me towards any step which I do not consider right.'

On another occasion, he wrote, 'There is not a sincere friend or sympathizer around. But even without them, may God keep on fortifying me.'

After 2 October, I got no letter from him. Those days he used to post a letter everyday, but it would be no surprise if they had been intercepted.

In October, he used to receive daily threats to his life by letter or telephone. One of these letters was found in his papers after his death.

Aziz Hayat Khan, who was one of the inmates of the refugee camp, told us that Mr. Kidwai would visit them everyday on his way to or back from office, listen to their troubles and sorrows and try to tackle them. A day before his murder, when he came he said, 'Today I have received a warning again.' We asked him what he was going to do about it. He laughed and said, 'Most definitely, I will not go away.'

Rampur House which was housing refugees had three thousand inmates out of which eight hundred were Kashmiris and Ladakhis. Some were labourers while others were also contractors whom the municipality owed thousands of rupees for the work they had done. On that day, they fell at his feet and prayed that their dues be paid so that they could go home. Shafi promised them that he would get them paid 'tomorrow'.

But when that day came, the Kashmiris wept bitterly that fate had deserted them (Shafi was killed that day). They did go back from Mussoorie but as penniless derelicts, to starve in their native land.

Shafi was then engaged in struggling against the communal partiality of government officials and the callousness of the majority community. All of them wanted to get him out of the way. On the other hand, he thought it his duty to confront them. This conflict cost him his life. How could he approve of their activities? Many feared that he knew too much and should be eliminated. Others wanted to prove themselves—protectors of their community, by killing him. But neither the insistence of his friends in Dehradun nor anxious letters from home could avert that fated day.

Now when I think of it, probably it was I who did not insist that he should come away. My brothers would say to me accusingly that if I put pressure on him, he would come away from Mussoorie. But who knew him better than me? With what face could I insist? When I compared his courage with my own cowardice, I felt ashamed.

To run away from danger, to retreat before opposition, to take any step against his own conscience was alien to his nature. He looked upon the country as his native land. He believed that he had as much right to live here and go about his business as any other person. The ruin of the country was his own ruin. He had to fight for this birthright. With this conviction how could he desist from helping the victims of the riots?

No one had been able to stop him from doing what he thought to be right, and neither did I. Sometime earlier, I had written to him in these words, 'I think no responsible person should leave his place of duty. It is possible that because of you some tens of human lives might be saved, and hundreds protected, or the sufferings of others relieved by your personal position.'

But the truth is that deep down within me I wanted him to come away or find some way to get to him. I longed to be consumed in the same fire with which he was playing. But I was helpless. Privately, I kept on praying for him and forbade my brothers to try to telephone or wire him. Once or twice I myself wrote to him: 'Deep in my heart I want you here. If you come away to Lucknow, it would be better. If only people here would allow me to leave, I would have been with you myself.' On 2 October, he wrote to me, 'Anis, do not weaken me. I will not move from here. Let the riots be over, then I will tell the truth to everybody. Otherwise whatever be my fate, only pray to God that I may remain firm.'

This reply enhanced my deep-felt respect for him. He could have run away and saved himself. In fact, that was what he was being advised to do. But he looked upon Gandhian non-violence as the biggest weapon against injustice and standing alone on the soil of Mussoorie he wanted to raise his voice of protest against the ongoing bestiality. How could I break his resolve when I was myself convinced of the truth in him?

With these thoughts I attempted, in vain, to calm myself. But God knows in what agony he spent the next three or four days. He was all alone. The siege of the foes was tightening around him with threatening letters and intimidating telephone calls and the steady steps of approaching death. My God, when I think of those days, I remember a couplet he recited while having his bath.

Kisi ke munh se na nikla
Mere dafan ke waqt
Ki in peh khak na dalo
Ye hain nahai hue'
No one should say at the instant of my burial,
Don't sprinkle earth on him for he is already bathed!

Such an ominous recitation! I lost my temper and quarrelled with him. He kept laughing, but never recited this couplet again in my presence. This incident keeps coming back to me.

In Dehradun, Mr. Khurshed Lal and others of their own accord got his berth reserved for 18 October and it was decided to send him to Lucknow. But fate had planned otherwise. Between 9.00 a.m. and 10.00 a.m. on his way to the office, he was waylaid and killed below Baharistan. Who was the peon with him? Who were the killers? Where did they come from? Why did the policeman who was posted for his protection only two days earlier stay at home and not accompany him? So many questions, but neither we nor the peon could answer them! The pistol which he had kept in his pocket on Khurshed Lal and Azad's insistence remained in his pocket. Since 1921, I had not seen him handling a weapon. When they gave him the pistol, he had protested, he did not know how to fire it. They tried to teach him and impressed on him to keep it in his pocket all the time. But at the moment of the fatal attack he did not consider it necessary to take it out of his pocket. Months later when we got it back, it had been cleaned up except for some blood spots, which put the seal on his innocence.

After having thrown off his heavy yoke, he must be very happy. He had lived through great hardships and self-denial. Hardly, one-twentieth of his income was spent on himself; he always gave precedence to the needs and wishes of others.

For once I was gripped by the fire of revenge but soon I regained control of myself.

Where thousands had been massacred, the thought that he died unsullied was enough to console me; he had never tyrannized, killed or ruined anyone and he paid the debt which his humanity owed to God and his people.

A friend asked why we hadn't demanded an investigation and made efforts to trace the killers. What could I tell her? I had no desire left. The arrow had been shot from the bow. How could it return? The wound in the heart would become a sore. In life's wilderness I would not know another spring.

Why should I help to get the killer caught and cause his wife to be widowed? Why should I be the cause of his children being orphaned? Perhaps, the killer has a mother. Why cause her to writhe in grief? Investigation and punishment for a crime was the business of the government. They did not need to request my permission to do it.

What had happened to me was nothing new. The same calamity had befallen thousands or rather lakhs and lakhs. How I wrestled with myself, explained to myself, and prayed that God give me the strength which Shafi had prayed for, for himself.

A week passed in this state? But how long could it go on? I was alive and for the world I had to present myself as a living person.

Therefore, I began to pull myself together. After four days of hard thinking I came to this conclusion: True, I could not join Shafi in Mussoorie. But I would go to Delhi and submerge my own agony in that sea of human suffering which was swamping Delhi. Gandhiji was there with his spirit in action. Delhi, which was an open book of India's past, which had been pulled out by the roots as many times as it had been replanted. Sometimes it had been ransacked by foreigners, sometimes it has been ravaged by its own people and sometimes by outsiders.

In its ancient book of history a new and bloody chapter began on 5 September 1947. In this storm-tossed city, I came to drown my deepest grief in the hope that I might find some clue to the future.

Jab kishti sabito—salim thi
Sahil ki tamanna kaon karey
Now in my broken boat,
Why should I want to reach the coast.

When my boat was intact and steady, I never thought of the coast, why wish for it now?

Translated from Urdu by A. J. Kidwai *

* Mr Anwar Jamal Kidwai (died in 1996), formerly Vice-Chancellor of Jamia Milla Islamia, was the younger brother of Begum Anis Kidwai.

Hindu-Muslim Social Relations
1935-47
ISHTIAQ HUSAIN QURESHI

There are quite a few eyewitness accounts of the communal holocaust that took place in Delhi. Nirad Chaudhuri's is one. So is Ishtiaq Husain Qureshi's (d. 1981). He was Professor and Head of the History Department in the University of Delhi, a leading exponent of the Pakistan movement, member of the Constituent Assembly and minister in the Pakistan Government from 1949 to 1954. He authored a number of scholarly books on medieval and modern Indian history. He also wrote pamphlets in the Pakistan Literature Series endorsing the two-nation theory. This is what he wrote to Jinnah on 14 June 1946:

'I am a wholetime servant of a Hindu-dominated university and it is not possible for me to take part in active politics. But I feel that I could perhaps render some insignificant service as a student of history and politics. . . .I am an ardent Leaguer, though my occupation prevents me from doing any active work. . . .'

In an extraordinary gesture of goodwill, St. Stephen's College, University of Delhi, has instituted memorial lectures in honour of him.

The purpose of this paper is to record my personal impressions of changes in the social relations of the Hindus and the Muslims that took place between 1935 and 1947. It should be remembered that by the year 1935 the idea of the establishment of a separate state where the Muslims would be in a majority had already been mooted but it had not evoked much discussion or response. It was around 1935 that the demand for Pakistan began to gather support and developed a momentum which led to its establishment in 1947. This change in the Muslim outlook could not have happened without accompanying changes in the social and economic relationship between the two major communities of the subcontinent. A

From *Miraj to Domes* (Karachi, 1983), pp. 59-71.

description of these changes by an eyewitness who can recall certain events and developments may possess some value for the historian. It may be mentioned that apart from the records of the political activities in support of and against partition and the communal riots which became such a feature of life in the twenties and even more so in the thirties, there is little on record to give a student of this period any information about the changing pattern of inter-communal relations. Obviously, therefore, the writer of this paper has to depend mostly upon his own impressions. These impressions are not scientific in the sense of studies based upon surveys and assiduously collected data and, therefore, their validity may rightly be challenged. Indeed such scientific accuracy is not claimed. Nevertheless, being based upon firsthand knowledge and experience this paper may not be devoid of all value.

Autobiographical material which would throw light upon this aspect of the question is extremely scarce. For the relations between the two communities during an earlier period we have an extremely good record in Nirad C. Chaudhuri's well-known book *The Autobiography of an Unknown Indian* (1951), but it does not even come up to 1935 so far as the theme of this paper is concerned. I have not come across any study of a similar nature by a sensitive and observant Indian or Pakistani regarding the years 1935 to 1947. In presenting an attempted description of inter-communal relations during this period, I have to rely only on my own impressions. A number of undocumented illustrations could have been given to illustrate the points made, but even if facts had been mentioned profusely they could not have added much in the way of providing a fully scientific basis for these observations. For this reason there is no justification for transgressing the limits of space that should be imposed on a paper.

It must be also admitted at the very start that within my own limited experience, even during a period of growingly strained relation, a number of facts could be found which might point in directions different from those indicated in this paper. However, I have chosen only such happenings as, in my opinion, indicated the general trend and to which the greater volume of happenings corresponded.

I have dealt with some of the psychological factors formulating Muslim attitudes in an earlier and fuller work, *The Muslim Community of the Indo-Pakistan Subcontinent* (The Hague, 1962), and do not intend to repeat all that has been said in greater detail there. Two points, however, must be mentioned. The Muslims in the subcontinent have always been anxious to preserve their separate identity. This has made them highly sensitive to any real or even imagined danger to their religion or culture. And then there's a certain amount of revivalism. Most of the manifestations of ill-will leading sometimes to riots and ugly incidents, were basically the result of revivalist feelings among the Hindus and the anxiety of the Muslims to preserve their identity. Relations were less strained when the two antagonisms did not have much impact upon each other and did not affect the masses to the extent of inciting them to violence. Here also the question of volume is involved. Small manifestations of Hindu revivalism would not have produced the same results as did larger attempts that embraced broader aspects of life. On the other hand if the Muslims had not been prone to look upon everything indigenous but not adopted by them to be a source of extreme danger to themselves, feelings would not have been exacerbated to such an extent as to make it difficult for the two communities to work harmoniously.

After the post noncooperation intensification of Hindu-Muslim antagonism which expressed itself in movements like *shuddhi*, *sangathan*, *tabligh* and *tanzim* and gave a high crop of riots, the situation was showing some signs of improvement around the year 1935, which was partly due to the fact that the Muslims themselves were not quite clear in their minds regarding their future destiny in the subcontinent. Politically-conscious majority opinion still thought that the best way would be to find a *modus vivendi* with the majority community and to form a unit of a multinational state. As this was considered to be the desideratum by the enlightened Muslims, they were not in favour of augmenting or keeping alive inter-communal friction in any manner. It was, however, difficult to press demands for effective safeguards and substantial autonomy without, in one way or another, creating in the Hindu mind misgivings of their intentions and, what was even more important, of their complete identification with Indian nationalism. The average enlightened Hindu looked upon all such demands as essentially anti-national, narrow-minded, based on prejudice and inevitably resulting in a weak state.

These feelings, however, was not very much on the surface, so far as social relations were concerned. The friction of the twenties had not died out. The economic and social repercussions of that friction were still visible, but it was at least felt seriously by a small number of thinking men and women that effort should be made to achieve harmony and friction should be removed so far as possible. This attitude, with the hindsight that we possess today, seems to have been a form of escapism for the well-intentioned because one does not find any efforts of a positive nature to bring about greater harmony. Either people pretended that the problem did not exist or they thought that it was best left untouched or did not consider it polite or pleasant to bring it up on social occasion.

It must be remembered that the intermingling of the two communities at the social level was meagre and confined to the more sophisticated westernized people who would meet one another in clubs. Club life was not popular amongst the Indians at that time and only an infinitesimal part of the huge population cultivated it. Relations at such urbane levels were still pleasant because of the general desire not to throw bricks in otherwise placid waters. This, however, did not mean that the people who met at such levels had no strong political opinions or that personal intimacy removed present or potential political hostility. It only meant that relations had not deteriorated to an extent that would have made social contacts impossible.

Indeed there was little on the horizon that would make feelings immediately exacerbated. The elections to the provincial legislatures in 1937 were fought, generally speaking, in an atmosphere of understanding. At that time, as is generally known, there was no friction between the stated aims of the Indian National Congress and the Muslim League. The scene, however, changed with the formation of the Congress ministries in many provinces. It is not intended to discuss here the policies of the Congress governments, nor is this paper the proper place to discuss the rights and wrongs of the Muslim feelings against the various Congress governments. What the formation of the Congress governments brought out in the open had been lying somewhat dormant below the surface. With substantial power being transferred into the hands of the people of the subcontinent, the innate tendencies could not but assert themselves. The resurgent nationalism of the Hindus started asserting itself in many ways which it considered to be legitimate. If there was to be a common Indian nation, it had to have a common language. This common language should have its roots in the Indian past and also perhaps in the common substance of Sanskriti origin in the field of vocabulary. This also applied to the script. Such a language could only be Hindi and not Urdu and because words are impregnated with history, culture and religion, therefore, the general culture of India inevitably was to be Hindu. It had to express and interpret the ideals of the majority, its traditions, *mores*, history and ideals. To the average Hindu citizen and politician it seemed only natural that it should be so. He felt puzzled that such a simple proposition was not accepted without opposition. And he could not, perhaps, be blamed, because the sophistication needed for sustaining a multi-cultural society is rare in even more politically developed societies. This attitude filled the average Muslim with alarm and he resented all attempts at Hinduizing the language, the culture and education.

It seems that this was a natural development and it is doubtful whether it could have been prevented. Even if the Congress had exercised the utmost wisdom, it could not have adopted the policy of going slow, but, to my mind, it could not have resisted popular pressures for any length of time. Similar Muslims, resistance to this process would also have ultimately come to the surface, even if the assertion of Hindu national instincts had been slow and cautious. Perhaps this resistance would have developed gradually. In the beginning it could have been less violent. Nevertheless at some stage or the other, the injury to deep-rooted Muslim feelings would have resulted in discontent and frustration.

The year 1937 is rightly considered to be a turning point in the history of the subcontinent. Its importance was magnified because of the lack of experience and foresight on the part of Congress leadership, but it would have remained a turning point in any case as fairly effective authority was transferred for the first time to the representatives of the people. Such transfer could not but raise their inner conflicts and psychological antagonism to the political level. There is the possibility that in case of a more gradual change Muslim sensitivities would have been dulled to a certain extent and perhaps if the possibility of lengthening the process had existed and been utilized, the Muslims might have made adjustments to the new order.

However, all this is mere speculation. Long nurtured ideas do not die so slowly and have an inconvenient habit of making themselves felt time and again. In any case because these antagonisms came to the surface and resulted in widespread and frequent communal riots, feelings were exacerbated and social relations now came to be affected because people's minds were greatly exercised not only by what was happening but also by the possibilities of what might happen in a not too distant future. The writer of this paper was away from the subcontinent from June 1937 to September 1939 when considerable intensification of ill-will took place. Perhaps the fact that he had remained away for two years from the scene gave him a vantage point. He could compare the conditions that he had left behind in 1937 with those that he found prevailing when he came back in 1939. Even though he had remained in touch with the happenings in the subcontinent through newspapers and correspondence he was amazed at the change that he witnessed on his return. The atmosphere was now surcharged with emotion and even in social gatherings statements were made which showed the extent of estrangement that had taken place. The Pakistan resolution was not adopted by the Muslim League until 1940 but the idea of Pakistan had caught the imagination of the Muslims like wild fire. They had come to believe firmly that they could not accept a common destiny with the majority community. The majority community in its turn had been exasperated to such an extent that any suggestion that parting company as friends might be the solution of an otherwise extremely difficult question was looked upon as treason to the ideal of united nationalism.

In view of this exasperation it could not be expected that there would be any attempt at understanding the point of view of the minority. There were a few exceptions here and there among the Hindus who saw some justification in the Muslim desire for separation, but such Hindus were extremely few. Their number sank into insignificance even when compared with that of the Congress-minded Muslims who still believed in a united nationalism and therefore, were called nationalist Muslims. The writer can look back with satisfaction and gratitude to the friendship which was extended to him by a number of his Hindu friends and even more by Hindu students who came into direct contact with him. What is being written hereafter is being done with the fullest consciousness of their kindness. The majority of these friends and students, indeed all of them, were quite firmly convinced that the Muslim attitude was not only deplorable but criminal, but they did not permit this feeling to affect their personal relations with me. On the other hand they never ventured to discuss the question of Pakistan with me, nor for that, did they get any encouragement from me. For the purpose of maintaining my social relations with Hindu friends, colleagues and students and not poisoning them by a discussion of my political convictions or theirs, I also scrupulously avoided any discussion of Hindu-Muslim relations with them. Political questions were invariably discussed by the Muslims with the members of their own community. Thus practically dialogue on the question of Pakistan ceased at the personal level. Only the press and the political leaders went on discussing the merits of the Muslim case or tearing it to pieces. There was more talking at each other than talking to one another.

In a situation like this it was quite obvious that positive efforts had to be made to maintain any relations. Indeed the worst of escapism was practised by everyone concerned in the sense that it was thought that the discussion of unpleasant topics must be avoided if relations were not to be poisoned. I do not blame either others or myself for this attitude because the Hindu and Muslim points of view were now clearly defined and there was almost a total acceptance of the views of the leaders of either side on these points. Besides the atmosphere was so greatly charged with emotions that it would have been impossible to carry on a discussion objectively or with restraint. Arguments would have carried no weight in the face of convictions held as strongly as religion itself.

This was the general pattern. There were, however, occasional outbursts in private meetings which did little to improve the situation. I remember several such occasions quite distinctly and my counterparts in the other community having to deal with Muslim colleagues and students might perhaps recall similar instances. In a weekly seminar held for the purpose of discussing the developments in the second world war a student blurted out without any provocation that the treatment meted out to the Jews in Nazi Germany was fully justified in view of 'their anti-national activities'. Up to now this remark, however deplorable, would not have created the ill-will that the sentence following it did. He added, 'if the minorities in India were not careful they would have to be dealt with precisely in the same manner.' There was no occasion for a remark like that and yet in a way it was quite natural because the Hindu mind was so much exercised by the likely role of the minorities, especially the Muslim minority, in a future independent India that the student's action was almost entirely involuntary. As an isolated instance it could have been dismissed as irresponsible behaviour of a student, but unfortunately it reflected a good deal of common thinking. I had to stop counter remarks by any of the Muslim students who formed a small proportion of the seminar. I simply ruled the remark out as irrelevant to the discussion.

I found a distinct decline in what was markedly a liberal atmosphere among the honours and postgraduate students. Up to the year 1937 liberalism was very much in fashion. I think that most of it was sincere so far as the university community was concerned. There was a certain schizophrenic tendency to keep the liberal and communal bias in watertight compartments, but, by far and large, liberalism was not openly questioned. From 1939 onwards I found that attitudes had become less liberal and there was a somewhat open adherence to the doctrine of intolerance for the purpose of national good. An incident would perhaps illustrate this point. I was informally discussing with a small number of students the desirability of basing domestic and foreign policies of a free country on the principles of fairplay and justice. We were not discussing any particular problem, nor was this really a profound discussion of social or political ethics. My surprise was therefore extreme when a student said rather excitedly 'What is justice?' and then he went on to add 'Is it just on Mr. Jinnah's part to demand Pakistan?' I responded mildly by saying that I was not prepared to discuss the justice or otherwise of Pakistan on that occasion but I said that I hoped that in principle it would be accepted that the only method of securing good and orderly government at home and peace abroad is an adherence to the principles of justice. The student then said, 'One gets a little tired of this word "justice", particularly when so many unpleasant demands are put forward in its name. In any case the word "justice" is so difficult to define that it cannot be accepted as a principle any longer in statecraft or international relations and even if it were accepted it would be difficult to determine where justice lay.' This, to my mind, was not an entirely indefensible remark, however morally deplorable it might be. I conceded that it might be difficult in certain circumstances to determine where justice lay, but I said that if one came face to face with a situation where justice was not difficult to define one should not shirk its consequences. 'When anyone comes face to face with justice,' said I, 'let him not turn his face away from it.' The next remark was, in my opinion, extremely revealing. He said, 'In certain instances where national interests are at stake, it is a patriotic citizen's duty to turn his face away from justice.' I was completely stunned. Such sentiments would have been impossible before 1935. This is by no means the most outstanding example of lack of liberalism, but coming from a comparatively intelligent, mild and decent young man it reflected a tendency that was frightening.

Such instances out of incidents witnessed by me—and they could be multiplied—would reveal that, in spite of excellent personal relations existing between the teachers and the students, social relations had a tendency to run into difficulties and the superficial pleasantness and the artificially cultivated smoothness of discussion could not truly hide—even in the academic atmosphere of a university—the fissures that had taken place underneath. As a matter of fact there had not been much co-mingling of ideas. Persons who were less willing to exercise caution and restraint in their actions and expressions of opinion were far too many even to permit a superficial avoidance of the unpleasant. So far as the Muslims were concerned they also tended to withdraw even more into themselves. They also scarcely could say anything which was perfectly honest and sincere—apart from the general banalities—which would not injure the feelings of others. Gradually the sole communication, so far as the Muslims were concerned, could exist between them and the non-Hindu minorities, where differences could be discussed in a somewhat dispassionate manner.

With the growing bitterness in the dialogue between the Indian National Congress and the Muslim League and particularly after the enunciation of the June 3rd plan, relations became extremely strained. This could be felt even in normal academic and official work. The university community could not escape from the effects of the poisoned atmosphere of the city of Delhi or for that matter of the subcontinent as a whole.

What was happening in the city was now a nightmare. Many quarters in the old city could be easily fortified by placing strong gates on the narrow streets providing ingress and egress. Very soon began a feverish collection of arms. A good deal of material from army disposals after the war surreptitiously found its way into the black market. The fortified *mohallas* (as the quarters were called) developed into arsenals. One could see that an undeclared and unofficial civil war was in the offing. It became the practice to organize parties of able-bodied inhabitants into groups who manned strategic places. At night the house tops began to bristle with armed men. This seems to have been a countrywide phenomenon and ultimately resulted in mass killings in many areas. The details of these pogroms are available in the newspapers and need not be repeated here. The killings were ghastly. A large number of innocent men, women and children were murdered. Feelings were inflamed by every story of rioting and killing that appeared in the press. It did not take long in cities like Delhi for groups to indulge in street stabbing. It became dangerous even to pass through the main thoroughfares of the city. People seldom ventured out at night; most of the killing was done in broad daylight. Stabbings were invariably cowardly because someone would emerge out of a narrow lane stabbing the victim from behind and disappear, once again, into the labyrinths of the narrow streets of the localities. These killers were sheltered by the inhabitants and could not be traced.

Under such circumstances the meagre social relations which had survived among the members of the two communities came practically to an end. Even the economic relations between the two communities were disrupted. In this the Muslims were the main sufferers. Delhi had a long tradition of Muslim craftsmen working for dealers in traditional materials. For instance, the makers of gold and silver laces (*gota*) were given materials by the dealers and their products were bought for wholesale and retail sales. The dealers stopped supplying materials or purchasing manufactured articles, resulting in great economic distress to the craftsmen. The same catastrophe befell the manufacturers of gold and silver leaf which was used in fairly large quantities for decorating sweets and dishes. A similar situation developed in handicrafts relating to brass and copper, brocades, ivory and certain decorative arts.

Then began a war of nerves and the nights were full of full-throated war cries raised by hundreds of men in one locality or another. Soon after Sikh and Hindu refugees started congregating in Delhi. Throughout this period militant organizations like the Rashtriya Swayamsevak Sangh were active. The Muslims had participated in the inhuman acts of stabbing and the blame for this can be apportioned to both the communities equally. The Muslims, however, did not have an organization like the Rashtriya Swayamsevak Sangh. Soon with the help of the ration dealers, more or less full lists of Muslims living in exposed and undefended localities were compiled. It was known almost with full accuracy how many persons were living in a locality and for that matter in a house. The ration trade was almost entirely in the hands of the Hindus. In such localities it became common for Muslims to find that their houses had been marked at night with the inverted Hindu *swastika* for pogroms which were being secretly organized.

Delhi became a prison for the Muslims. Trains were searched and Muslims were killed in cold blood. Buses and cars met with no better fate. The most ghastly killing took place when the Grand Trunk Express going to Hyderabad and Madras was stopped and every Muslim, man, woman and child was slaughtered. News now started pouring in from the surrounding villages and townships of large-scale killings. The Muslims could not help noticing the coincidence that the Sikh deputy commissioner who was now always surrounded by leaders of the Rashtriya Swayamsevak Sangh would visit a village one day and the very next day its Muslim population would be exterminated. I had known him earlier. He was sociable and had visited me in my house once or twice quite informally. He had admired my collection of Mughal miniatures. After my house had been looted, rumour has it that they found their way to his house.

I lived on the campus of the university. In close proximity was Jawahar Nagar which was a Rashtriya Swayamsevak Sangh stronghold. The camps of the refugees were also quite near. The arrival of the refugees naturally raised a wave of sympathy for them. I tried my best to accommodate and help refugee students because it would have been inhuman not to try to mitigate human suffering. The feelings of the Hindus and the Sikhs were greatly embittered for which no blame could attach to them. Soon after armed Sikhs and others were seen roaming in and around the campus. As I had been elected to the constituent assembly on the Muslim League ticket, I was now an enemy for all but my own circle of friends and students. My movements were watched, throughout the day and the night. Some agent of the Rashtriya Swayamsevak Sangh was posted at a vantage point to keep an eye on all those who came to see me. A student whom I knew to be a Rashtriya Swayamsevak Sangh member came a little too often to see me. Some Muslim friends pointed out to me that I was in a precarious situation, but there was little I could do. There was a small Muslim community on the campus and if I had left, their morale would have collapsed.

At last the inevitable happened. The Muslim inhabitants of Timarpur, which was within a mile of the campus, were attacked. Stabbings around the campus became common. One day a Muslim recluse living in a deserted mosque nearby was killed. The next day the male members of my family went to the nearest mosque to offer Friday prayers but found it locked and deserted. About a mile away from the campus were located orchards which extended for miles. As the fruit trade had been a Muslim monopoly, the orchards were peopled by Muslims who worked there. By Friday afternoon Muslim refugees from these orchards began to pour in towards the university because many had been murdered. That night was full of terror for us. We could hear screams of men, women and children who were intermittently being killed in their homes. Next morning the campus was attacked. There was no loss of life, but all Muslim houses were looted, one by one. Muslim students and teachers were evacuated with difficulty. We escaped in our car. Women hastily put on Hindu caste marks on their foreheads and put on Hindu clothes. I took them to the Pakistan High Commission. The streets were littered with dead bodies. My nine-year-old son looked up and said simply, 'Father, are you afraid?' I said truthfully, 'No.' I had no emotions at that time. Our house was looted soon after.

I lost all I had except the clothes on our bodies and the money in the bank. I did not mind that, but the loss of my personal library containing some rare manuscripts and miniatures, quite a few of them heirlooms, was difficult to bear. I had two of my own books, one in manuscript and the other in typescript ready for the press, both of which were irretrievably lost.

The following day, I sent my family into the Old Fort, where the Muslim refugees from the city had congregated, and plunged into rescue work. There were many memorable incidents, but the most significant of these was that I brought Dr. Zakir Husain, later President of India, from his house at the Jamia near Okhla, at that time several miles out of Delhi, and we two went and saw Gandhi. We did not have to tell him much because his workers were reporting events fully and truly. There was no effort to hide the truth from him. I said to him that only he could stop the carnage. For a moment he grew thoughtful and promised simply, 'I will put my best into the effort.' And I think he did keep his promise. Otherwise he would not have been assassinated.

From the Valley of the Jamuna to the Valley of Hakra

MASUD HASAN SHAHAB DEHALVI

Unlike Josh or Khwaja Ahmad Abbas, Masud Hasan Shahab Dehalvi is not a prominent figure in Urdu literature. Standing apart from any ideological position or political movement, his is the voice of one who spent his childhood and youth in the old city of Delhi, a symbol of mixed living and composite culture. For this reason his impressions gain significance here.

Like many others who went to Pakistan, in this excerpt from *Delhi ki Bipta,* he reflects on the aspects of Delhi's life which were intellectually enriching. The underlying nostalgia is widely shared by people of his background.

The city of Delhi, situated in the Jamuna valley, always fascinated the Hindu rajas and Muslim *badshahs.* That was probably why they made it their capital. The rajas named it Indraprastha; Raja Dehlu called it Delhi and Shahjahan named it Shahjahanabad. *Auliyas* and *Shaikhs* graced this city and called it the home of the twenty-two *Khwajas.* No one knows how many times this city was devastated and how many times was it resettled. Muslim kings ruled over Delhi for a thousand years. The British flag flew over it for more than a hundred years. It was here that the flagbearers of freedom faced an alien government boldly, and shot or hanged to death.

On a day in the month of August 1947, the sun rose heralding the dawn of India's Independence. Delhi too breathed the air of freedom. But this freedom brought with it the message of death and destruction for the Muslims. All through the freedom struggle they were often subjected to the tyranny of an alien government. But now they were attacked by their own people. The old, the young and the children were killed mercilessly. Women lost their

'Wadiye Jumna Se Wadiye Hakra Tak', from *Delhi ki Bipta* (Bahawalpur: Maktaba Ilhaam, 1987), pp. 5-6, 12-24.

husbands, children became orphans. Homes were ransacked and plundered. The Muslims were driven out of their country. Their crime was that they had demanded a separate, independent country for themselves where they were in a majority, where non-Muslims could not exploit them and where they were free to lead their lives according to the tenets of Islam. The whole of India had become independent, but the areas where Muslims were in a majority were now called Pakistan. The erstwhile India was divided into two regions. One continued to be called India, while the other—Muslim India—assumed the name of Pakistan. There was no provision for compulsory migration of Muslims from areas which did not form a part of Pakistan at the time of independence. The city of Delhi was one such area where Muslims had lived side by side with Hindus. But the bigotry of the Hindus forced them to leave Delhi and go to Pakistan. Those who were not prepared to leave the country were told at the point of dagger that there was no room for them in India. People who refused to listen were promptly sent to Pakistan.

The sight of people being murdered was extremely disturbing. I had got married on 4 May and had just begun to experience the joy of marriage. These joyous moments were completely overshadowed by violence and suffering. My maternal uncle and aunt, whose daughter I had married, had come all the way from Bahawalpur for the occasion. The marriage ceremony was still to be performed when the riots broke out, and they faced great difficulty in returning home to Bahawalpur.

Thanks to these riots, even my marriage was solemnized during the curfew hours. I had to procure curfew passes for the guests. Zahirul Hasan Fitna, the elder brother of Nazish Haideri, who wrote humorous poetry, said in his laudatory poem in praise of the bridegroom, i.e., myself, which ran somewhat like this:

The groom has chosen this time for his marriage.
Because he knows the whole town is under curfew.

Only a few days after my marriage, bloody riots broke out. Because of them we had absolutely no idea how the great occasion of Independence was celebrated in the city. September turned out to be especially gruesome for us. The place where we lived, Bhojla Pahari, was situated behind the Hindu locality. Close to the Hindwara was a predominantly Hindu area. Initially we kept hearing of riots in Subzi Mandi and Paharganj. But they soon spread to the streets and lanes of the walled city. A couple of incidents also took place in our locality. A newly-married person who had gone up to the roof of his house was shot at and killed by a Hindu. Another unfortunate man who came out of his house was shot down by a soldier. The poor fellow was still alive after he was hit by the bullet and was groaning with pain when a soldier thrust a bayonet into his chest and belly and killed him.

This incident took place in the lane right in front of our house. The other members of our family also saw this ghastly scene. But no one could muster courage to go out and stop the soldier from doing that. They knew that by doing so they would jeopardize the security of their family.

After witnessing this incident, my mother lapsed into complete silence. Other members of the family were also terribly shaken. Seeing that our area was unsafe, I persuaded my people to move to my office, which happened to be very close to the Juma Masjid. From there I took my wife and went over to the residential quarters located in the neighbourhood of Niyariyan where my maternal grandmother lived with her younger son, Tajammul Husain. We planned to go to Lahore by air and then overland to Bahawalpur. I had already bought the tickets for the journey a few days earlier because I knew that was the only way I could take my wife there. But unfortunately our tickets were cancelled at the eleventh hour. After a couple of days one of my maternal uncles, who happened to be the son of Khan Bahadur Bahauddin, and lived in Kucha Pandit, came and told us that if we wanted to go to Pakistan, a truck would pick us up and take us to the Old Fort. We discussed the matter, considered the situation in Delhi and concluded that it was better for us to go to Pakistan for the time being. When the situation would return to normal we would come back. The following day the truck arrived. We boarded it, along with other people of the neighbourhood. We were accompanied by our maternal grandmother, younger maternal aunt and her baby daughter. Tajammul Husain was employed in the Railway Clearing Accounts Office. Having opted for Pakistan, he had already left for Karachi. Our maternal grandmother was old and frail. She could not walk and had to be carried by one of us. The result was that we took just a few essential things with us, and reached the Old Fort leaving our house and our entire belongings at God's mercy.

There was complete confusion when we reached the Old Fort. Every one was engrossed in his own problems. The whole area, spread over a few miles, was teeming with people from Delhi. It seemed that the entire population of Delhi had shifted to the fort. We too selected a spot hoping that God would look after us. A large number of people had reached the Humayun's Tomb, which had been converted into a refugee camp. Ever since I had come to the Old Fort, I was constantly reminded of my parents and brothers whom I had left in my office. In the circumstances it was impossible to leave Delhi without taking them. I wished that if I left Delhi, all of them should go with me. Later, I gathered courage and went from the Old Fort to Juma Masjid. I told my parents how we reached the Old Fort and asked them to accompany me because that was why I had come.

My mother and brothers agreed, but my father kept saying: 'You take them with you. I will join you later.' But I prevailed upon him with great difficulty and persuaded him to come with us. Mother left us for a while to fetch some essential things and food from home. As soon as she returned we took a *tonga* and reached the Old Fort. The whole place was in the grip of complete confusion. The women who had never stepped out of their houses were going around without bothering to cover themselves properly. The food that mother had brought stood us in good stead. The men of the family had to fetch water. Some water taps were installed in the Fort, but it was an arduous task to fill up even half a bucket. The water carriers raised the rates of a single leather bag to Rs 5. We were helped with fuel for cooking our food. Lots and lots of building timber, belonging to some contractor, was lying outside the Old Fort. He allowed us to make use of precious wood worth lakhs of rupees.

Two days after my family moved to this place, we came to know that special trains were being organized to take people to Pakistan. All those who wanted to go were asked to board the truck the next morning and reach the railway station. These trains were to start from Basti Nizamuddin. The following day my brothers and their children boarded the trucks, reached the railway station and left for Pakistan. After that we waited for our turn to leave. We then heard that all the trains for Pakistan were waylaid by rioters and their passengers butchered. We cancelled our plan to go by a special train and, instead, decided to travel by air. But the problem was that only government servants and their families were allowed to travel by air. My father—serving the Delhi Municipal Committee—did not fall in the category of government servants. Somehow, we contacted a close relative who didn't have a family of his own and persuaded him to take us with him. The next day we reached the airport with him. When the staff at the airport checked our tickets, they found that we had an extra child with us. Actually one of my younger brothers, Zahirul Hasan (now Deputy Director, Information), was still a small child, and the other one was my maternal uncle's daughter. (Thank God the two are now wife and husband). We had bought half-tickets for the children and were expecting the seats to be allotted accordingly. But the airport officials told us that a full seat had to be allotted to even those with half-tickets. So we could take only one child with us. It was a tricky situation. My father, who had heard this, offered to drop out so that the others could proceed. His suggestion posed a greater problem. We feared that if left behind, no one would be able to bring him to Pakistan. Suddenly I thought of a solution. I took the Captain of the plane into confidence and asked him to announce that an extra seat was available in the other plane. One of us could occupy it. Father was pleased to hear this and said to me: 'All right, you sit here with your wife. I will go to the other plane.' Now that would have exposed the truth. So I told him that I was willing to travel in the other plane because of the company of some friends on board. . . .

The plane took off. I was left alone. I returned to the Old Fort where I waited for three more days to catch the next flight. I was able to fly to Rawalpindi. I grabbed the opportunity with God's name on my lips. After reaching Rawalpindi, I went to the railway station. The whole city seemed devastated and deserted. Even though I had not seen it before, I could not imagine that it would be like that. Actually here, too, the rioters had caused havoc and ruined a flourishing city. Anyway I reached the station and bought a second-class ticket. When I stepped on to the platform, I found the place so densely crowded that it was difficult to spot the train. People were hanging on to the train; some sat right on top of the compartments. My misfortune was that my wife's suitcase had been left behind with me. It had her precious silk suits. I had to carry it myself. A noble person saw me and asked where was I going. I told him that I wanted to go to Karachi via Lahore. He told me that the route to Lahore had been closed because of floods. The trains were now going to Karachi via Lyallpur. My idea was to first go to Lahore and ascertain if my brothers had arrived there safely or else find out what had happened to them. Only after confirming this would I proceed to Karachi. But when I learnt that this was no longer possible, I accepted the will of God and decided to go to Karachi. The gentleman who had offered to assist me said: 'You stay where you are. Let me go and see what I can do for you.' He went and came back after some time and made me get into a compartment, saying: 'You sit here in comfort.' In the circumstances, finding a place like that was nothing less than a miracle. But soon after, the railway guard and ticket checker arrived and took me to a compartment which had no seats. Mail bags were scattered all over. I sat on one of the bags and the train started. It was a night's journey. I hadn't slept for the last so many nights. With all my near and dear ones gone, I had not slept at the Old Fort in Delhi.

I was sitting in that uncomfortable position when sleep began to overpower me. Just then some people entered my compartment brandishing naked swords. They told me that they were out to wreak vengeance on the non-Muslims for uprooting and driving out Muslims from their homes in India. The swords they were carrying had been snatched from the non-Muslims. Now they were on the way to Lyallpur to hunt down more of them. They consoled me by saying that 'now that you have come to your home, you don't have to worry about anything.' The net result of their talk was that I felt a little more reassured, and feeling relaxed, went to sleep. I had put on many clothes, one on top of the other. I had a West End watch, with an alarm in my overcoat pockets. When the train reached Lyallpur my hand went into my pocket to take out the watch. But it wasn't there. I looked for it all over the compartment thinking that I might have dropped it somewhere. But it was nowhere. Most probably I had been relieved of it by the crusaders of Pakistan who had come to give me the good news that the people who made me suffer were being punished by them. I suddenly thought of the cash I had with me. I had divided it and stuffed it into different pockets. When I searched the cash too was gone. Only my ticket and the change saved from a hundred-rupee note were still there in an inside pocket. The crusaders had proved their great skills!

It was in this state of penury that I reached Karachi. But the tragedy was that I had not noted down the addresses of any of my relations in Karachi while leaving Delhi. A notebook with my father had the addresses. After getting down at the Karachi railway station, I looked around thinking that I might see someone I knew. But I was disappointed. It was Sunday and the offices were closed. So, it was not possible to ring up the office of a relative and inform him of my arrival. I was at my wits' end when I remembered that Jamil Wasti could be contacted at Sind Madrasa College. He might have the addresses of some of relatives. When I enquired about the location of the college, I found it was close to the station. So I found a coolie to carry my luggage and reached there. The Principal's bungalow was nearby. I met him and enquired about Jamil Wasti who was Vice-Principal of the college. He told me that Jamil lived in Fikri Mansion in the Sadar area. I asked him to send his peon to fetch a victoria (a horse-drawn coach) for me. He did so and told him to go with me to Wasti's house. When the victoria arrived, I told the peon to explain the route to the coachman. He did this and sent me on my way. The coachman was a cunning fellow and wanted to take advantage of my being a stranger in the city. Each time he covered a short distance, he would stop and tell me that the fare had now gone up to this much. Then after travelling a little further, he stopped and said: 'After all, where do you have to go? I won't go any further.' I understood his game. He wanted to get more money out of me. I pretended that money was no problem and said to him: '*Baba*, don't worry about money. I will give you whatever you want. Just take me to my destination'. Hearing that he took me straight to the Fikri Mansion. I had still to locate Wasti's flat when the coachman came to me and said: 'Here is your luggage. Now give me my money.' Just then Jamil Wasti emerged from somewhere. When he saw me, he asked what was going on and then turned to the coachman and said: 'You wait. I will just call the sergeant. He will tell us how much we owe you for a journey from Sind College to this place.' Hearing this, the driver simply vanished. When I entered Jamil Wasti's drawing room, he was reading a letter he had just received by post. He placed it in front of me. An acquaintance had informed him that his father, mother and brother had been killed. I felt the earth slipping from under my feet and thought 'what bad luck to enter his house at a time like this!'

Jamil Wasti was the brother-in-law of my paternal aunt's son and was a regular contributor to my publication, *Ilham*. I offered my condolences and said that I had come to him only to find out if he could give me the address of one of my close relatives. He took out a notebook and told me that anyone who came to meet him after Pakistan had come into being, put his address down. It was quite possible, he said, that the book would have the address of one of my relations. He found the address of Noor Ahmad, my brother. It was just the place I wanted to go to. He was the son of my mother's sister who later served as the deputy director in the department of broadcasting and information at Islamabad. My father and other members of the family too were to stay with him.

Let me tell you that the news about the death of Jamil Wasti's father M. A. Ghani, ex-principal of Islamia College at Lahore, was not true. Both of them moved to Bahawalpur. Anyway when I set out from there after taking down my brother Noor Ahmad's address, I met with a few familiar faces. Noor Ahmad lived in the locality of Jetland line. When I got there everyone was delighted. They had given up all hope of seeing me again. To begin with, they kept waiting for the other plane which was supposed to bring me there. Then, my father kept going to the airport for a couple of days to see if the other plane had arrived from Delhi. When he couldn't gather any information, he resigned himself to fate. My arrival gave a new lease of life to our family members.

Our plan was to go to Bahawalpur. We had to take my old maternal grandmother to her son and my father-in-law, Ajmal Hasan, who was employed there even before the birth of Pakistan. My wife, who was unable to meet her parents after our marriage, also wanted to go there. So we left Karachi and travelled to Bahawalpur. Once there, we stayed put. My maternal uncle advised us to settle for good and stop thinking of going elsewhere.

That is how this land, called the valley of Hakra and the centre of one of the most ancient civilizations and cultures, became our permanent abode. Forty years have elapsed since we settled here. Now we are a part of this country, but memories of Delhi still linger.

The heart still yearns for Delhi's literary gatherings. What a wonderful time it was! What marvellous people! The anxiety to provide for our daily needs was very much a part of life even then. But despite this burden, people did not deprive themselves of the other pleasures that life offered them. After the day's long, hard work and the rough and tumble, when evening descended, these people dressed, came out of their homes and set out for the Juma Masjid to refresh themselves. The Juma Masjid had the distinction of being the cultural centre of Delhi. People from all walks of life gathered there. Its steps were converted into veritable *bazars* where anything from grilled fowl to especially prepared festive food, from sweet ices to all sorts of sweetened, cold drinks were offered by the hawkers. Here and there one also came across caged-birds and hen coops. Situated in front of the eastern gate of Juma Masjid were the tombs of Hare Bhare Shah and Sarmad, the martyrs, around which one could see the dervishes dancing to the tune of *Dam Mast Qalandar*. The water carriers moved around with their leather bags, clinking their water bowls to attract people's attention. It is said about Sarmad, the martyr, that he was a Jew who later embraced Islam and after attaining mastery in both spiritual and temporal realms, achieved sainthood. He wandered around naked. They say he was infatuated with a Hindu lad, but later that love was transformed into the love of God, and a stage came when he began to say, 'I am the Truth.'

The *ulama* of the time objected to this and petitioned the Emperor Aurangzeb to declare him a heretic and order his execution. They say that before he was executed, he recited the following couplet:

My beloved severed my head from the body,
That put an end to my suffering; else the headache was too
severe.

According to the legend, it is said that after his execution he picked up his severed head with his own hands and reached the stairs of the Juma Masjid saying: 'I am the Truth.' Alongside his shrine was the tomb of an outstanding leader of the struggle of independence, Maulana Shaukat Ali, the elder brother of Maulana Mohamed Ali. Not far from it was the Parade Ground where hoards of precious stones and medicinal herbs were sold.

One came across groups of people crowding around a quack selling his miraculous cures. These quacks harangued the people and made such extravagant claims that their listeners gasped with wonder. Located in this complex was the grave of Maulana Abul Kalam Azad. (He became the Minister of Education in independent India.) At some distance stood the tomb of Shah Kalimullah Jehanbadi. There was much hustle and bustle around it every Friday.

People who were fond of listening to *qawwalis* and seeing enraptured individuals going into a state of trance came there in droves. Before the establishment of Pakistan, Mustahsan Faruqi, editor of *Aastana*, had to look after this place, which he did with complete dedication. He had the whole *khanqah* repaired and reconstructed. Hazrat Shah Kalimullah lived at the time of Emperor Farrukh Siyar. He had succeeded to this spiritual seat from and with the blessings of Qutab Medina, Sheikh Mohiuddin Yahya Madani. A celibate all his life, he attained perfection in innumerable fields of learning. Amongst his writings, *Sawa-al-Sahil* and *Tasnim, Ashra Kaamla, Quran-a-Quran* and *Muraqa Sharif Aur Kashkol* were considered the Chishti guides for good conduct. Of the people who preceded him in this religious office, Hazrat Maulana Nizamuddin Aurangabadi was a highly esteemed Chishti saint. The Chishti order was strengthened in India by Khwaja Fakhruddin Fakhar, son of Maulana Nizamuddin. Khwaja Nur Mohammad Mahaswi was also one of the famed spiritual successors to this office. Punjab was indebted to him for his spiritual dance. His *khanqah-i-Chishtian* in district Bahawalnagar is even today a place of retreat for the common people.

Situated adjacent to Shah Kalimullah·Jehanbadi's tomb was a place for recreation called Edward Park. An equestrian statue of King Edward was installed there. The *karkhandars* (workers in workshops around Juma Masjid) of Delhi made fun of it by saying that was exactly like him, the Englishmen would run away from India. After Independence this statue was replaced by one of Subhas Chandra Bose who played a prominent role in India's struggle for independence. It was he who raised the Indian National Army. Many Indians joined it and fought against the British.

Edward Park was a popular meeting place for those who were fond of strolling or wandering in search of amusement. One could see groups of people sitting around. Poets gathered to recite their works. Such impromptu poetry meets were held almost everyday. On occasion some senior poets of Delhi would join such sessions to encourage up and coming poets. To the north of this area was the famous Urdu Bazar. It was lined with bookshops from one end to the other. A large number of writers and poets, often famous, flocked to the area in the evenings. The shops of Wali Ashraf, the brother of Ashraf Sabuhi and Maulvi Samiullah, the son-in-law of Mufti Kifayatullah, were the two main meeting places for writers and poets. Visiting writers and poets too congregated here. The office of the Urdu monthly *Peshwa*, edited by my brother Hassan, was in Urdu Bazar. The office of the Daily *Ansari* was also located in this area. Hilal Ahmad Zuberi was its editor.

Many tea-shops and restaurants crowded in the same area to the north of the Juma Masjid. Masita's famous *kebab* shop was a part of this complex. This gentleman was a master cook and a highly principled man. No one was served out of turn at his shop. The *kababs* were prepared and handed over to his numerous customers on a first come first served basis. Even the most important people had to wait for their turn.

Two hotels were located to the north of this complex from where the *bazar* turned to Chitli Qabar. One was known as Saeed Hotel and the other by the name of its owner, Hafiz Shah. One could always spot a poet or two among their regular customers. My office was situated in the upper storey of the Hafiz Hotel. My preceptor Khayam-ul-Hind Haider Dehalvi had made it his permanent office. It was here that I first met the late Raza Ali, member of the Viceroy's Council. Sirajuddin, Inspector of Schools, often visited the place. One of his sons later became secretary to the Government of Pakistan. No poet in the country who visited Delhi failed to come here.

The bustle of the Juma Masjid area could be observed from the office verandah. The tram station directly in front of our office was always crowded. On Friday, the day of prayer, the whole place was filled with people; row after row prayed, reaching right up to our place. At times the devotees spilled over and had to be accommodated in our office and on the roof of the two hotels.

That reminds me of an interesting incident. Once, on a Friday, our office was getting ready to take in these people when my preceptor suddenly picked up his stick to go out. I asked him: 'Where are you going? Aren't you going to say your prayers?' He replied: 'Now that Allah has seen this house it is better for me to leave.' Next to our office was the locality called Chatta Sheikh Manglu, from where one could go towards Churiwalan. The office of the periodical *Din Duniya* was located in this area. The Ansari Printing Press, owned by Hilal Ahmad Zuberi, too was there. My paper was printed at this press. Nawab Aziz Ahmad, who was the honorary magistrate of Delhi, also lived here. He was a very elegant and cultured person and maintained excellent relations with the people. No one had ever seen him coming out of his house unsuitably clad, i.e., in *topi* and *achkan*. Syed Murtaza Ali, who occupied a high post in the office of the Commander-in-Chief, lived opposite Nawab Aziz Ahmad. He was also related to me. Once or twice I met him in connection with my job. He was a tall, lanky fellow, deeply interested in literature. Jigar Moradabadi, the famous Urdu poet, always stayed with him. Directly in front of my office were the junk shops. At the end of the street was Hakim Dilbar Husain's place. Further down to the west of Juma Masjid was the post office and the office of Mustahsan Faruqi.

The people of Delhi were very fond of merrymaking. As soon as clouds appeared in the sky and the weather turned pleasant, groups of them headed straight for recreation spots. Humayun's Tomb, Qutab Minar, Okhla Madrasa and Roshanara Gardens were some of the most popular picnic resorts. On such occasions people dressed in beautifully embroidered muslin *kurtas*. They carried boxes full of delicious food which included *parathas*, minced meat and mangoes. They relished sweets and spicy preparations. Special orders were placed with sweet sellers for sweets like *andarsas*. The festival of flowers (*Phool Walon Ki Sair*) and the festival of staffs (*Charion Ka Mela*) were held at Nizamuddin and Qutab Sahib, respectively. Kite-flying and rearing pigeons were the most popular pastimes.

I am reminded of an incident of my childhood. A kite, cut loose by someone, passed over the roof of our house. I started running after it. By chance, a gentleman who lived in our locality was passing by and was surprised to see me doing this. He stopped me and said gently: 'Imagine the children of our gentry chasing two-penny kites like that. What degradation?' His words left such a deep impression that thereafter I never left my house to grab a kite. Actually, the neighbours cared for the morals and manners of the locality's children more than their own parents. We, on our part, greatly respected the elders of the neighbourhood.

Translated from Urdu by A.S. Judge

My Ordeal as a
Citizen of Pakistan
JOSH MALIHABADI

Cast your steady and loving stare at poesy's Laila.
Well past lexicons and glossaries, can you get a glimpse?
Meanings do not flutter over the heads of syllables
You have to descend inside the bosom of words to feel
the experience.

Shabbir Hasan Khan (1898-1982), popularly known as Josh
Malihabadi, would rank, along with Mohammad Iqbal, Faiz Ahmad
Faiz and Firaq Gorakhpuri, among the great Urdu poets of this century.
He was the *Shair-i Inqilab*, the poet of revolution, a nonconformist,
an iconoclast and a relentless crusader for social justice, human dignity
and equality. His poems (the first collection was published in 1921)
have, in the words of the noted critic Syed Ehtesham Husain, 'all the
heat of fire and his ideas all the force of a volcano'. In his patriotic
and revolutionary poems, including 'A Dream of Prison-break' and
'Address to the Sons of East India Company', he enunciated his theory
of revolution for reconstruction, clearly expressed in these lines:

Behind the facade of the destruction of this fossilized man
The work of creating a new man is in progress.

Josh was editor of *Aaj Kal* and adviser to the All India Radio before
migrating to Pakistan in 1956 against Jawaharlal Nehru's advice. He
was tormented by the decision. A loner in Pakistan, he missed his
friends from Hyderabad, Bombay, Delhi and Lucknow. His eclectic
and unorthodox ideas were severely criticized. At the same time, the
'unselfconscious candour' of his autobiography reveals the

'Pakistan Shahriyat' from *Yadon ki Baraat* (Delhi: Shaan-i-Hind Publishers,
Reprint 1992), pp. 284-298.

opportunism, fickleness and, above all, vulnerability of a great literary mind.

It was probably around 1948 when I dropped the idea of selling vegetables and reached Delhi. I went to Panditji [Jawaharlal Nehru] straightaway who talked to Sardar Patel over the phone and fixed up a job for me. He also agreed to arrange a pension for me from some of the states. He then asked me to meet Mian Azim Husain [son of the Punjab Unionist Party leader Fazl-i Husain], secretary of the Information Department.

Mian Azim Husain turned out to be a gentleman. I was impressed. He told me that I would receive a monthly salary of Rs 1,100, but wondered if this paltry sum was sufficient to make both ends meet. I told him that Panditji had promised to organize a literary pension.

When I stepped into the crowded hall for the interview [editorship of *Aaj Kal*], I noticed a large number of applicants [*lashkar*, or army, in the original]. The expression on their faces changed when they spotted me. They were haunted by the prospect of being rejected. For this reason I was deeply upset. I wish I hadn't come and caused such disappointment to so many. I was reminded of the verse of Urfi [Persian couplet of Urfi Shirazi omitted]:

I entered the interview room and noticed Mian Azim Husain, Ajmal Khan and four or five other persons who were not known to me. I made myself comfortable and took out my *paan* box. Just then, a Madrasi-looking gentleman told me in English to refrain from chewing *paan*. I protested indignantly. 'You are free; yet you adhere to the norms laid down by your erstwhile colonial masters. I'll not stop. Chewing a *paan* is like breathing. If you don't approve, I leave. I was just about to do that. That is when Mian Azim Husain and Ajmal Khan intervened and told me to go-ahead.

Thereafter, probably Ajmal Khan said to me: 'How do we interview you, Josh *Saheb*? Please recite your poem against the Nizam' [of Hyderabad]. I replied: 'Ajmal Khan, what's the use? My poetry won't go down well with people who are still influenced by British manners [and customs].'

In response, Mian Azim Husain, Ajmal Khan and several other people said in one voice: 'Please do recite your poem. We are your admirers.' I did so and the interview was over thereafter.

After joining *Aaj Kal* as its editor, I went over to meet Panditji. He asked if I had met Sardar Patel, the minister of my department. I told him I hadn't. Nor did I intend meeting him. Panditji wanted to know the reason. I replied in English: 'Because he has got a criminal face.' [*Is liye ke unka chehra mujrimon ka sa hai*]. Panditji burst out laughing. 'No, no, you must meet him. I'll fix a meeting.' He did just that. I was asked to go across to his [Patel] residence immediately.

Clad in his *dhoti*, Sardar Patel stood in the porch. 'Sardar *Saheb*', I said to him after the handshake, 'I was keen to meet you for a very special reason.' He was a hard nut to crack. 'Special reason?' He understood and asked why was I so keen to meet him. I replied: 'The reason is that I've heard very many comments against you'.

He led me to a room. After we settled down, he said to me in English: 'You would have heard that I am an enemy of the Muslims. I know you are brutally frank in your conversation. So am I. That is why I want to say to you clearly that I respect Muslims like you whose ancestors came from outside India and settled in this country. But I don't approve of those *shudras* and lower-caste Hindus who embraced Islam under the influence of the Muslim governments. Such elements are, in actual fact, extremely prejudiced [*mutaasib*], wicked [*sharir*] and troublemakers [*fasadi*]. They are a minority; yet they want to keep the Hindu majority under their thumb'.

I said: 'Sardar *Saheb*, first and foremost, the entire humanity belongs to one race. I have no faith in the caste system at all. Secondly, how does it matter if somebody's ancestor was a *chamar* two or three hundred years ago? Do you think his station in life has not been transformed? Is he still a *chamar*?'

He was about to reply when his secretary reminded him of his appointment with the Maharaja of Patiala.

I ran into Maulana Azad as soon as I came out of Sardar Patel's house. He stopped his car and called me over. And when I got off my car and went over to him, he had a pained expression on his face. 'Josh *Saheb*, you and Sardar Patel.' I bowed my head, while he read the verse. [Persian couplet omitted].

The Maulana departed after reciting the verse, but I was greatly troubled. After all we've made such sacrifices to achieve independence. What for? To sound the death-knell of Urdu? To leave Muslims confused and bewildered? I recalled the words of Qazi

Azizuddin, the prime minister of Datia state, who had said to me: 'Josh *Saheb*, did I not tell you that Hindus would slaughter the Muslims the day India is free?' Another thought came to me. Why didn't the architects of Pakistan consider the fate of those Muslims who were destined to remain in India? Why did they not take every single Muslim along with them to Pakistan? I then comforted myself with the hope that mutual hatred and prejudices would be overcome. A socialist government would be formed, one that would put an end to the divisive forces. That is when religious collectivities [or fraternity] would be replaced with universal brotherhood [*insaani biradari*].

Ye ek shab ki tarap hai sehar to hone do
behisht sar pe liye rozgaar guzre ga
Faza ke dil me purafshaan hai aarzooai ghubaar
Zaroor idher se koi shehsawaar guzre ga.
This is the agony of the night, let the dawn come
Paradise will descend on earth
Desires spread wings over heart's domain, for the dust to rise
A chevalier will surely pass by.

In 1955 I went to Pakistan for the third time to take part in a *mushaira*. Then, as also on previous visits, my friend Syed Abu Talib Naqvi (chief commissioner of Karachi) invited me to settle in Pakistan. But on this occasion he was more insistent than before.

I was not prepared to live in Pakistan. But I didn't want to hurt Naqvi by saying so. In order to avoid any further discussion, I agreed to consider his request.

Naqvi organized, while I was still in Pakistan, a gathering at his house and invited the elite of the city, including Iskander Mirza. My *musaddas—Husain aur Inqilab*—was recited. Everybody present, including Iskander Mirza, insisted that I settle in Pakistan. By God, I was convinced that I would not do such a thing but ended up by agreeing to consider the suggestion.

'Josh *Saheb*, how long will you keep on thinking?' Naqvi persisted in getting an answer. I was exasperated. How long could I postpone a decision? [*Aur bedudh ka baccha paala rahun ga*]

One day he turned up at the Metropole Hotel to secure a firm commitment from me. I said to him: 'You know that I love you and that I would be prepared to give my life for you. But ...'

'Now, don't you say no.'

I kept quiet. Naqvi moved from his sofa and sat next to me. 'So, when are your coming to Pakistan?'

I braced myself for the occasion, lowered my eyes and told him: 'How can I come to Pakistan so long as Pandit Jawaharlal Nehru is alive!'

Placing his hand on my shoulder, Naqvi asked: 'And what will happen after Nehru? Have you thought about this?'

'I pray to God that I don't live to see that day.'

Naqvi said: 'A poet's greatest misfortune is that he tends to weigh the serious problems of life in the scales of emotions. I want to know if you've considered your future in the event of Nehru's death during your lifetime. Who will admire you in Hindustan? What would happen to your job, your leisurely life, your prestige? Even if you are treated well, you must consider the future of your children. What happens to them after you? They would be at large and without a patron. So far I've been discussing the material aspects. The cultural [or *tehzibi*] dimension is also important, nay, alarming. Your children will be made to read Hindi and not Urdu. They would read translations of your poetry in Hindi. Indeed, they would have no links with your cultural and intellectual heritage. Such is the likely scale and magnitude of the impending social and cultural transformation. Are you prepared to accept the massive destruction of a tradition? If you don't settle in Pakistan, it would simply mean that you are ready to sacrifice your family interests in order to serve your personal ends.'

I was stirred to the depth of my heart by his long, sentimental, coherent speech. What would happen to my pampered children who are accustomed to a comfortable life-style? And my wife with her aristocratic temperament? Of course, my children will not be able to do well in India.

I told Naqvi that he had shaken me up but I needed more time to decide. 'I'll let you know my final decision at this time the following day.'

I turned to Nasir Ahmad after Naqvi was gone. He agreed with every word spoken by Naqvi.

Raising his forefinger in the air, he said emphatically: 'If you don't migrate to Pakistan, you will repent all your life. 'You and your ancestors have ruled over Malihabad for many generations. Your *ryots* tremble in your presence, bow before you, salute you. The children of the same lot [*usi do kauri ki riyaya*] will preside over the lives of your children. They would make them wear *dhotis* and grow *chotis*. God willing, may we not live to witness that day.'

I woke up in the morning, had a bath, went over to Naqvi's house, and conveyed to him my readiness to migrate [*hijrat*] to Pakistan. He was delighted. At that very moment he directed the deputy commissioner to allot a plot of land on Jehangir Road for a house and a cinema hall, and 50 acres of land (I don't remember the name of the place) for an orchard.

I gained possession of the land. My *chaukidars* built their *jhonpris* and started living there.

With the formalities over, Naqvi asked me to travel to Delhi, secure an emergency certificate and bring my family over to Pakistan. The cinema hall, he told me, would be built after my arrival. His secretary Rabbani found me a small house in the Sind Muslim Housing Society. I then took a flight to Delhi.

I reached Delhi. Panditji was out of town. He was expected to return after two or three days. I went to see the Maulana straightaway. He had already read a newspaper report in a that Pakistan was trying to rope in a Hindustani poet. He promptly pointed towards me. 'Probably, you are the one.'

'Yes, Maulana, I'm the poet.' I narrated my story, repeating every word of Naqvi's speech. 'Now Maulana, what's your opinion?'

He asked a few questions and understood the problem and its various facets. 'Your *hijrat* will be a source of embarrassment to us. But, I believe, you should go for the sake of your family. Naqvi was right in saying that after Nehru's death you will not be well looked after. Why just you, nobody would care for me either [*ap to ap khud mujhe koi nahin puche ga*]. I tend to view problems from a logical [or pragmatic] standpoint. Not Jawaharlal. He is intensely emotional and would not agree to your going [*hijrat*].'

On the third day I reached Palam airport, greeted Panditji, drove back with him to his house and explained everything to him. He was visibly distressed to hear Maulana Azad's reaction.

'Josh *Saheb*, you've placed me in a difficult [or awkward] situation. In my opinion, you wouldn't have considered abandoning your country but for the narrow-minded patriotism of the Hindus. Anyhow, this is a very delicate [or sensitive] matter. Let me think for a couple of days. I will also seek the Maulana's opinion.'

I went back to Panditji after two days. I noticed the relaxed, bright expression on his face, an expression that comes naturally to those who have solved a knotty problem. Beaming and smiling, he announced that he had come up with a solution.

'Is it not true that you are going to Pakistan to safeguard the material and cultural interests of your family, and to promote the cause of Urdu?'

I agreed. 'There is no second reason.'

'In that case your children can be Pakistanis. But you stay put in India. Make a trip to Pakistan for four months each year and serve the cause of Urdu. The government of India will grant you leave and pay your salary for the period of absence.'

I jumped at Panditji's suggestion. I told him that I endorsed his idea wholeheartedly. In this way I would have the best of both the worlds.

Panditji was delighted and hugged me.

The very next day the media men cornered me. I explained my discussions with Nehru. My interview appeared in the English and Urdu newspapers two days later.

PAKISTANI CITIZENSHIP

*The going of Prince Gulfam in the fourth direction only to be surrounded by demons and evil spirits.**

Before I turn to the evil spirits, let me tell you that Naqvi *Saheb* dampened my spirits when I revealed my future plans in the light of discussions with Panditji. He made it clear that no land allotment could take place unless I agreed to be a Pakistani citizen. Nobody would build a cinema or raise an orchard. 'Your children are dear to us because they are yours', he said.

Naqvi added: 'Besides, to which country would you belong to? In Pakistan you will be treated as an Indian, whereas the Indians would be suspicious of you because your family members are citizens

---

* All the Princes in our folktales were called *Gulfam* (resembling a flower). they were always told by the mother to hunt only on the three sides of the jungle and avoid the fourth side, the side inhabited by evil spirits and demons. But people are so often drawn towards the forbidden area. So the *Gulfams* did the same. As a result, they found themselves surrounded by evil spirits and demons.

of Pakistan. And haven't you decided to spend four months in
Pakistan? Josh *Saheb*, you can't cross a river with your feet anchored
in two boats. Mind you, your credibility would be undermined in
both the countries.'
    I was rudely shaken by what Naqvi said. He was realistic and
talked sense. I accepted his arguments and became a citizen of
Pakistan.
    Now, about the evil spirits.
    Soon thereafter, there was a massive outcry in Pakistan. All hell
broke loose in Karachi. It seemed as if the bugle announcing
doomsday had been proclaimed [*goya sur-i qayamat phoonk dya
gaya hai*]. Urdu and English newspapers came out into the open
and declared war against me. So did intellectuals, poets and
cartoonists who acted in tandem against me. [*tamam adba wa
shuara aur cartoon-saazon ne apne apne qalmon ki talwaren niyam
se nikal kar mere khilaaf mazameen, qataat aur cartoonon ki
bharmaar kar di*].
    There were noisy and uproarious scenes everywhere, as if the
great Mughal—Abul Talib Naqvi—.had divided Pakistan into two
and handed over one part to me. People belonging to different
groups forged a common front and united against me. For example,
the Wahabis, the Barelwis, the Deobandis, and the Qadianis. The
Sunnis and the Shias set aside their long-standing differences of
1,400 years to act in unison and declared war against me.

chaman me kya gaya goya dabistaan khul gaya [Ghalib]
As I stepped into the garden, it became a school, as it were.

My going to Pakistan was like a dreadful dacoit ransacking the
treasures of Qarun. Or Abraha laying siege to the Ka'aba. Or
Kamdev sneaking into the palace of the virgins. Picture the virgins
running helter-skelter and repeating the name of Allah —*Hai Allah!
Hai Allah!*
    News of the uproar reached the ministry of external affairs. Naqvi
was asked to give an explanation. Realizing that I was the source
of his difficulties, I quietly surrendered the plot of orchard land and
the cinema.
    In those days Chaudhri Muhammad Ali was the Prime Minister.
Naqvi fell out with him. He took on the prime minister on the
strength of Iskander Mirza's backing. But the Mirza turned his back

on Naqvi. He was removed from office. Naqvi's downfall was the last straw. I was left high and dry.

I thought of returning to India, but did not do so to protect my self-respect and dignity. I asked myself, 'Khan *Saheb*, what next?' My heart told me not to give up. 'If there is a thorn one can make a bouquet' [Persian line].

Some people suggested that I secure a license and get into the import-export business. I got into the act only to realize later that I was not fit to be a trader. I would leave in the morning, return to the house in the afternoon, rest for a while, and then set out again. Running around was a nightmarish experience.

My state was reduced to the *alam* that is taken out by the village people during Muharram. Amidst the din and clatter of drums, the *alam* is placed in the courtyard of every household, taken out in a procession, and then brought back to the house amidst the same din and bustle.

My running around was unrewarding. Yet I came across directors, secretaries and ministers only to experience their demeaning behaviour and conduct. They were a pathetic lot, arrogant, crude and ill-bred. I concluded that there was no place for a man of letters in this community [*qaum*]. Every writer and poet should commit suicide. It is true that the Hindu officials are often pretentious, but, *Allah-o-Akbar*, when a Muslim becomes a head-constable he starts acting like a *Haamaan* and Pharaoh. Once in power, children of domestic servants and street vendors regard themselves as a Kaiser and a Darius.

Consider, [the litany of my complaints] the list of my failures:

1. I voluntarily surrendered the cinema plot at Jehangir Road, along with the orchard land.
2. I made a bid for a cinema plot, but failed to pay its price.
3. The deputy commissioner of Karachi, Hashmi, gave me 50 acres of land for cultivation. Altaf Gauhar confiscated it.
4. I was given a permit for cycle-rickshaws, but their prices crashed in the market.
5. I was allowed to build a cold-storage but the financiers were told to back out.
6. Likewise the financiers were prevented from investing in another business proposition that was worked out with Wajid Ali Shah.

7. Secured a license for the sale of leaf tobacco, but could not stand the behaviour of the official. I said unpleasant things to him and came home in a huff.
8. The minister was removed when I was about to receive the permit for the equipment of the cinema.
9. The minister changed when I was about to receive permission to start a textile mill.
10. The minister was removed just before he was to give his assent to my printing press.
11. The secretary in the fisheries department who issued a permit to me was removed.
12. My attempt to buy a petrol pump proved abortive.
13. A house was allotted to me but I have yet to occupy it.
14. My application for a job in the department of village upliftment was rejected.
15. I could not find a publisher for my books.
16. I was allowed to start a restaurant in the corner of Friar Hall. The concerned officer was transferred.
17. I was not paid remuneration for the work I did for the Sindhi Adabi Board.
18. An officer in the rehabilitation board allotted me land for building a house. But he did not extend to me the courtesy of rising from his seat; so I tore up the letter of allotment in his presence.
19. The chief minister of Punjab, Qizilbash, was to give me permission to start an industry. Just then the army staged a coup and his ministry was dismissed.

Jis jagah hum ne banaya ghar sarak me aa gaya

I was completed disoriented with these unending failures. I was acutely depressed and poverty-stricken. The thousand rupees loaned to me by Naqvi every month was inadequate. To make both ends meet I used a friend to sell off the jewellery.

How long can one sail in a paper boat? My wife asked me to cut down on expenses; so I gave up drinking. I was like a child from whom milk is taken away. To overcome my craving for alcohol, I had an early dinner. But I continued to be restless. I picked up a book but found it so very hard to read. Alphabets slithered like snakes and words appeared like scorpions with their sting-tails up.

I would keep tossing and turning in bed. Not a wink of sleep. My body used to itch a lot and I would scratch myself for hours. I was in acute pain and my agony was like that of the severed tail of a lizard. And when I looked into the mirror in the morning for my daily shave, I would be shocked to see my gnat-like face crumpled by sleeplessness. I looked like a pauper sitting on the stairs of Delhi's Juma Masjid flashing his teeth and begging for alms.

If I was lucky enough to get a wink of sleep on a day or two, I would wake up with unpleasant and disjointed dreams. The tick-tick of the clock—like the blows of a sledgehammer—would add to my agony . . . .

Translated from Urdu by Mushirul Hasan

Delhi in Mourning

KAMALADEVI CHATTOPADHYAYA

When Kamaladevi Chattopadhyaya was a little girl, her mother took
her to meet Annie Besant. She asked Mrs. Besant to bless her so that
she also grew up like her, with the same zeal and enthusiasm to bring
about changes in our society and the position of women.

Kamaladevi (d. 1990) did grow up to be one of the women leaders
of the Satyagraha Movement, having joined the Non-Cooperation
Movement in 1921. She was also a member of the Indian National
Congress, and in 1926 was the first woman to stand for elections from
Mangalore. Although a founder-member of the All India Women's
Conference, she resigned in 1930 to work full-time in the Civil
Disobedience Movement. Arrested several times, she was gradually
drawn to socialism while in jail, and in 1934 she joined the Congress
Socialist Party.

After Independence, Kamaladevi devoted herself to the revival of
handlooms and handicrafts. She is remembered today as much for her
work in this sector, as she is for her political activism.

The birth of freedom on this *elevated* day did not bring India any
such ennobling benediction. On the contrary the country was
shaken by a volcanic eruption.

All Delhi seemed ablaze waking up ghostly memories of bygone
invaders who pillaged and looted this beautiful city. Fires raged right
and left as bloodless hands ripped what they could lay hands on.
Streets were strewn with loot. Women cried, children screamed. We
rushed where we thought succour could be given. Pandit Nehru
was often seen dashing into these turmoils, which provided the
greatest moral boost. The very sight of him against the flames with
us following, brought out even some of the timid, the wary, the
doubters, the unbelievers (some of whom may have been with the

. From *Inner Recesses Outer Spaces: Memoirs* (New Delhi: Navarang, 1986),
chapter 10, pp. 306-10, 313

evildoers in spirit). I think it was Pandit Nehru's most elevated moment, as also the darkest, when he saw the concept of secularism in tatters, its rising edifice in flames. He fought with desperation. None of us wanted this to be a rearguard action, rather, an onward leap through this very baptism. Alas the evil is still with us. Not just a shattered dream, but a haunting ghost.

Secularism was one of the concepts we wanted to wear more as a jewel on our chest with conscious pride rather than practice as an article of faith. We flaunted it rather than practice it. No wonder it came to mean so many different things to different people. But that did not worry us—each to his own. We rather puffed with pride, even though religious rituals kept intruding into so many of our national functions. We played down the fact that what are called communal conflicts were on the increase. In short there is hardly a time now when we are free from them.

I wonder how many can really define a true secular state as a concept of a passionate adherence to the ideal of freedom of thought, conscience, to profess and practice the faith of one's choice or even choose not to practise any faith, that the State as such would not identify itself with or be controlled by any particular faith or its laws be dictated by the fundamentalism of a particular religion. When we characterized this new state when it was formed as secular, we presupposed not an atheist or anti-religious State but one consisting of people who believed in and accepted the spiritual dimension of each personality, to rise above his or her own narrow emotional orbit to integrate into a multi-dimensional harmonious fellow-feeling.

As I watched this unbelievable turmoil descend on us at this long-fought-for hour of liberation, a spark ignited in the darkness. Why not make something worthwhile emerge out of this agony? I decided to apply myself to the rehabilitation of some these uprooted families, though the very thought weighed heavily at the sheer magnitude of this colossal task.

To me the appropriate answer lay along the cooperative path. To these families torn away from their age-old homes who now faced the challenge of remaking new homes, modelling new vocations, all in unfamiliar settings, equipping themselves to meet unaccustomed challenges, in such a context, cooperation to me was the mechanism. The resources, equipment, experimentations could all be *shared* therefore with less hazard in their struggle, and convert despair into hope and on to achievement. But for this an organization was called for. I drew up a blueprint for a cooperative body that could plan, generate action and coordinate functions.

I was at a loss whom to consult, whose aid to seek. Under this frightful emergency all concentration was on *immediate* relief. Long-term plans seemed unreal. My thoughts flew to Gandhiji. So I took the blueprint to him. He was one person I was confident would take it seriously. And he did, even as he glanced over it. I explained I had already initiated a few preliminary tests. I had visited some of the refugees and several of them were ready to form cooperatives if they got the land, they assured me. I would get the organizing body registered as the 'Indian Cooperative Union.' Would he in the meantime secure land for them? He kept my draft with him to enlist supporters. I was soon called by him. He greeted me with a broad smile. I saw his old alert self again. He had liked the project, felt it should work. In his enthusiasm he had commended it to Pandit Nehru. But the latter however characterized it as utopian, one of those impractical newfangled plans the socialists would think up— and with this crisp comment summarily dismissed it. Gandhiji did not seem too concerned, then he proceeded. 'I shall help and identify myself with the venture. But on one condition. You and the cooperative farmers rely on your own earnest labour, and not lean on the administration. For as you know the first principle of cooperation is self-reliance.' I readily concurred, but reminded him that we would have to get some land, for all evacuee land was in government possession. Thinking for a while he said he would approach Govind Ballabh Pant, as there were sure to be evacuee farms in U.P. bordering on Delhi. 'You go ahead with your promotional body,' he ended on a most optimistic tone. That was Gandhiji. In this dark hour of his agony, caught in the cruelest turmoil of his life, he had time to spare for an ordinary worker, a novice, found time to study my fumbling project paper, tried to help me. Tears trembled in my eyes.

The framework of the Cooperative Union was unacceptable to the Delhi State Cooperative Department as it had been independently set up. An independent cooperative body was an anachronism and a deadly challenge to its established authority.

The usual procedure was for it to sponsor it (a cooperative), appoint its office-bearers, give loans, make its budget, in short, run it departmentally. Gandhiji heaved a heavy sigh when I reported this to him. Then he continued in a low, sad tone: 'I am glad you thought of trying to help rebuild torn lives. Because of the decisions we made, thousands of poor innocent people have to bear hardships. I myself feel it wrong to live in this palatial building. Bhangi Colony, which was my chosen abode, is chokeful of refugees. I am troubled by the thought of families with children out in the cold.' There was great agony on his face, his eyes, his voice.

I never realized then how much of the responsibility for this he took upon himself, that he had erred somewhere down the line for this to happen.

I went to very few of those memorable prayer meetings of his— they were truly fantastic, drawing all sorts of people like a magnet— some hardly aware why they went. At one of these I got a hint in his discourse when he confessed he must have made a mistake somewhere and the mistake must be now having its effect.

I hesitated to visit Gandhiji frequently. Apart from the communal upheavals all over the country, there were internal political conflicts too, and I was hesitant to add to his burden. When I finally went one day I was shocked by the change in him. He looked physically weaker and mentally disturbed. He was being besieged all the time by crowds in distress. There were also piles of letters, papers. I heard him say firmly he must read every single letter, and every letter must be carefully answered. The heavy air however was occasionally crackled and lightened by his unfailing witticism, mostly jokes against himself.

He finally called me to his side. 'Why have you not come for such a long time? I have spoken to Pantji and also to some private individuals. Keep your end ready.' I explained, 'I hesitated to come often as you are very busy . . . .' He abruptly cut me short. I am never too busy to see those who wish to see me. The trouble with you perhaps is you cannot forget you are Kamaladevi, extra sensitive. Look at all the crowd here, they come when they want to.' I was shaken out of myself. Yes, I was too self-conscious. These people were may be simple. As I was ruminating, he broke in on my thoughts: 'You make amends for the past. Come when you feel you want to, just do that.' I was so emotionally moved, I leaned forward and touched his hands as I moved away, a thing I had never done before.

The next time was never to be for the very next evening he was gone. As I stood beside his body that fateful evening, I could not believe he was dead. I touched those very same hands I had said farewell to for I felt I was alone in a vast empty void, with nothing I could hold onto, nothing I could look up to. I had no stomach to watch the funeral. Minoo Masani was taking Jayaprakash who had just arrived to watch the last journey and he persuaded me to join them.

As I do not listen into radio news, I was not prepared for the sight that met me. Gandhiji's body being taken on a gun-carriage on its last journey—to me an unbelievable sight! It was with some effort that I could control myself. Jayaprakash and I looked at each other in painful silence. To me this was adding insult to injury. What slaves we had become to completely alien, irrelevant impacts, adopting ways and manners inimical to what the occasion demanded, outraging our finer fibres.

He died even as he had lived, adhering to his principles, no matter what the cost. He entertained an innate respect for every individual whose dignity he must not violate. To uphold that principle he had ultimately laid down his life.

What a different world we live in now. The public today is universally suspect. The more important a public function the more ferocious the display of weapons, *security* as it is called. Our innate sensitivity has by now been corroded to complete bluntness. Even the invitation, no matter how imposing its appearance, will contain stern warnings of the various *Don'ts* (*sic*) to be observed.

How had it all happened. As I had watched the weird funeral procession, people were standing in dead silence, too stunned, bewildered, dumb. Occasionally some voice would shriek: "Mahatma Gandhi *amar raho—Bolo*,' but the shriek would vanish into the fading light. For no answering voice would come-not even an echo. The million throats stayed dumb, making everything eerie, weird, unreal.

The past few weeks before it one had been persistently hearing of threats to the Mahatma. More tangibly while I was in Bombay. Then came the bomb explosion. Still it did not carry reality. Who would want to kill one who was an embodiment of love and compassion.

When it happened many blamed the victim himself, for he sternly forbade any *security* measures. In fact he openly condemned the very thought of it. At public places, more so at his own prayer meetings, he could not restrict peoples entry. The prayers were open to all. To him threats to those wishing to come, were abhorrent. Whoever wished to come to see him he simply would not bar. He had to be allowed to come freely. For him his life was not worth it if it was to be guarded by weapons. If such a moment came, it meant it was time for him to go. He could live only if he could serve and his service was welcomed. Those who came to him were his honoured guests. Imposing restrictions on their entry to him was barbarous.

These were the sentiments he gave expression to. They showed up the fine fibres he was composed of. Was all that he tried to live up to in vain?

I mused over this catastrophe and wondered how it had come about. Reminiscencing over the times since the advent of the British into India, picture after picture kept floating before my eyes. Immediately preceding the gigantic revolt of 1857, the Muslims had been in the forefront of the anti-British forces. Though the various early Muslim rulers who made heroic efforts to rid India of the British grip, were those whose forefathers had originally hailed from outside, *they* had become one with this country and their patriotism was genuine and exemplary. [. . .]

How then did this catastrophe occur. Now partition hangs on our horizon like a perpetual question mark, tantalizing us.

The concept of partition as a solution to multi-cultural and multi-religious problems has haunted us since that ominous partition of 1947. The British have been using this weapon wherever one of its colonies strove to come free of Britain's colonial coils. Though we in India asserted that we did not believe in the two nation theory, by acquiescing in the partition at the behest of those who forced it on us, we seemed to have accepted it.

The subcontinent was carved as a sop to one man's insatiable ambition, setting a pattern into motion, paving the way to many more splits, goaded by similar bouts of inordinate personal ambitions but under the romantic banner of linguistic states, which neither served any regional language nor developed any regional culture. The country is periodically threatened to be torn apart by such cataclysms. The chain reaction generated in 1947 still continues to spin. We have before us two similar tragedies: Ireland and Palestine.

Several world personalities were seen around after Gandhiji's funeral. How did they materialize, no one asked. It seemed natural they should be there and one kept meeting them both by design or happy accident. [. . .]

The Ganges in Mourning
ARUNA ASAF ALI

Aruna Asaf Ali (1909-1996), a legend in her lifetime, was once described by Jawaharlal Nehru as 'a symbol of these changing times . . . a disturbing and disconcerting individual to many.' Crusader, rebel (in 1928, at the age of 19, she defied convention and married M. Asaf Ali, a prominent Congressman), freedom fighter and staunch supporter of women's rights, an active engagement with politics, it seems, was the organizing principle of her life.

She participated in every phase of the freedom movement, beginning with the Salt Satyagraha of 1930. In the early 30s she moved to Delhi and began working with the Women's League, affiliated to the All India Women's Conference. But 1942 transformed her, and her struggle against the British became markedly militant. In August of that year, she went underground, organizing country wide resistance to British rule.

Secular and socialist by conviction, Aruna Asaf Ali's involvement with the women's movement has always been part of her wider commitment to social transformation.

In 1954, she helped found the National Federation of Indian Women as a radical alternative to more middle class organizations, organizing working-class women in fields and factories.

The noise and fever of existence is never the same from year to year. Patriotism unites a whole people. Its blaze draws within its arc of light the entire mass. Parochial and tribal passion also resembles it and imparts to the group the same intensity and cohesiveness. But in the one case the war is against a common enemy. In the second case the war is a family war. Incalculable and unanalyzable forces work during an internal strife and cruelty rises from screech to screech. Whether the enemy is real or imaginary it

From *Fragments from the Past: Selected Writings and Speeches* (Delhi: Patriot Publishers, 1989), chapters 25-26, pp. 171-9.

hardly matters. In moments of frenzy, the eye is blinded, reason quite blunted and that most hateful of all passions—fear—holds supreme command. If one could only banish her, purge the body, the obsessed mind of all its concomitants and instill instead fearlessness, national and group hysteria would cease to convulse man. If a formula to exorcize the animal fears that haunt individuals as individuals or collectively as masses could be found, these periodic strifes would not injure mankind as wantonly as they do today. How to embolden the spirit of man? Give him confidence that is born of strength and he ceases to be a coward. To create in him the assurance that he will be his own enemy if he is *afraid*, requires a revolution in psychology, environment and above all a sublimation of the *life-instinct*. The will to live is healthy; biologically it is the only urge that is important for race continuity. All the other instincts stem from it and spring out of its main steam. To seek to destroy it is to suggest race suicide. But when craven fear grips man and reduces him to something abject *because he is afraid to die*, race-interest demands that a sublimation, an alteration in the quality of the urge to hold life dear, takes place. On the borderland of this love of life there must be many another urges supporting it, almost acting as scaffolding for the safety of this main drive. If fear of death could prevent death its purpose might have had a healthy aspect. Actually it encourages mortality and all the evils which man is heir to ever since he gave up living in the wilds. Wilderness-living is no solution, quite true. But the chaos and immorality implied in a warring, wrangling and mutually destructive society is hardly civilization.

Lessons learnt in the school of life are not easily forgotten. They teach one volumes even if they leave one shell-shocked and stupefied at times. One must explore before one can analyze. One must analyze for coming to conclusions. There is wear and tear involved in this journeying for knowledge and experience. The world and the antics of its living creatures and man, more than others, are undoubtedly exciting experiences. But when men and women complain incessantly of crimes committed against them, of pain and death and evil that harasses the body and soul, the mind grows sick. Self-imposed burdens sit lightly as a rule, but in moments which confront the mind with pictures of suffering and sorrow, the load weighs heavily. The spirit to be strong must be serene. And serenity is the first casualty when you sit watching men talk of fear-gripped man's cruelties, his acts of cowardice, lust and avarice. Resentment at our inability to control and guide human passions, unable to alter the facts of race and social heritage, faced with problems beyond solution unless possessed with limitless power, one's will to serve wilts. And helplessness and a sense of defeat cast their shadow around one. But can we live under a shadow for long?

Calcutta is under a shadow that is long and depressing. For almost eight weeks its people have lived in fear. What they have seen and heard has affected them deeply. It is not all for the worse. Much wisdom has come to many whose outlooks have been changed as a result of the actualities they have witnessed. Indulging in generalizations about superior and inferior culture is impossible for one who has known men of learning and breeding behave as the unlettered, prejudice-ridden fanatic or gangster behaves. Mob fury again is known to be uncontrollable. Stories are common of furious mobs suddenly calming at sight of extreme helplessness. Marooned in a hostile locality, families have been rescued at great personal risk by men belonging to the hostile community. Hindus and Muslims have helped each other because for generations they had lived as good neighbours and friends. Non-aggression pacts were entered upon and evacuations took place under such pacts. Whenever groups defended themselves by organizing their locality and the much described pitched battles were fought, casualties were few. Group resistance, it was found, was most effective because it meant organized defence and therefore matched the aggressor's preparations for attack. Wherever this was possible, gruesome forms of revenge were not perpetrated. Wherever the victims were isolated and defenseless they suffered death and much worse than death. Stories of heroism, though few and far between, as compared to tales of sordid crime and beast-like behaviour, are rich with significance. That despite the gravest provocations there were individuals in both the affected communities whose sense of honour and humanity did not desert them is heartening news. Class solidarity played its own part in so far as the middle classes were concerned. But lower down the scale this was not so. Strangely enough common sufferings born of a common economic condition did not make the common men of either faith brothers in facing a situation dangerous to both. They fell a prey to the incitements of those imported from elsewhere. They killed each other instead of saving one another.

Religious wars in history are full of instances of acts committed in blind anger. And such wars, we must know, have raged in Europe more than elsewhere. The Catholics and Protestants of England and Europe generally fought each other savagely. Power politics have exploited religions throughout history. This phase of religious bigotry in our country is in its last stages. Before extinction the flame always burns at its brightest.

It is inconceivable that the common Indian will not see through quite soon the cunning of which he is the victim. Out of this deluge of human suffering a new awareness is registering itself—the awareness that to the Muslim wage-earner Pakistan today means no means of earning a living and to the Hindu employer boycotting the Muslim means paying higher wages to labour and is therefore not sound economics even if it is good retaliation.

Furies roused by the politician-demagogues of the Muslim League's hatred-dispensation in Bengal initiated this communal war. Had the Government not been a party, the course of action followed by the inflammatory antisocial gangster stuff in Calcutta could have been checked. Counteraction, began in a spirit of self-protection rather than aggression, became violent and brutal and in some instances extremely savage.

This and much more will be revealed. But a postmortem analysis will scarcely justify the sacrifice of men and women who have paid with their lives. It must pay a dividend. It must lead us out of this gruesome phase in our social relationships. Congressmen have been accused of inaction on the one hand and of actively sympathizing with the counter-killing on the other. When faced with a situation such that prevails in a religious war those whose nationalism is synonymous with religion are placed on the horns of a dilemma. If they withdraw into their shells waiting for the storm to subside their integrity is questioned. Their private sanity pitted against public madness is tested severely. Congressmen fail to rise to such occasions not because they lack courage. Their hesitation to appear on the scene is not because their values have been distorted. I am of the opinion that our greatest handicap is the inadequacies of organization. Faced with a crisis when the State is content to be a nuisance, the Congress machinery fails it (sic). Helplessness and inability to function during such conflicts make Congressmen ineffective, good targets for its well-wishers and enemies. Therefore, it is time that we looked at ourselves from 'the inner platform of ourselves' and small as we are, we feel personally obliged to make the Congress strong, conscious of its sovereign power because it has the moral support of men and women who alone can confer sovereignty.

Analyzing, testing and experimenting are the scientists' method of arriving at conclusions. This must be our method also if our enlarged responsibilities are to be discharged with efficiency and to some purpose. All the grace goes out of our persuasive efforts when we are unable to follow up our advice with material help. Protect the weak, organize for self-defence, mobilize against antisocial attacks on the defenseless, respect, irrespective of caste or creed, the sanctity of the non-aggressive individual. These are platitudes if we cannot provide organizational means of effectuating good advice. A disciplined volunteer organization trained to observe a code of ethics based on equalitarian principles and drilled into physical fitness and physical fearlessness would meet the demands of today. The Congress is expected to fulfil functions that are state functions. Its machine must either be strong enough to break the old State or must assume parallel responsibility. Information, courier and ambulance services must form auxiliaries of the volunteer service if during emergencies it is to act as the people's supreme organization.

On the way to Calcutta I witnessed an experiment on the above lines. Curfew and other restrictions on citizen's liberties in Allahabad had been imposed to check antisocial elements from destroying the peaceful way of life. In broad daylight the city's streets were deserted because the 20-hour ban on movements was relaxed late in the afternoon and early in mornings. I was reminded of descriptions of a besieged city. Here and there military vehicles swooped around posting pickets on point duty. It was sad to contemplate that such should be the first fruits of the power transference process. Nevertheless there was at least in this very city an experiment in progress on the success of which would depend real freedom. The Students' Congress Officers Training Camp with 55 trainees from districts in United Provinces was an oasis in this silent, deserted, tense city beside the Jamuna. Practical military training, its science and arts imparting political information were subjects with which the 15-day course was planned. Alert and brisk, the officers to be were being remoulded.

As the sun went down in the west the young men took by turns their certificates and in their eyes I found a look that was unseeing.

They looked beyond you, uncommunicative, almost forbidding. This neutral gaze had behind it firmness and the determination not to surrender to weakness. 'Not to be taken unawares' is one of the motives behind this type of training. If every young man who seeks to serve causes other than his own receives training with this objective heavily underlined, maybe our adventures in search of utopia will end not in bloodshed but a reign where fear will be outlawed.

DEATH FESTIVAL

The last fortnight has been made up of days of anguish, suspense and helplessness for the people of Noakhali District. In every corner of the country men and women are aghast at the capacity of the unscrupulous to hate innocent folk. Men and women quite ignorant are asking why the merciless should suddenly descend upon them demanding submission of body and soul. Compassionlessness had reached a point that defies understanding. A general state of stupefaction prevails and normal life is suspended in East Bengal. The reckless elements in that part of the province have gained the upper hand. To curb men whose purposes are criminal and methods ruthless, organized force—violent or nonviolent—is necessary. The State should be the repository of such sanctioned force meant to protect and defend the average citizen. The problem for the terrorized sections in East Bengal is this: who will protect the helpless when the State is hostile to their aspirations? Who will save them when the State's resources are utilized against their well being? Openly and through agents provocateurs they feel the State is assaulting and terrorizing them.

In the Indian scene the British have flourished largely because they found willing instruments to act for them. When rebel Muslims had to be crushed Hindus were cajoled into helping them. When Hindu India became the spearhead of mass rebellion Muslims were brought into action. The agent is either a dupe or a calculating miscreant. The machinery that regulates his activities is elaborate and cleverly constructed. It oils its engines with diverse lubricants. Greed, bigotry, brute instincts, nothing is too evil for it particularly when the power it subserves, apart from being foreign and alien in spirit, is numerically inferior and qualitative of a different calibre to those it has overpowered. The British have flourished in India and elsewhere by making a fine art of this special branch of the science of ruling men in foreign lands. They foresaw years ago the value of making a systematic inroad into the unifying forces in India's social fabric. A series of cunning devices were initiated. The deadliest of these was encouraging religious bigotry. Having realized that the Indian mind was sensitive to religion it took advantage of the existence of different faiths in our country. It exploited the readily inflammable stuff that makes the orthodox a bigot and set about lighting fires with it wherever necessary. Contrasted with Akbar's endeavours to overcome the religious bar between ruler and ruled the British rulers' efforts strike one as barbarous and devilish. The one brought together Muslims, Christians, Buddhist divines, so that a universal religion could be founded. Every student of Indian history knows this. What he does not know perhaps is that under Muslim rule forcible conversion was considered a crime. No less an authority than Maulana Abul Kalam Azad believes this. As he points out, had Mughals or their forerunners embarked on a campaign to convert the masses to Islam at the point of the sword, in the United Provinces of Rohilkhund and Oudh and the area around Delhi, men of the Muslim faith would have been in an overwhelming majority. Occasions in our pre-British history when religion became the plaything of politics and flared up are rare. Since the advent of the British they are frequent. British rulers took with them the Christian missionary wherever they wanted to plant their domination. They did so in India. Consequently the Christian religion with possibilities of political advantages attached to its followers, became a menace. Efforts were made to prevent the faithful from breaking away either from Islam or Hinduism. This in its turn became material for helping the British policy of encouraging religious divisions. Fanaticism was deliberately though cleverly encouraged. The majority were made to believe that they had a right to rule ruthlessly and the minority told to expect nothing but insecurity and exploitation from a majority.

Camouflaged as a communal war a civil war is being precipitated. Lest it should be too late, even in a matter of months, British agents in India were called upon to release immediately forces that would stop the liquidation of British power. From Waziristan to the easternmost shores of the Bay of Bengal there is enough evidence that the masterly policy of giving up power and straining with every means to retain it, is working. Newspaper statistics of dead men and women may or may not be accurate, but the fact that the Hindu minority of Eastern Bengal are being terrorized by an inhuman group of gangsters hired for this specific purpose is established beyond doubt. Two hundred and perhaps more villages have been besieged in the districts of Noakhali and Tippera. In Ranigunj, Lakshmipur, Begumgunj and Senbag *thanas*, in the former and the Chandpur and Faridganj *thanas*, in the latter a terrified minority is living in constant danger. Always an area where communication between district towns and villages are not easy owing to flooded fields and rivulets roads have been broken and the small railway stations burnt by armed leaders of this campaign of terror. Indifferent for two months to warnings of their preparations, the Government of Bengal helped the organizers to perfect their plans.

The immediate object of these organized attacks is to enforce Pakistan in India. Its other incentive is to rain revenge on the Hindus of Noakhali for the death of Muslims in Calcutta. Utilizing an ignorant and fanatical section of the peasantry to act as his crusaders a notorious leader of dacoits is trying to work out a private programme of political revenge. This led to his not receiving a Muslim League ticket in the last elections. Lest his unlawful manner of earning a living be exposed and incidentally to wreak vengeance on the present Ministry of Bengal this man declared war on the peace-loving docile men and women of East Bengal. In the name of Pakistan he is actually having his own back on the Direct Actionists for Pakistan. Working for the downfall of the present Ministry is among his first objectives—so that he may be revenged. Also he told his 'followers' to take the law into their own hands because, after all, it was League Raj. This sounds complicated, but we would do well to trace these wheels within wheels. The Government of Bengal is now becoming aware of these facts. Hence the recent note of firmness in its pronouncement.

All efforts to create eleventh-hour resistance groups by the threatened failed because their opponents had cut off all means of rushing help. Wherever the brave died resisting, the moral effect should have affected the heart of the aggressor. But it was wherever the brave resisted and held out, that they were overawed. The State's apathy on the one hand and the people's unpreparedness on the other have caused death on a big scale and panic on a bigger scale. Relief and rescue work is engaging minds of the elderly. There is on the other hand a strong move to launch a movement against the government and have it replaced. Men and women of Bengal whose political consciousness is keen are moved to the depths of their being. The cradle of revolution in India will be turned into a graveyard, they say. Drives for forming volunteer and guerilla squads are being made. The lessons that Noakhali teaches are many. Unless the Congress can take to the masses its programme of a social revolution they will be puppets in nefarious hands. Unless plans of the socialist state for which social revolutionaries are working are unfolded the misled Mussalman peasant and worker will go on taking one suicidal step after another. They have to be saved from the ugly politics of a party that has neither a human outlook nor a social programme of mass well-being. And finally we must not let momentary hysteria cloud our vision. A compromise with first principles means the betrayal of the future. Our ancestors made many such compromises. We are paying the wages of their sin. And their sin was fear. Hence for a thousand years or so foreigners came and overpowered them. A fatal lack of union was their primary weakness. It is ours also. Not a unity of religious faith so much as a unity of the humanist and the equalitarian must spring into being. "The world is a bridge; pass over it, but build no house thereon". But what if the bridge goes down?

The City Of Djinns
BADRUDDIN TYABJI

Badruddin Tyabji (1907-1996), one of India's leading diplomat and administrator, belonged to the distinguished Tyabji family of Bombay. His grandfather was one of the founders of the Indian National Congress, and presided over its third session held in 1887 in Madras. His father Justice Faiz B. Tyabji was a distinguished jurist of his time in Muslim Law. He was a leading lawyer in the Madras and Bombay High Courts. He was politically identified with Liberal leaders like Tej Bahadur Sapru, M.R. Jayakar and Hriday Nath Kunzru.
Badruddin Tyabji joined the Indian Civil service in 1932 and held senior diplomatic positions until 1967. He was vice-chancellor of the Aligarh Muslim University from October 1962 to February 1965. He wrote newspaper articles on India's Muslims and authored a number of important books, including the two volumes entitled *Memories of a Egoist*. He held liberal and secular positions in public life.

Through my association with the work of the Constituent Assembly, my acquaintance with Pandit Nehru began to grow, and soon a personal relationship was established. His views on present as well as future problems came closest to mine, and his personal qualities evoked my warmest admiration. In the troubled days of the interim government, and the even more critical period that followed Independence and the partition, he and Mahatma Gandhi seemed to me the only two leaders in whom an Indian Muslim could unreservedly place his faith.

Sardar Patel was the Home Minister, in direct charge of law and order, and in control of the apparatus for dealing with refugee movement between he two new nations. It should therefore have been his prime responsibility to give the minorities in India the

From *Memoirs of an Egoist*, volume one 1907 to 1956 (Delhi: Roli Book, nd.), pp. 177-185.

confidence to believe that they had an equal place in the country; that their life and honour would be protected; and above all, that the government was determined to ensure this. He seemed little concerned about this; indeed the few occasions on which he did speak about it, he did it in such equivocal language that he made them more anxious than ever about their future. He encouraged their exodus instead of arresting it.

It was Panditji and the Mahatma who went about the country rallying the broken-down spirit of the left-over minorities. They risked their lives to inspire faith in the new India that would come into being, whatever happened across the border. The other Congress leaders, while uttering no overt expressions of discrimination against Muslims, preferred to follow the Sardar's lead in this matter. Their whole attitude towards the problem seemed to be governed by the principle of reciprocity, by what was happening in Pakistan. They altogether forgot that the Congress had always claimed that its ideals were national and far superior to those of the Muslim League.

In the years previous to Independence and the partition, New Delhi had been very much just an official city. Its social life, particularly for officials, had largely revolved round the houses of their colleagues, British and Indian. The few nonofficial social centres then so far as I was concerned, included those of Sir Shri Ram and his brother Lala Shankar Lall on Curzon Road, the newly built house of Nawabzada Liaquat Ali Khan on Hardinge Avenue (Tilak Marg) and Sir Sobha Singh's mansion on Queensway. Mr. Jinnah also had built a fine house on Aurangzeb Road (now the Netherlands Embassy) but it was more a political landmark than a social centre.

Lala Shankar Lall's house was a great meeting place for people of every kind, from all communities and political persuasions, as it was there that Mrs. Sarojini Naidu stayed during the Legislative Assembly sessions. She was a magnet that drew old and young alike, binding them all to herself by her gift of friendship, love of laughter and appreciation of good food. She had no prejudices in any of these matters; only an insatiable appetite for all of them.

Looking back on those days, what seemed socially and aesthetically to have distinguished the city most was the wide, and on the whole worthy, representation of a variety of cultures, ways of living, and characters. The fusion of the British or rather Anglo-Indian element in it undoubtedly played strange tricks with it; perhaps it palyed too dominant a part in shaping the society that was on top at the time. But even that had by the end of the war years begun to diminish, to be Indianized, to use the current jargon. The cult of the 'Brown Saab' was already on its way out. Well heeled samples of the species were looked down upon rather as figures of fun; certainly not as models to be emulated.

The variety to which I refer was established by Muslim, Hindu, Parsi and Sikh families who were accepted as leaders of Indian society both on the basis of their means that permitted them to entertain liberally, as well as on account of their manners and culture that made their society agreeable to the wide variety of their guests. This was despite the fact that political tensions and the sharp divisions of opinion on the future of the country between the Congress and Muslim League had already begun affecting the general pattern of society in the capital.

I knew leading personalities in both the camps intimately, and could see the corrosive effect of politics that was beginning to affect social relationships, and even distort established reputations. In the old days, the Liaquat Ali Khans used to draw into their circle practically every lively young officer and his wife posted in Simla and Delhi, irrespective of his race or religion, provided that he was agreeable to converse with, appreciated good food and drink, and best of all if he was also a fair hand at bridge, a game the Begum loved. At the house of Ghulam Mohammed (subsequently Governor-General of Pakistan) one would constantly meet all the up-and-coming officers belonging particularly to his own Indian Audit and Accounts Service. He was kind and hospitable to all of them, and was considered more or less a guru in his service. The same could be said of another prominent Muslim officer of the Finance Department, Zahid Husain, later on Pakistan's High Commissioner to India.

All this now began to change with an ominous sense of inevitability under the pressure of political developments. A sharp ideological cleavage first separated, and then began to poison the social relationships between the supporters of the Muslim League and the Congress. And as the day of freedom from British rule drew nearer, physical violence of the most brutal kind between the two sides became the order of the day.

During the tenure of the interim government, formed jointly by Congress and Muslim League representatives at the Centre in September 1946, the situation worsened. And after 15 August 1947, when the two new independent dominions of India and Pakistan came into being, the violence rose to a crescendo.

From Delhi itself, hundreds of Muslims were daily leaving for Pakistan by rail, road, and air. A much larger number were fleeing from their homes in terror and seeking shelter in refugee camps, a notable one being in Purana Qila, the Old Fort. When we ourselves were uprooted from our house, our two Muslim servants—a cook and a bearer—had also to seek shelter there. Merely paying them an occasional visit to see how they were getting on was itself a harrowing duty not devoid of risk. What it must have been living there, I cannot imagine.

The Hindus and Sikhs who were pouring in from the Punjab as refugees, were also regrettably; though not inconceivably, seeking revenge for what they had been made to suffer on the other side. Mass communal hysteria had been aroused, and once that happens people do not stop to consider the logic of their actions. Hindu and Sikh refugees from the Punjab sought to revenge themselves on the Muslim population in India, and to turn as many of them into refugees as possible. It was a ghastly situation—a vicious circle in the true sense. The only two clear unequivocal voices raised in public against this madness were those of Pandit Nehru and Mahatma Gandhi.

I was also inevitably sucked into this mad whirlpool. We were living in a house in Tughlaq Lane. Soon things came to such a pass that I had to get my guns out to protect ourselves from mobs of gangsters who were going round, breaking into every Muslim home they found unguarded, looting it, and often killing the occupants. We took such comfort as we could from the knowledge that we were both good shots, and whoever attacked us would first have a price to pay for it.

Out neighbours at the time were the P.R. Nayaks. He belonged to the Bombay ICS cadre. I had known him as a most efficient and understanding Under-Secretary in the wartime Supply Department. I shall never forget the kindness and consideration that the Nayaks showed us at a time when we felt absolutely isolated in the locality, and did not know where to turn.

Eventually, some of our friends suggested that we should leave our house, and go and stay with one of them. We did so, and stayed for some days with our old friends, the Bijju Nehrus. Fory Nehru's mother (a Hungarian Jew who had gone through similar or worse trials in Nazi Hungary) was also staying with them then. The strain on the old lady from our presence in the house as refugees and liable to be attacked on that account was so great that we soon decided that my wife and children—Adil, my second son and Laila, my daughter, only a few months old—should leave Delhi and go to Hyderabad to stay with my wife's parents. My eldest son Hindal was in Welham School, Dehra Dun, and remained there.

The family's drive to the airport in a military jeep in command of the then dashing young army Capt. Tutu Bhagat, escorted by another armed military vehicle, was an experience in itself. One was constantly hearing then of Muslim families, some of whom we knew, being waylaid on their way to the airport, and done to death.

Fortunately, my family got safely to Hyderabad. But I stayed on in Delhi, accepting the kind offer of my old Punjab friend, Diwan Chaman Lall, to live with him. He was then a member of the Constituent Assembly and lived at 8 Windsor Place. His wife, Helen, and young son, Rahul, were away in Simla. His house was already full, both with Muslims, who were seeking shelter there before they could get away to Pakistan, and Hindus and Sikhs who were seeking refuge in India.

I have a vivid recollection of the eerie feeling I had sleeping there the first night. At dinner, we had been regaled with grisly tales by the Sikh refugees on how they had fought their way out of the Punjab, how many Muslims they had killed, the butchery they had seen, and what they felt about the Pakistanis. At night, they slept with their swords by their side. I confess that I could only sleep fitfully with one hand feeling the bulge of my little automatic pistol under my pillow.

Before we left the house in Tughlaq Lane we packed up some of our valuables in trunks and cases, and locked them in its storeroom. There were however a couple of trunks that we were anxious to deposit elsewhere for greater safety. We took them across to a friend who lived opposite us. I can still recall the chill that came over me when he, with obvious embarrassment, declined to help. His wife feared, he said, that the fact that they were guarding Muslim property would become known, and they might be raided by Hindu fanatics.

I did not press the point, and hastily withdrew. I do not know what the sentiments of my friend's wife really were, but I could see from his face that he was himself terrified. It would have been sheer cruelty to put pressure on him. We therefore drove over to another friend, Kalyan Sundaram (ICS, Law Secretary and subsequently Election Commissioner). The remembrance of the joy and relief that I felt, when he, without the least hesitation, gave orders to his servants to take the trunks out of our car and have them put inside, is still a cherished memory. His simple and natural gesture brought home to me in a vivid manner the realization that in the topsy turvy world of the time, there were still people who put their principles above temporary personal considerations. I have never forgotten it, though when I try to analyse it I find it difficult to understnad why I particularly remember it, when I have forgotten so much else. It was the spontaneity of the action, and the look of concern on Kalyan's face at our predicament. It made all the difference in the world at the time to a person like me, who suddenly found himself a fish out of water though still in the very pond in which he had, like a treasured carp, been showing off only the other day. It reinforced my own belief in my ideals.

A day or two after I had moved to Chaman Lall's house, I received a telephone call from Jerath (then the Postmaster General), who lived very near our house in Tughlaq Lane. He said that some persons had broken into my house, and were carrying off things from there. I immediately got into my car, and accompanied by Khairati Lall Malik, a young Hindu friend of Chaman Lall, drove there. On entering the gate I saw a Sikh soldier in uniform with his gun suspended on his shoulder carrying off my silver Bidri *hukka* in one hand, and some other articles in the other. On seeing us he put the articles down and advanced towards us. He came right up to me and pointing the gun at my chest enquired who I was. Automatically, almost involuntarily, I replied that I was a Muslim. I felt that my last moment had come. I think I closed my eyes, awaiting the shot. Then suddenly my companion intervened. He caught the barrel of the gun and tried to push it away. At the same time, he began upbraiding the soldier, asking him what he thought he was doing, whether he realized the consequences of his behaviour, etc. The crisis passed. The soldier suddenly put down his gun but sternly told us to go off as he was guarding the property. I confess that I had no fight left in me at the time. There was no one else in sight, and it seemed foolish to attempt to grapple with an armed soldier. I drove immediately to the nearby Tughlaq Road police station. It was practically deserted. Most of the policemen were on duty elsewhere. As a matter of fact, the Delhi police force as such (formerly to a large extent Muslim) had practically disintegrated. Most of its Muslim officers had left or opted for Pakistan, and the Muslims in other ranks themselves feared for their lives. I remember the pathetic story related by some of them earlier, when they came to me seeking moral support. They said that Mr Jinnah had taken away all their officers, and left them bereft of leadership.

The Tughlaq Road Sub-Inspector was most considerate and sympathetic, but he expressed his inability to leave his post. Telephone calls were constantly coming and there was no one else there to answer them. A little later, however, a couple of policemen turned up, and taking them with us we went back to my house. We found it deserted. The Sikh soldier had left, taking away the things that we had seen on him and some other articles. Inside the storeroom, besides the pilferage committed, a lot of glass and crockery had been wantonly smashed. We did what we could to put things in some order and locked up the place again. I then returned to Diwan Chaman Lall's house in a mood compounded of relief at having escaped assassination, but depressed beyond measure at my helpless situation. The complete breakdown of law and order in the country that had even affected the discipline of the armed forces took my memory back to the accounts of the 1857 war of independence.

Sometime later that afternoon I received a message that Panditji had heard of the incident and intended visiting the spot. I found him there along with some police officers. He asked me what had happened, and on learning it, expressed his sorrow and anger. He then pensively picked up a bit of chalk that was lying there, and symbolically put his initials on the remaining boxes in our storeroom, instructing the police officers to take good care of them. This action of his—his immediate response to my difficulties—had an indescribable effect on me. I felt again that I was an accepted member of the Indian family, that the problems affecting any of its members would be faced jointly by us all, without distinction or discrimination.

This drew me closer than ever to Panditji. Soon it became a regular routine for me to look in at his house at 17 York Road (now

Motilal Nehru Marg) where he lived until he moved into the former British Commander-in-Chief's house (now Teen Murti House and used as the Nehru Memorial Museum). After Panditji left 17 York Road it became the Italian Embassy, which it still is.

In the early days, there was very little protocol or security formalities at the Prime Minister's house. There were some guards around, but once they knew one, it was possible to go in and out without any fuss. The personal staff of the house was also very small. Usually, there were only Mr M.O. Mathai and a servant or two about. The Prime Minister's daughter, Indira Gandhi, used to live in Allahabad then with her husband, and only paid visits to Delhi. On more than one occasion Panditji asked me to stay on for dinner. I dined alone with him, sharing the frugal meal that his servants used to provide him. Food was generally in short supply at the time in Delhi due to the disturbed conditions in the city and its neighbouring areas. But even then Panditji's meals rather astonished me, and I was not surprised to learn from some of his friends that he was not being properly looked after and badly needed a housekeeper.

One incident of this period is particularly vivid in my memory. Jai Kumar Atal (Makhi) of the ICS (subsequently of the Indian Foreign Service and Ambassador of India) was then Maulana Azad's Private Secretary. Though much younger than me, he had come up to Balliol from Winchester during my probationary year, and we became friends. I knew his grandfather, Sir Tej Bahadur Sapru, who was my father's friend. He was very fond of his grandson and came to Oxford to see him frequently during the days when he was in London for the Round Table Conferences. As I was much older than Makhi, he had asked me to keep an eye on him. A special friendship grew between Makhi and me that lasted for years.

Now once again Makhi and I saw a great deal of each other. Makhi had been given some patrolling duties by the district authorities and he and I used to go about in a jeep armed with shot-guns to help keep the peace, and intervene in the event of trouble in the areas of New Delhi that had become notorious for stabbing and looting incidents. One of the most troublesome spots was around Minto Bridge. Muslims fleeing from Old Delhi had to pass over it on their way to the refugee camp in the Old Fort. They were frequently waylaid by bands of miscreants who rushed out from the Minto Road area and stabbed and looted them.

We related this to the Prime Minister and were discussing with him what remedial action could be taken. To our surprise the Prime Minister suddenly dashed off and then came back with a pistol in his hand, looking very pleased and excited. He said it had belonged to his father, Motilal Nehru. Then he made the astonishing suggestion that all three of us should disguise ourselves as refugees, and stroll down Minto Bridge. Our appearance and apparent helplessness, and the articles that we would be carrying would attract the gangsters. They would try to get at us and when they did we would shoot them down!

It was only with great difficulty that we were able to persuade the Prime Minister that the adoption of such tactics was foolhardy and hardly worthwhile. Some less hazardous and more effective method for putting an end to this kind of crime should not be too difficult to devise. We were careful not to mention what was uppermost in our minds, that it was unnecessary for the Prime Minister himself to play such a personal role in dealing with it.

It was during this time that I really got to know Panditji's family and household. I particualarly remember the period when Sheikh Abdullah and his family came down from Kashmir on a visit. The difficulties of making arrangements for them to stay in that comparatively small house along with the rest of the Nehru family, with their very different style of living and eating habits, were considerable. Indira Gandhi had to cope with them, with such help as she could get from her aunts, Mrs Vijayalaxmi Pandit and Mrs Krishna Hutheesingh. M.O. Mathai was then Panditji's principal Private Secretary in the real sense. His official secretaries were Tarlok Singh, ICS (later a member of the Planning Commission) and V.S. Coelho, IAS. It was then that the fateful decisions about the accession of Kashmir to India and the flying out of Indian troops in its defence were taken.

Who Killed India?

KHWAJA AHMAD ABBAS

As a student at the Aligarh Muslim University, Khwaja Ahmad Abbas (1914-87) was the chief organizer of the Students Federation on the campus. A law graduate, he took to journalism first in Delhi and later at Bombay where he had a column in *Blitz,* the English weekly. He wrote a number of novels and produced many films, including *Saat Hindustani* and *Shehar aur Sapna,* which bore the stamp of his personality and reflected his socialist convictions. *Ajanta* is one of his well-known stories. At the time of partition, his family was trapped in Panipat, but 'thanks to the compassion and humanity of a man named Jawaharlal Nehru who sent a truck with an armed escort to bring them to Delhi, the lives and honour of my mother and sister were saved.'

I Am Not An Island: An Experiment in Autobiography was written in 1975 and published two years later. He declared, 'Isn't it enough that one has lived, lived for sixty-one years, lived fully, experienced the richest emotions, witnessed the exciting events of one's times, participated, to whatever humble extent, in the great drama of human existence?'

Once upon a time was a man who built a house in a forest, even as his brother had built a house in another part of the same forest.

To make the place secure, he built a high wall around it. To ward off robbers and thieves he kept a squad of dogs, and bought a rifle.

One day he had a feeling that there was a robber in the forest.

He was afraid the robber would surprise him with a sudden attack. So he loaded his gun, and went out to search for the miscreant.

From *I Am Not An Island: An Experiment in Autobiography* (New Delhi: Vikas, 1977), pp. 276-99.

He felt the intruder rustling in the grass. He saw footprints and went after them.

He thought he saw him at last—or at least his substantial shadow. So he fired at the intruder.

There were two shots fired. Two people lay dead.

The brothers, each of them suspecting a marauder, had killed each other.

I don't know why, whenever I hear of a communal riot, or of Indo-Pak tension, or an Israeli-Arab conflict, this story comes to my mind.

Fear leads to hatred—hatred leads to violence of language and of temper—violence leads to mutual slaughter of the two brothers!

Towards the end of 1945, once again Bombay was gripped by a series of what are called communal riots which continued upto August 1947. The city was divided between 'Hindu Bombay' and 'Muslim Bombay,' with no communication between the two. Fear gripped not only the minority but even the majority. Trams passing through Bhendi *Bazar* would empty at Crawford Market at the southern end, and at Byculla Bridge at the northern end. No Muslim would venture into Girgaum or Kalbadevi, Lal Bagh or Parel or Dadar. But I, who regarded myself as neither a Muslim nor a Hindu, but an Indian, made a point of visiting both sides. The poor poorbi *doodh-bhayyas* and the Muslim bread sellers were among the people who had to criss cross the unseen lines for their living and, sometimes, had to pay with their lives.

I have personally seen some of these killings—their gory details, haunted my dreams for years. I had experienced the sense of shame and helplessness at being a witness to the cold-blooded murder of innocents and yet be able to do nothing about it.

Once, from the balcony of my friend Sathe's office in front of Harkisandas Hospital, I saw a bizarre killing which inspired (or provoked) one of my stories *Main Kaun Hoon?* It was a 'Hindu' area, and a *goonda* spied a man in *kurta* and *pyjama* walking by the side of the road. He followed him, and taking him to be a Muslim, stabbed him in the back. The knife pierced some vital spot and the man lay dead. The *goonda* wiped the blood on the knife on the clothes of the victim, and as he was doing it, a doubt seemed to cross his mind. So he tugged at the pyjama cord, opened it, saw that the man was not circumcised, and then clasping his knife, uttered two words that would haunt me for years. He said, '*Mishtake ho gaya*'.

And I felt like crying out from the balcony, 'Yes, you are right. You have made a horrible mistake—and the mistake was that you killed your own brother—not because he was an uncircumcised Hindu, but because he was a man, someone's son, someone's husband, someone's brother, your own brother.'

For several months a death wish obsessed me—I would take unnecessary risks, I would don khadi clothes, and put on a Gandhi cap, and take a tram through Mohamed Ali Road and Bhendi Bazar, stopping at book shops near the J.J. Hospital, hoping to be mistaken for a Hindu—and killed or, at least, stabbed. In my overheated imagination I wanted that earlier '*mishtake*' to be equalized.

I was running repeated risks for, during curfew hours, with my Press pass, I would detrain at Dadar station and, since no buses were running then, I would walk across the road to Shivaji Park sea-front where my flat was. My wife knew the risk I was running, but it was typical of her that she never frightened me or discouraged me. A time came when the Shivaji Park area was taken over by the RSS, everyday the saffron flag would be put up, and their volunteers would be drilled and made to listen to anti-Muslim harangues. One by one, the dozen or so Muslims residing in that area migrated to 'safer' localities in the city—and ultimately I and my wife, my servant were the only three Muslims left in Shivaji Park.

After *Dharti ke Lal*, I had been to Lahore to make a film, but the film could not be properly finished due to the riots, and I had to come back without completing it. (It was later patched up in Bombay, and also released somewhere or the other, but I never got to see it.) But I had seen enough of the riot-ridden Punjab. In Rawalpindi the Muslims who were in an overwhelming majority, were clearly the aggressors, though there were humanist exceptions where Muslims did save the families of their Hindu and Sikh friends and neighbours. In Lahore, where both sides were about equally balanced, it was not a riot but a civil war which was being fought with burning and looting and killing. In Amritsar, and other places in the East Punjab, it was the obverse of Rawalpindi, and Muslims were the victims of violence.

I was in Amritsar when Pandit Jawaharlal Nehru toured the place, and I saw with my own eyes a whole bazaar burnt, including several bookshops, and burnt-out copies of the Vedas, the Gita, the Holy Quran and the Granth Saheb lying side by side, among the cinders.

On 3 June 1947, I and Sathe were at the house of the Maharashtrian actor-director-producer, the late Master Vinayak, discussing a film project which was to be called, significantly enough, *Naya Admi* (The New Man) when the radio announced that in a few minutes the speeches of Lord Louis Mountbatten, Pandit Jawaharlal Nehru, Mr M. A. Jinnah and Sardar Baldev Singh would be broadcast. Literally millions all over the yet-united India, sat glued to their or their neighbours' radio sets, for the fate of India was to be decided that day. From Peshawar to Travancore, from Karachi to Shillong, India became an enormous collective ear, waiting for the broadcasts breathlessly, helplessly, hopelessly. Never before in the history of the world would the destiny of so many depend upon the words that would fall from the mouths of so few.

Pakistan and partition had been in the air for too long for any one to be surprised by the content of these speeches. The 'special correspondents' and their 'sources close to Whitehall' had for once been quite correct in their forecasts. When we sat down to listen in we knew exactly what was coming. And yet when it came, one could hardly believe one's ears. And, as one after another, the four speakers of the evening reiterated their acceptance of the fact of partition, the thought kept hammering at one's mind: can these four people, or even greater ones than they, conjure away the oneness of India and divide it into two separate countries—Pakistan (truncated) and Hindustan (non-*akhand*)?

The tones of the speeches were significant—you might even say symbolic.

Lord Louis Mountbatten was confident, complacent, patronizing. He knew he had achieved a rare miracle, and he expected compliments and congratulations, which were soon forthcoming from the three who followed him—a Hindu, a Muslim, and a Sikh! Yes, Mountbatten had reduced the redoubtable secularist, Jawaharlal Nehru, to a mere Hindu!

Jawaharlal Nehru was choked with emotion, rhetorical rather than (as was usual with him) conversational, indulging in the professional writer's weakness to cloak inconvenient facts with a pretty turn of phrase. He talked of Indians 'being on the march', of 'the goal', and 'the journey's end', of 'months of sore trial, difficulty, anxiety and, sometimes, even heartbreaks' and of his abiding faith 'in the great destiny of India which takes shape, even though with travail and suffering'; he commended 'the vital change affecting the future of India'. And he concluded with the salutation that would sound hollow at least on that day: *Jai Hind!*

If Jawaharlal Nehru had still to acquire a conversational, informal, radio manner, Mr Jinnah was just a voice before the microphone. But his sense of triumph and elation came through, even if (like all new broadcasters) he messed up his words now and then.

Sardar Baldev Singh had nothing much to say, and he said it badly. He was included, I suppose, to placate the valiant Sikhs and to reassure the *jawans* of the army, navy and air force.

It would have been all so amusing, even funny, if it were not for the tragic implications of what was said. Jawaharlal Nehru's words might well have been the theme song of the moment—'With no joy in my heart!' There was no joy even in the hearts of his listeners. I saw tears in the eyes of the people listening in along with me. Death is final, inevitable, yet every time someone dear to us passes away, human sentiment protests, revolts, bursts out in a flood of tears. How does one mourn the death of a country, one's country?

Who killed India? I asked in my next 'Last Page'. Yes, indeed, who did?

Was it the work of an insane individual, a stab in the back as in a communal riot; or the diabolical conspiracy of a gang? Was it a case of slow poisoning? Or, as it might be, was it a more diabolical, a more cunning master plan, in which the victim himself was hypnotically induced to commit suicide. . . .

India was killed by Britain. The first blow was struck when the British (after ignoring and neglecting them for half a century after the events of 1857) instigated and encouraged the Muslims to demand separate electorates and then conceded it. That was the first step towards Pakistan, however copious tears Lord Mountbatten may now shed over the mortal remains of United India.

India was killed by the British and their 'Divide and Rule' policy. But not by the British alone. India was killed by fanatical Muslim Leaguers who played upon the community's apprehensions and fears to produce in them a peculiar psychosis which was a dangerous combination of inferiority complex, aggressive jingoism, religious fanaticism, and fascistic *Herrenvolk* legends.

India was killed by the fanatical Hindus, the Hindu fascists and Hindu imperialists, the dreamers of a Hindu empire, the crusaders of Hindu *Sangathan*, who provided the ideological fuel for the fire of Hindu communalism and fanaticism.

India was killed by the Hindu communalists, the believers and supporters of Hindu exclusiveness . . . . who yet masqueraded as Nationalists and Congressmen, who prevented the National Congressmen and the National Movement from becoming a fully representative, completely non-communal front of all Indian patriots.

India was killed by the Communist Party of India which (during the days of its 'People's War' and 'pro-Pakistan' policies) provided the Muslim separatists with an ideological basis for the irrational and anti-national demand for Pakistan. (Phrases like 'homeland,' 'nationalities,' 'self-determination' etc. were all ammunition supplied by the Communists to the legions of Pakistan.)

India was killed, and stabbed in the heart, by every Hindu who killed a Muslim, by every Muslim who killed a Hindu, by every Hindu or Muslim who committed or abetted, or connived at, arson and rape and murder during the recent (and earlier) communal riots.

That an imperialist power planned the dismemberment of our country in the very hour of our freedom is not surprising. The wonder, and the tragedy is that India should have been killed by the children of India. . . .

Gandhiji was the only leader of note who refused to bless the concept of Pakistan with his approval. In any case he was busy in Noakhali and Bihar, quenching the fires of intercommunal hatred and violence.

But why did Jawaharlal the secularist, Maulana Azad, the apostle of unity, and Sardar Patel, the nationalist, agree to this partition? According to Durga Das, the author of *India from Curzon to Nehru and After*, they were old men who 'were too weary to carry

[1]Durga Das, *India from Curzon to Nehru and After* (London: Collins), p. 255.

on the struggle any further and were, in their heart of hearts, anxious to grasp power and enjoy its fruits without further delay.'[1]

Another theory which I have heard advanced by a knowledgeable person is that Nehru, when questioned about partition, said, 'It is either that—or back to jail!'

I am inclined to doubt the veracity of this quotation from Nehru. This is not his language. It is possible that he did say something which might be misunderstood or misinterpreted as his weariness of jail-going. He was tired not so much of jail-going—as much as of the unyielding stone wall of the Muslim League which was not willing to agree to unity on any terms. And the British, the clever monkeys, were unwilling to part with power without nibbling at freedom which was divided between the two hostile camps—or cats—of the Hindus and the Muslims. Moreover Nehru, as the head of the interim government, had experience of heading a ministry of the Congress and the Muslim League and knew the combination was unworkable and would always lead to more and more trouble.

But why did Mr M. A. Jinnah agree to a truncated Pakistan— yielding Hindu-majority districts of Bengal and the Punjab to India? Here the testimony of an ex-officer of the CBI seems plausible— Mr Jinnah had just come to know of the cancer from which he was suffering. He had not long to live and couldn't postpone the realization of his cherished dream of carving Pakistan out of India. For him it was either this or a period of struggle, agitation and, perhaps, armed conflict for which he was not in a physically fit enough condition.

An interlude of sanity and unity—the wedding of my friend V. P. Sathe and Leela Purandekar in Poona. Quite a few of us made the night trip to Poona, leaving Bombay after midnight and arriving early next morning in Poona. Quite a few Muslim friends were present—Dilip Kumar (Yusuf Khan), the film star, Najmul Hasan Naqvi and Mohammad Hassan, both film directors, who were eventually to reach Pakistan, and my old friend Manmohan Sabir, my wife and I, of course!

In a small way, this wedding—and the casual manner in which Sathe and his father—did away with the communal orthodoxy undid the partition for me, and helped to repair the mood of depression that had settled over my soul.

Mountbatten's 'Calendar of Partition' was fluttering away, as the two sides bargained about the division of assets. So many days before

15 August, when independence would come to India and a day earlier, to Pakistan. Meanwhile the riots ceased in the two would-be new countries—their place was taken by massacres and murders on a mass scale, of the Hindus and Sikhs in Pakistan; of Muslims in India.

My family was in Panipat, but there were also parts of my family in Delhi—my cousin and his wife—i.e., my sister—and their children in a flat on Babar Road; my cousin sister and brother-in-law were in the Jamia Millia in Okhla. One day the RSS boys came to the Babar Road locality in trucks to carry away the Muslim property. A minute earlier a kindly Sikh gentleman hid my cousin and his family in the interior of his house, and when the looting began, the Sardar's children joined in the process, and brought home much of the household articles which, they claimed as their neighbourly right! Asked as to where the 'Musallas' had gone, they had no compunction about the virtuous lie they told—that they had run away to a refugee camp. If somehow the looters had come to know that they were there, not only their lives were in danger, but also the life of the old Sardarji who was standing guard over them holding a drawn sword in his hand. (It was this incident which inspired the story of *Sardarji* many month later!)

My young friend Manmohan whose family was somewhere in Shaikhupura was staying with me in Shivaji Park, and through him I could well imagine the plight of the Hindus and Sikhs who were trapped in Lahore, Peshawar, Rawalpindi and Lyallpur in what was to become Pakistan. Sometimes he would have nightmares in his sleep, and give out bloodcurdling yells at night. Another friend, a shaved Sikh, Harbans Singh, living alone in the Shivaji Park area, and waiting for the safe arrival of his parents from Rawalpindi, would come every night to my place and he and Manmohan would sleep in the drawing room, while I and my wife slept in the bedroom. To these two friends I owe my safety during those murderous days.

One day I was returning home at night from the office, and passing through the curfew-bound roads. The situation on that day was very tense. Several murders had been reported from different parts of the city. The Hindu and Muslim *goondas* used to keep the score even—as in the mischievously-devised cricket pentangulars, when there was the crucial match between the Hindus and Muslims. If five Hindus were killed and against that six Muslims were killed it was a point of honour (or dishonour) for the Muslim *goondas* to equalize the score. There was no particular issue in Bombay—it would remain in India, in any case. Killing Hindus or killing Muslims was a sport of the ungallant gladiators.

As I was walking home, thinking of the unfortunate situation and the gory developments of the day, I heard the sound of footsteps behind me. Who was he? I thought as the steps came nearer. In Shivaji Park, at that time it could only be a Hindu? But was it a peaceable householder returning home like me? Suppose it was not, suppose it was a *goonda*? There was not a soul anywhere in sight. Only two men walking, one after another. Death never seemed so near as on that day at that time. Should I run for my life? But he might overtake me. So I slowed down so that he might overtake me and pass on in front of me. Suppose he stabbed me in the back—I had a twitching sensation in my spine. I died and lived several times during those seconds, while the footsteps also slowed down. That man was not going to pass me and go ahead. Was he also afraid of me? Or was he taking out his dagger to slash me in the back? But he continued to walk slowly just a few paces behind me. At last the suspense was too much to bear. Let the worst happen! So I stopped and took a step back. He was afraid of me. I was afraid of him. The two brothers stalking each other in the forest that was curfew-bound Bombay.

But in the light from a street lamp, he recognized me and felt relieved.

'Abbas *bhai*,' said the man.

I also recognized him as a neighbour of mine.

'Bhaskar Rao, where are you going?'

'I'm going to attend the first meeting of the *Swaraksha Dal* that we are forming for the defence of Shivaji Park. Are you coming?'

I was not abreast of local politics and did not know that a *Swaraksha Dal* was being formed in Shivaji Park. So I said, 'Yes, let's go.'

There were about fifty or sixty residents of Shivaji Park, gathered in one of the sports clubs in the park. I sat inconspicuously in the background, but several people recognized me and urged me to come forward. Somebody was voted to the chair and the meeting began. The first item was the election of an executive committee. I was surprised to hear the first name proposed—it was my own name. Bhaskar—the man who, a few minutes earlier, I was suspecting, was going to stab me—proposed my name. Much to my surprise, I, a Muslim, was unanimously elected. The meeting dispersed soon after the election of the executive which would meet the next day in the flat of Seth X Chand.

I took leave from the office the following day to be able to attend the meeting of the executive of the *Swaraksha Dal.* Still, when I arrived, a heated argument had already begun. One of the members was outlining the strategy.

Twelve men had to be appointed to guard against a sudden attack from the Mahim side. The secretary had proposed to recruit twelve ex-INA men. The proposal had received universal and enthusiastic support, as it was said it was our patriotic duty to provide succour to the unemployed INA personnel—till the names of the twelve men were read out.

Then it was found that a 'Pakistan fifth columnist' had smuggled himself in the group. One of the twelve had a Muslim name—some Qureishi or Farooqi or Usmani!

Then all hell broke loose.

'How can we entrust the defence of our locality to a Muslim?'

'No. No. You tell the INA people this man is not acceptable.'

'But,' the secretary interjected, 'INA people will supply their men only if we will keep the whole lot. There are five Hindus, six Sikhs and only one Muslim.'

'*Arey, ek machhali saray talab ko ganda karay hai*' [One fish sullies the whole tank], one fat man said.

Then a lean man, with hungry looks, added, 'How can we entrust the safety of our sisters, our daughters and our wives, to a Muslim?'

He said it, and then looked at me. '*Abbas Bhai ki baat aur hi hai,*' [with Abbas *bhai* it is different] he added apologetically.

I came away from the meeting on some excuse. I walked in a rage. No wonder they were asking for Pakistan! No wonder they had got their Pakistan! Who killed India? If the Muslim communalists were guilty, their accomplices were also such Hindus? So Muslims had their Pakistan, and Hindus had their Bharat. Where were the Indians like me to go? There was no Indian then! Even Jawaharlal Nehru had become a Hindu! Even Maulana Azad will have to go to Pakistan!

That day was the nearest I came to abandoning India. That day I had to go somewhere—away from Bombay. I couldn't go to

Pakistan—it was betrayal of one's country, of one's principles of secularism. so I went *back* one thousand and five hundred years—to Ajanta! I and my wife and my friend Sathe. We took a train to Aurangabad, reserving the seats in our true names—Mr and Mrs. Abbas and V. P. Sathe!

For three days we wandered over the caves of Ajanta and Ellora, marvelling at the art of Buddhist painting and mediaeval sculpture. Ellora, being carved out of stone, was much better preserved. There were Hindu gods and goddesses carved out of the same rock, and the serene countenance of the Buddha and his apostles, and the Buddhist legends.

I was astonished to learn that several generations of artists had worked on the sculptures of each cave, which had taken between two hundred and fifty to four hundred years to complete. And none of them had carved their names or even their initials. To work was its own reward. To work devotedly, dedicatedly, anonymously! I could even hear the hammers hitting the chisels, slicing the rock in the unfinished cave. Then I knew what the caves of Ellora were saying to me.

I went to Aurangabad railway station to take the train back to Bombay. Both I and my wife felt spiritually renewed and rejuvenated.

So I came to Bombay and, on the very day of my arrival, went to the meeting of the *Swaraksha Dal.*

'After you left that day,' one of my colleagues informed me, 'we had a big debate about the INA personnel and we persuaded the two or three nervous and non-secular types that the INA members were above communal considerations, and whether he was a Hindu, a Sikh or a Muslim—he was, as a member of the INA, above all else, an Indian! So we have appointed the INA people to guard Shivaji Park.'

There were tears of happiness in my eyes, I felt choked with emotion.

At the meeting that day I found all the members agitated about the prospects of an attack from the Muslims of Mahim.

'We will all have to be on our guard at night with *lathis,* and whistles and torches. They might not come by the road which is likely to be patrolled by the police, but they are likely to march along the sea-front.'

That night, with a ridiculous *lathi* in my hand I joined the other members of the *Swaraksha Dal* in patrolling the sea-front. It was a moonlit night and there was no possibility of an attack. Moreover, I knew some of the people in Mahim, and I knew they must be as scared of an attack on them from the Shivaji Park Hindus as we were afraid of them.

During the patrolling, I broke away from my squad and went walking down the beach towards Mahim. There, I could see silhouetted figures with *lathis*, patrolling. My heart started beating wildly. I had reassured all about the unlikelihood of an attack from Mahim side. And here I was seeing them coming with *lathis*—or, who knows, spears? I turned back to see my people but they were already lost in the shadows.

Meanwhile, I was apprehended by the shadows from Mahim.

'*Kaun hai?*' one of them shouted, and I could detect a note of fear mixed with alarm and apprehension.

I said I was Khwaja Ahmad Abbas, who had come to talk to the people of Mahim.

'What do you want to talk about', said one of them.

I replied, 'We hear that you are going to launch an attack on us in Shivaji Park? Is it true?'

'On the contrary,' he replied, 'we hear the Hindus of Shivaji Park are going to attack us, the Muslims of Mahim. We saw some *lathi*-armed Hindus coming this side to launch a sneaky attack on us in the night. So we also took our *lathis* and came to defend ourselves! You have armed INA people to lead the attack.'

'I am not a Hindu but a Muslim—there is also a Muslim among the INA people. So you have two guarantees that the people of Shivaji Park will not launch an unprovoked attack on the people of Mahim.'

Soon a short, slim caricature of a man came forward, looking like Sancho Panza with a *lathi* twice as high as himself.

'Abbas Saheb.'

'Khan Saheb.'

That was the late Rashid Khan, the pocket-sized actor of the radio, the IPTA's *Dharti ke Lal*, and then of the screen. He embraced me which was difficult because of our two *lathis* coming in the way.

So I threw my *lathi* on the ground.

He did the same.

'What are you doing with that *lathi*?' I asked him at last. 'The same as you are doing, Abbas Saheb. Remember the dialogue I spoke in *Dharti ke Lal*.'

I remembered it very well. After all I had written it. There, as a teacher who had gone mad after the death of his wife, the wild-haired man, hugging a street lamp, makes the final comment on the human condition. So I intoned the dialogue: '*Suna hai insaan pehlay bunder tha! Ab taraqqi karte karte kutta ho gaya hai—kutta!*' [Human beings were monkeys before! Now progressing step by step they have become dogs—dogs!]

'Yes, you are right. I don't know why but I remembered that dialogue today as with *lathis* in our hands, we were patrolling the beach and hiding in the shadows, expecting an attack from the Shivaji Park side.'

I made an appointment with him and others for the morrow at noon at the police check post on Ghodbunder Road. I would bring half a dozen men from Shivaji Park and they should do the same.

Next day the twelve of us—six from each side—met at the police check post which was a barrier between Mahim and Shivaji Park. The Hindus were discouraged to cross over into Mahim, and the Muslims were afraid to enter the Shivaji Park area.

We talked of the rumours that each side was fearing an attack from the other, and now that we were there face to face, we laughed at it. That seemed to ease the situation and soon there were more and more people—mostly shopkeepers who got up from their shops—came to the check post to look at Muslims (or Hindus) from across the barricade. Enquiries were made of the market prices prevailing on either side. Old acquaintances greeted each other and enquiries were much about each other's health. Even the police were relaxed now and took part in the conversation. At last someone—I forgot from which side, or did the suggestion came simultaneously from both sides? suggested that the police lift the barrier. The police officer looked from one party to the other, then with one movement of his hand, the barrier went up, and now the amazing thing happened— Hindus and Muslims who were supposed to be thirsting for each other's blood were embracing each other, laughing and some were weeping, too!

This experiment in restoring normalcy and cordiality between the two communities inspired the Indian People's Theatre Association and the Progressive Writers' Association to come together and mobilize all the progressive cultural associations and organizations of Marathi and Gujarati, Hindi and Urdu writers, artists, film workers, artists of the Prithvi Theatre and various theatre groups in Bombay. I remember that in all fifty-two associations were mobilized to take out a unity procession that would parade from Bori Bunder to Bandra, passing through the exclusively Hindu areas and Muslim areas, thus removing the unseen barriers that were dividing Bombay into little bits of 'Hindu Bombay' and 'Muslim Bombay'. The procession was a great success. We had different trucks—one with Prithviraj Kapoor, the doyen of film industry, and his teenaged sons—Raj Kapoor and Shammi Kapoor—beating the drum. The IPTA truck had Balraj Sahni and Prem Dhawan and Chetan Anand and Dev Anand. The Urdu Progressive Writers were represented by Sajjad Zaheer, Ali Sardar Jafri, Kaifi Azmi, Sahir Ludhianvi and Majrooh Sultanpuri.

There were my friends, V. P. Sathe and Inder Raj Anand and Manmohan Sabir. There were Marathi writers and artistes, including the veteran Mama Warerkar, and the younger Anant Kanekar. There were Gujarati writers and artistes including Gulabdas Broker, Jithubhai Mehta, and Ojha.

This massive caravan moved slowly through the streets, and a whole concourse of people marched with it. There were speeches and songs, and poems were recited and slogans were raised. The denizens of the ivory tower and the artistic dovecotes had descended to the earth, and the people were amazed and happy.

When we reached the J. J. Hospital corner of Bhendi Bazar, a young Muslim Leaguer taunted me from the sidelines: '*Kyon, Abbas Saheb, aaj bohat din ke baad nazar aae ho?*' [Well, Abbas Saheb, how come we see you today after so many days?]

I shot back through the loudspeaker, '*Par aaj akela naheen aaya hoon. Ek lashkar leke aaya hoon!*' [But today I haven't come alone I have come at the head of an army.]

Bombay—15 August, 1947.

As I woke up early in the morning, my first worry was whether it would rain on that memorable, historic day.

The morning papers were full of last night's transfer-of-power ceremony in New Delhi. Jawaharlal Nehru's 'tryst with destiny' speech had been made, and duly reported, and to read it even in cold print was an exciting experience.

Long years ago, we made a tryst with destiny, and the time comes when we shall redeem our pledge. . . . At the stroke of the midnight hour, when the world sleeps, India will awake to new life and freedom . . . it means the ending of poverty and ignorance and disease and inequality of opportunity. The ambition of the greatest man of our generation has been to wipe away every tear from every eye. That may be beyond us, but as long as there are tears and suffering, so long as (*sic*) our work will not be over.

I did not know then that as he was uttering these stirring words he carried in his *sherwani* pocket the telegrams from the Punjab, from UP, from Bihar and Bengal about the atrocities that continued to be committed against Hindus and Sikhs, and against Muslims.

As I dressed in *khaddar* pant and bush shirt, I knew it was for the last time. I was wearing khaddar till that day.

Now, I said, India is free and khaddar would become identified with the Establishment. All sorts of people, for all sorts of reasons— not all honourable—would now don what till then was the livery of the army of freedom.

Having read the papers, and after a perfunctory breakfast during which I had little time to worry about the riots and the transfer of population which meant that my family was trapped in Panipat; twenty-five thousand Muslims from this town of thirty thousand men were under orders to be forcibly evicted and sent to Pakistan, while my family was anxious to come over to Bombay!, I took a tram to Gowalia Tank, where the 'Quit India' session of the Congress was held in 1942, and from where the mammoth procession was due to start today which would end in the afternoon at Flora Fountain.

On that day, quiet reflection and introspection was not possible. There was too much excitement. All Bombay was at Gowalia Tank *maidan* and at last the procession started. There must have been a million people in the three-mile long procession. I never saw the whole of it. I was not an island. I was a drop in the ocean, and I wondered if a drop can see the ocean as whole.

I was one of a million performers in the greatest drama of our century, and was I proud of this moment? Elsewhere intercommunal killings were going on, but I did not know it, I did not want to know it. For the time being, the ugly and grisly news had been pushed out of the front pages which were exclusively devoted to news of the freedom celebrations. What if a few hundred thousand people were killed in the two new dominions, so long as four hundred million—we were only that many then—were free at last. Free. Free! It didn't strike us that along with the few hundred thousand people, the values of humanity, compassion, unity and freedom were also being killed or grievously injured.

I was in the group of writers and artistes in that procession. Everyone was singing, and everyone was dancing to the rhythm of the drums that were being played by a number of artistes, including a young film star. And I, too, danced on the streets—believe it or not—with some dancers of international reputation!

On the way, there was a slight drizzle—then it was clear—and then there were more showers. But by the time it all ended we were soaked more in our own perspiration than in the rain water.

The slogan-shouting, the speeches, the songs, the dances were over—for the time being at least. A great depression seemed to fall over the million dispersing participants in the freedom pageant. For now they were not knit by the unifying fact of freedom. Now they were mere individuals worrying about how to reach home.

It was about 8 p.m. when I reached my little flat—that was still in Shivaji Park—and found a telegram waiting for me. It had been sent three days ago from Panipat. It read: 'Situation Critical. Arrange Our Safe Journey To Bombay!'

MY LONG LOVE AFFAIR

Despite his stirring "tryst with destiny" speech, I was not happy with Jawaharlal Nahru.

The fact of partition—and, more so, his acceptance of it—rankled in my throat. He had made too many compromises. Was dominion status what our martyrs like Bhagat Singh and B.K. Dutt and Jatin Das had died for? Mountbatten was to be our first governor-general. Why? Pakistan had at least chosen Jinnah. Did our Jawaharlal have to demonstrate his friendship with the Mountbattens? None seemed to protest, or to show him the right path, to remind him of his own speeches, of his promises and pledges to the people—not Sardar Patel, not Maulana Azad, not Pandit Govind Ballabh Pant!

They all seemed in (What appeared to be) indecent haste to share the fruits of office and power!

Or (another disturbing thought) had we the people betrayed our leader—by indulging in mass massacres which besmirched the fact of freedom with blots—or, rather, pools—of blood? It seemed that, out of all the millions of India, only two decent human beings had remained. Gandhiji was celebrating the advent of freedom by tramping the villages of Noakhali and Bihar to take the message of peace to the Muslims and the Hindus. For him at least humanity came first—freedom came last. And Jawaharlal Nehru was daily risking his own life to restore peace in Delhi. Had he not snatched the naked sword from the hands of a would-be murderer of Muslims? He spent days and nights by driving in a jeep, with but a single guard-driver sitting beside him, going where the trouble was. Did he not rush to the Jamia Millia at Okhla when he heard that the great store house of Urdu books—which significantly and symbolically included Urdu translations of Gandhiji's *Experiments with Truth* and his own *Autobiography*—had been reduced to cinders? Was it not said of his friend Zakir Husain, when Jawaharlal Nehru asked him to estimate the loss, saying, "We have been able to get a lakh worth of books today?" Perplexed and puzzled by Zakir Saheb's peculiar statement Nehru exploded, "I heard you have lost books worth lakhs in this fire!"

"True!" the great-hearted doctor of philosophy replied, "But when I heard of the fire I had written off all the books worth five lakhs. If books worth a lakh have been saved, that is a net gain for us. It's a way of looking at things—you can be a pessimist or an optimist. I prefer to look at the bright side of things."

At last despite the tension and the strain, the shame and the anger that he felt, Nehru relaxed and smiled and at last chuckled.

To this bad-good man, whom I had loved and hated simultaneously, in those days of horror, I turned in my hour of need when the lives and the honour of my own family were involved. I sent him a long wire, telling him about the plight of the Muslims of Panipat, the majority of whom wanted to live in India but they were being forced to evacuate to Pakistan because of the rising pressure of Hindu and Sikh refugees from Pakistan. I told him that my family had decided to come to Bombay, where I would be available to provide for them, and that at least they should be helped to come to some safe place in Delhi from where I would make arrangements to fly them to Bombay. I sent the telegram, and then waited. That was what millions of people were doing on both sides of the Radcliffe Line.

Meanwhile, my friend Manmohan, after months of silence and suspense, received a letter which was addressed to him in the handwriting of his father. His hands were trembling, there were tears in his eyes, and he could not bring himself to open the letter. He did not know what message it had to communicate—his father might be writing to give him the news of his mother's and sisters' death while coming from Pakistan to India. At last I opened the letter and gave him the good news that both his parents and sisters had been saved by their Muslim neighbours, and helped to cross over into India. Now they were living in a refugee camp.

At last after waiting for a week I got a letter from my mother that they had safely arrived in Delhi and were staying in the upper floor room of *Bara Dawakhana*—a Unani pharmacy my father had founded while he lived—in Lal Kuan. They had many adventures (both pleasant and unpleasant) but, thanks to the kind intervention of Pandit Jawaharlal Nehru, they had arrived safely in Delhi and were waiting for me to arrange for their air journey to Bombay as, they had heard, trains were still unsafe.

The "adventures" to which my mother referred in her letter were harrowing enough to ladies who had led a sheltered life behind the purdah. Pieced together from accounts told by her and my sisters later, this is their story.

No one in Panipat understood the true nature and implications of Pakistan. The few white-collared employees in the government service had opted for Pakistan in the hope of getting quick promotions in the Islamic state, but they never bargained for setting up permanent homes in the far-off and unfamiliar cities of Pakistan—like Karachi, Lahore, Montgomery (where the bulk of the Panipatis were settled in the homes of Hindus and Sikhs who had migrated to India and been settled, of all places, in Panipat!). Why couldn't the Muslims of Panipat stay on in Panipat and the Hindus of Montgomery stay on in Montgomery?

Two cousins of mine had a large, modern-style house—a *kothi*—with extensive gardens and orchards near the Panipat railway station. They received very attractive and lucrative offers from the local Lalas for the house and garden in June and July but they wouldn't part with it. It was built by their father, and they were sentimentally attached to it.

"But, Khwaja Saheb," the would-be purchasers argued, "after all you are going to Pakistan. Why not sell your property while the going is good?"

"*Abay, pagal huwa hai?*" (Idiot, are you mad?) My cousin remonstrated with the would-be purchaser, "*Aur jab naukri chhore kay, pension lay kay aaengay, to hum kahan rahengay?*" (And where shall we stay when we return after being pensioned off?) That was the simple-minded attitude of the bulk of the Muslim employees of the civil secretariat. Pakistan was a kind of new province, with favourable employment chances for Muslims where one could go—and return to India to live, when one got pensioned off!

As for the working class Muslims—mostly weavers—of Panipat, they had no fascination for Pakistan which they neither understood nor approved, except as a remote place where Muslims would go, as on a pilgrimage.

As soon as the trains started bringing Hindu and Sikh refugees from Pakistan—many of whom had suffered at the hands of the Punjabi Muslims—curfew was imposed on the city, ostensibly for the protection of Muslims. But the police inspector in charge of the thana was a *refugee* who had personally suffered at the hands of some Muslims of Lahore or Rawalpindi, and wanted to take his revenge on the Muslims of Panipat! So he would relax the curfew only for an hour or two, when the Muslims were to make their purchases. But there was no meat to be had—as the goats and sheep were brought from the villages. For more than a month all the women and children of our family subsisted on boiled *daal* and *chapatis*. My mother was a regular *pan*-eater, and *pans* had become a rare luxury. The price went up from four *pan* leaves per pice to one rupee for a single *pan* leaf, which my mother would divide into ten little pieces for consumption. There was no male member—except little children who were already showing signs of malnutrition, as milk was not to be had for love or money.

It was in this state of siege that, one late evening, the police came and knocked on our door.

"A military lorry has come for you from Delhi—we can give you half an hour to be ready. Take with you what you can carry with you, as there is no transport. The lorry is standing near the *tehsil*." That was nearly two miles from our house. So the ladies

and children had to pack the small suitcases and portable bundles
to carry on their heads. The women had to discard their *burqas* for
the first time in their lives. (I had talked *purdah*, but I felt sad to
hear the circumstances in which, to save their lives, *burqas* had to
be discarded by my mother and sisters).

Before leaving the house, my mother had nailed to the door
two signboards which she had got prepared beforehand. They said
that this house belonged to Khwaja Ahmad Abbas, and his mother
and sisters were going to him in Bombay, *and not to Pakistan*. They
had every intention of returning to Panipat. The signboard was in
Urdu, Hindi and Punjabi.

Having done that, they locked the doors and left in the starlight,
their footsteps sounding eerily in the cobbled lanes and by-lanes.
Before long they heard the distant sound of metal striking metal.
My mother did not like to believe that the locks of our house could
be broken open, had been broken open.

Later, when they boarded the lorry, the south Indian military
driver and the guards saluted the ladies and, when on their way,
asked them who they were for whom the Prime Minister was so
concerned. He had himself instructed them to bring the family safely
to Delhi. My mother told him that I was known to Pandit Nehru,
and had sent him a telegram.

"So you are not going to Pakistan?"

"God forbid!" My mother used the Urdu phrase "*Khuda na
karay*," and added proudly that her son was a nationalist.

They lived for fifteen days in Delhi, while I went about
scrounging money to bring them to Bombay by air. All my
friends, impecunious as they were, contributed their mite. The
air fare in those days was Rs 112 per ticket. That was just
enough for them to fly back, I would have to go by train. That
very day news appeared that in the states of Rajasthan through
which the Frontier Mail would be passing, Muslims were being
dragged out of trains and massacred. I was too well-known to
pretend to be a non-Muslim—also I had my own self-respect
and scruples about hiding my identity. So again my friend
Manmohan came to my rescue, he volunteered to go in my
place and to bring back the luggage by train, and to send the
women by air.

When I saw him off at Bombay Central, little did I know that
from his own compartment some helpless Muslims would be

dragged out at the Bharatpur station and beheaded just outside the railway premises. That ghastly sight, and the sense of shock that it could lie *my* fate, gave Manmohan the jitters and the shivers. By the time he reached Delhi, he had high fever!

The day my mother and the rest of the family arrived, I and my wife were at the airport. We were taken aback to see the rickety condition of the children—specially of six-year old Anwar Abbas, my nephew, who is now an Air India executive, but whose physical weakness and proneness to a variety of illnesses, and his surprising nervousness in planes in flight, are all directly traceable to the lack of nutritious food during those days. My mother was frail as before, but in good spirits. I had imagined her to be in tears about leaving Panipat, about having been compelled to discard *purdah*, and about all that she had suffered. Perhaps she was. But she never let a word of complaint escape her lips. She said to me after embracing me with more than normal warmth, "I like this travel by aeroplane. I am always going to travel by air. One feels so much nearer God."

Two days later, I wrote a long letter to Jawaharlal Nehru, thanking him on behalf of my family, for his kindness and consideration, and telling him of what Manmohan had seen at Bharatpur station. That was the only letter to which I did not get a reply. Perhaps I should have written about my own family which he had been able to save, and not about the Muslims at Bharatpur whom he could not save. There was only one Jawaharlal, and there were too many swords in India—and in Pakistan—for him to grab.

I felt no hatred for Pakistan or Pakistanis. How could I when there were my relations, my friends whom I admired and loved? But (contradictory as it might seem) I was dismayed by the concept of "one religion, one country" which was at the root of Pakistan. I felt instinctively antagonistic to this concept, and whatever the rationalizations of the *fait accompli*, I would never be able to make peace with this concept. I know there are Pakistanis-in-*dhotis*—the RSS, the Jan Sanghis, and the DMK which would like to have a Tamilian "Pakistan" in the south of India! While I wished Pakistanis all luck in building up their country, it became a secret obsession of mine to try and bring back at least some intellectuals who belonged to Indian areas, but who had been persuaded by family considerations, or by political compulsions, to migrate to Pakistan.

In 1948 I wrote an "Open Letter to Sahir Ludhianvi" in the now-defunct *India Weekly* in which I appealed to this young Indian poet to return to India. I reminded him that so long as he did not change his name, he would for ever be regarded as an *Indian* poet, unless Pakistan invaded and conquered Ludhiana. To my surprise, some copies of the paper did find their way to Lahore where Sahir read it. And, to my considerable surprise and joy, he (along with his late old mother) came back to India and, after initial difficulties, made a name for himself as a distinguished literary influence in films, while retaining his progressive ideology.

I was anxious, likewise, to recall Syed Sajjad Zaheer also, but he was under instructions from the Communist Party to stick it out there. When in the Rawalpindi conspiracy case he was detained for an indefinite period, along with his friend, the poet Faiz Ahmad Faiz and others, I thought the door was closed for ever on his likely return. But after years, when he was released from jail, once again I was anxious for this amiable and soft-spoken communist's return. The communists, too, felt like recalling him but the trouble was that their relations with the Nehru government were not as they would be later. Who would give him a visa? Who would give him a nationality? There was only one person—Jawaharlal Nehru, and I undertook to broach the subject with him.

I went to Delhi and sought an appointment with the Prime Minister.

I asked him if he knew Sajjad Zaheer.

He said, "Of course, I have known him since he was a boy—he was in the AICC secretariat when I was first President."

I said he was in Pakistan and ill and needed the care and attention that only being with his wife and children would ensure.

"Who asked him to go to Pakistan?" He asked, rather sharply.

"I suppose his party sent him to organize the Communist Party in Pakistan."

"He and his Party—they are all a pack of fools!" He exploded not with malice but affection. "Syed Sajjad Zaheer—our *Bannay Mian*—the aristocratic poet from Lucknow, was supposed to teach communism to the Punjabis and the Baluchis and the Sindhis!" The very idea, according to him, was ridiculous and preposterous. Then he added abruptly, "What do you want?"

I said I wanted him to come back to India and to be an Indian again, to live with his family and to be useful to his country.

"Hoon!" he thoughtfully said, "So you think so?"

I knew it was not a question, still I said, "Yes, Panditji."

"How many times I have told you not to call me 'Panditji.' I don't believe in it—nor do you!"

And that was the end of my interview.

I never broached the subject again. Yet, within a few months Sajjad Zaheer was given a visa to come to India, and within a year, he was an Indian citizen again. He published *Roshnai* (Ink), a monumental history of the Progressive Writers 'movement in India, revived the Progressive Writers' movement, started the Afro-Asian Solidarity Committee, and, though still a member of the Communist Party of India, his urbanity and scholarship, even his poetry, won him a long list of friends and admirers in all parties and among no-party intellectuals. He died in 1973, in Tashkent, of a heart attack, while attending a meeting of the Afro-Asian Solidarity Committee....

But I have been anticipating events and giving a chronological "flash-forward."

Actually, we are at the beginning of 1948, and Gandhiji had just been assassinated. I was one of those who were expecting something of the sort to happen—either to Mahatma Gandhi or Jawaharlal Nehru. It happened to Gandhi, martyrdom suited a saint. It was also appropriate that Gandhiji should have been killed by a Hindu. Nathuram Godse represented the worst features of Hinduism.

That evening, I was taking tea in the Parisian Dairy when I heard of the three fatal bullets having been fired at Gandhiji. The identity of the murderer was not immediately revealed, and when it was, I heaved a sigh of relief. Thank God, it was not a demented Muslim who had done the deed. Thereafter I could find peace only in a newspaper office, and though I had left the *Bombay Chronicle* and transferred even my "Last Page" to *Blitz* (where I was paid better, had more freedom to write as I felt, and where my byline appeared every week). Still in a time of crisis like this, I could think only of a daily paper like the *Bombay Chronicle*. I was one of those who had prepared a whole big file on Gandhiji's obituary three years earlier when he was fasting and death seemed imminent. Gandhiji survived his fast, toured Noakhali, Bengal and Bihar, saved thousands of Muslim and Hindu lives, survived another fast for peace, and finally succumbed to the assassin's bullets fired at him from point blank range.

I joined the group in the *Bombay Chonicle* that was feverishly bringing the obituary up to date. Someone had brought a portable radioset, and I could hear the tearful speech of Jawaharlal Nehru: "Friends and comrades, the light has gone out of our lives and there is darkness everywhere. I do not know what to tell you and how to say it. Our beloved leader, Bapu, as we called him, the Father of the Nation, is no more...."

I worked the whole night and the work helped to assuage the grief and sorrow I felt at the passing of Gandhiji. Muslims (of India and even of Pakistan) had particular reason to mourn his loss as it was for them that he had given his life. My mother, I found next day, had spent the night on the prayer-carpet, praying for the soul of Mahatma Gandhi . . . .

So Freedom Came

D. F. KARAKA

D. F. Karaka (b. 1911) was educated in Lincoln's Inn, Oxford, where he first heard Gandhi during the Round Table Conference. According to him, Gandhi 'made no appeal to sophisticated Oxford. Intellectually, they were left unsatisfied. Emotionally, they were moved. . . .' He was Founder-Editor of the *Current*. Among his publications are: *I Go West, The Pulse of Oxford* and *Out of Dust*.

There was something different about that August morning. I could feel it as I lay in bed in the small hours between sleeping and waking. It was our last day of bondage. I counted the hours that were to pass before we became free people in the eyes of the world.

The day itself was a normal working day like any other we had known. It was the thought of the morrow which made it so exciting.

From early in the afternoon a brisk movement was noticeable in the streets. There were sounds of festivity in the air. It was difficult not to be conscious of the moment towards which we were moving. 'At the stroke of midnight,' Nehru had said, 'a new India will be born.'

It was nearly 5.30 p.m. when I finished my day's work, cleared my table of all the grievances and grouses that pour into a newspaper office, and said good-bye to my colleagues. More than a day was ending; an era was soon to pass away. We would meet again in a new land, even though geographically it was to be the same. The impact of freedom appeared to make that difference.

The crowds of office workers returning home were gay. On government offices, some of the larger commercial houses, the Secretariat, and the big hotel, a handful of workmen were putting the finishing touches to the illuminations. Floral arches spanned the main thoroughfares. Festoons were strung across streets and lanes.

From *Betrayal in India* (London: Victor Gollancz Ltd, 1950), pp. 35-43.

Colourful bunting and streamers waved everywhere. The smaller roads and bylanes had been swept clean of the usual litter of rubbish.

Huge, lumbering lorries with full loads of workmen rolled past. Slogans flew in the air. From one of these lorries they greeted me lustily and for a moment I wondered why. Then my eyes fell on the press label stuck on the windscreen of my car, and at the same time I heard them shout 'Long live the pressmen who kept our fight alive.' The people were in a mood to cheer. Everyone was happy.

The vehicular traffic moved slowly along the crowded streets for all were returning home. That evening they would bathe and anoint themselves as for a holy fiesta. Caste and out-caste, capitalist and labourer, city man and peasant all had the same idea.

As I came home I smelt the smell of rich Indian food. My servants told me they were gathering for a little celebration of their own. They had pooled their rations, bought chickens for a *pillau* and a large salmon which was dressed with onion and garlic.

As I bathed and changed for the evening, I took stock of the years that had passed and recounted the days of the struggle, the anguish of our people, the hopes and fears which had punctuated this great, nonviolent movement for freedom.

My mind went back to my school days, when I had first learnt how India had passed into subjugation with the granting of the Charter to the East India Company by Queen Elizabeth. The Battle of Plassey accelerated the process whereby a commercial nation gained control of a country which was almost a continent and was able to lord it over a people who numbered one-fifth of the world.

My mind went back to the events and men who had made this day possible for us. From Dadabhai Naoroji, one of the first crusaders for freedom, to Mohandas Karamchand Gandhi, some of the finest of India's sons had dedicated their lives to the cause of freedom. They had endured physical chastisement, spiritual bludgeoning and had suffered humiliation and privation so that this country of ours could be free.

It was a Scotsman or, as we called him, a 'Britisher' who helped pave the way, an ex-secretary of the Home and Revenue Department, Allan Octavian Hume, who, ironically enough, was responsible for starting an institution 'to promote a better understanding between natives and whites.' The institution was to become the Indian National Congress. This was in 1885.

At the turn of the century there came the great Maharashtrian, Tilak, who first raised the cry of swaraj, a word which was to inflame young men with patriotic enthusiasm and conjure up a vision which was their inspiration.

Then came Gokhale, Motilal Nehru and his son Jawaharlal, Pandit Madan Mohan, Lala Lajpat Rai, Mohamed Ali and his brother Shaukat Ali, Vithalbhai Patel and his brother Vallabhbhai, Srinivasa Sastri and a whole galaxy of Indian personalities who played their parts in this nonviolent revolution.

In 1942, climaxing half a century of battling for freedom, Mahatma Gandhi, who had by then given this revolution its distinctive shape, decided upon another movement calling upon the British to quit. The two words 'Quit India' sounded the death-knell of British imperialism.

All that seemed past and over. The fight was done.

That night I dined at the Taj Mahal Hotel. The Mayor of Bombay was my host. Ours was just a private party like many others in the room. At our table was a young Muslim Begum, a Hindu Congressman, a Parsi jeweller, a Polish Jew and his English wife, an American couple, Nehru's younger sister, a couple of newspapermen, one of whom was my host's son, and an industrial magnate—the half-French, half-Indian head of Tatas.

As it neared midnight, when the room would be darkened and the new flag illuminated, they called me forward to say a few words. I moved to the dais and said: 'Today we join the community of the free people of the world. The flag which was once the symbol of rebellion has become the flag of the people. Let us hope that under it this country of ours will find peace, dignity and greatness again.'

As the lights came on, free Indians greeted each other with fond embraces, not knowing in the excitement what was the correct greeting of the moment. I noticed an elderly Hindu, wearing a red and gold turban, joining his hands in *namaskar* and bowing humbly to the flag. Then he sat down in his chair and wept.

Outside the streets were chock-a-block with people. That wide open space between the Taj Mahal Hotel and the Gateway of India was one solid mass. The bright lights of the illuminations fell on them. From the harbour the ships were throwing searchlights on the land. So freedom came—like all the New Years rolled up in one!

What a night that was! With the crowds refusing to go home, with men in dinner-jackets dancing with men in *dhotis*, with Englishmen cheerily singing Auld Lang Syne, with Gandhi caps being tossed into the air and British army berets perched on Indian heads, with Indians speaking pidgin English and Englishmen replying in equally bad Hindustani, with Indian women, not many years out of purdah, caring little who saw their faces, with the hotel band leaving their rostrum to play to the crowds below, and the crowds yelling 'Jai Hind' to the tune of Tipperary. So the night passed—one long hour with the shouting dying as the morning light came.

With the dawn there came the more sober realization of the greatness of the day. It was raining heavily till late in the afternoon when there was a great parade of elephants and horses, tanks and guns, followed by men, women and little children. Thousands of people walked in a procession from Gowalia Tank to the tune of 'God Bless the Prince of Wales'. Probably too embarrassed to play 'God Save the King,' the band apparently decided to settle for the nonexistent Prince of Wales. It was the spirit that mattered, not the technicality! In the first flush of freedom, flags were hoisted upside down and sometimes even at half-mast. No one seemed to care for little details like these.

It was the same all over the city and what was happening in our town was happening all over the country.

In Delhi, as the great day approached, the enthusiasm and excitement grew. Then, for some inexplicable reason, a religious spirit spread over the capital. The *Time* magazine in its report said: 'As the great day approached, the Indians thanked their various gods and rejoiced with prayers, poems, hymns and songs.'

Even Pandit Nehru, who had never been known to frequent the temples or to indulge in much religious ceremony, consented to have the blessings of the religious *pandits*. From Tanjore there came emissaries of the head priest of *sanyasis*, an order of Hindu ascetics. It was traditional in ancient India to derive power and authority from the holy men. Pandit Nehru yielded to all this religious ceremony because it was said of the kings of India that this was the traditional way of assuming power. The mood of New Delhi had become almost superstitious.

In the evening the priests walked ahead of these religious processions. They carried the sceptre, the holy water which they had brought with them from Tanjore, and rice. They waved their gifts about the Pandit's forehead and the priests gave him their blessings.

Later, at the house of the President of the Constituent Assembly, Dr. Rajendra Prasad, who was also President of the Congress, Pandit Nehru sat round a holy fire; around it the women of the house were chanting hymns. The oldest woman among them made an auspicious *tilak* mark on the forehead of all the ministers and constitution-makers.

All then left for the Constituent Assembly hall which was gaily decorated in saffron, white and green, for the occasion. Here Pandit Nehru said: 'Years ago we made a tryst with destiny and now the time comes when we shall redeem our pledge, not wholly or in full measure, when the world sleeps, India will awaken to life and freedom.'

'At exactly the twelfth chime a conch shell, traditional herald of the dawn, raucously sounded through the Chamber. Members of the Constituent Assembly arose, pledged themselves to the service of the people. Delhi's thousands rejoiced. The town was gay with orange, white and green. Bullocks' and horses' legs were painted in the new national colours and silk merchants sold tri-coloured saris. Triumphant light blazed everywhere, even in the bhangi (untouchable) quarter. Candles and oil lamps flickered brightly in houses that had never before seen an artificial light. The government did not want anyone to be unhappy on India's independence day.'

In the general celebrations that followed, all political prisoners, including Communists, were freed. All death sentences were commuted to life imprisonment, and all slaughter-houses were closed. Little children were given free sweets and there were fireworks for them all over the city .

The grace shown by Britain in handing over the reins of power was reciprocated with like grace by the common man of India who, forgetting a political fight of a quarter of a century, rose to the occasion and gave Lord Mountbatten, the representative of the British in India, a cheer reserved only for our own leaders. They shouted in a great roar which echoed through the capital 'Mountbatten ki jai'. It was a singular honour for an Englishman in India.

Mountbatten had earned this for himself with his polished diplomacy, his compelling sincerity and his courage in implementing the British pledge. Human contacts came naturally to him. In two months he had won over not only the Congress and the Muslim League; he had also succeeded in converting the Tory diehards of England.

Soon after the Constituent Assembly broke up, Jawaharlal Nehru and Dr. Rajendra Prasad went over to Lord Mountbatten and asked him if he would consent to become India's Governor-General, so that thirty-two minutes after Mountbatten had ceased to be Viceroy of India he became free India's first Governor-General.

In spectacular fashion the Mountbattens drove through the Delhi crowds in their open carriage, drawn by six bay horses. Normally, a Viceroy was only to be seen from a distance, and certainly never touched by the people, but on this occasion the people crowded around Mountbatten's slowly moving carriage and they shook hands with him all the way. Two little Indian urchins seemed to live in a fairy tale as they drove in the same carriage with the King's representative.

No one, however, was oblivious of the fact that the chief architect of our country's freedom, Mahatma Gandhi, was not to be found in the capital. He was in troubled Calcutta on that day, mourning because India had been divided. That very morning he had moved into the Muslim quarter of Calcutta to bring courage and strength to this suffering minority. He spent the day in fasting and in prayer. Angry Hindus stoned his house and broke up his prayer meeting because of the harbour his presence was giving to the Muslims.

Sadly he remarked: 'If you still prefer to use violence, remove me. It will not be me but my corpse that will be taken away from here.' 'For this disillusioned Father of Indian independence,' *Time* magazine remarked, 'there might be some consolation in the rare cry he heard from Muslim lips, Mahatma Gandhi zindabad.'

But the sombre note which Gandhi struck died amidst the bursts of fireworks, the singing, the bells and the conches. There seemed to be an atmospheric change all over the country, like the smell of earth after the first showers of rain. Freedom had come to four hundred million people, three hundred million in India and one hundred million in Pakistan. From every flagmast in the country now flew the tricolour of the free Indian people—the flag of deep saffron and dark green with the white central belt and the dark blue *chakra* (wheel) in the centre, a replica of Asoka's wheel of Sarnath. Asoka was a great king who lived in the golden era of Indian history, when India was closest to being a nation, whole and strong. The flag was, therefore, associated with the tradition of the land. The three colours once formed the flag of the Indian National Congress. The one difference was that the spinning-wheel had given place to the wheel of Asoka.

This had been a point of much controversy. The spinning-wheel was introduced by Gandhi for the economic betterment of the villagers. It had become the symbol of the poverty-stricken masses of the country and spinning, which had its justification primarily in economics, became the symbol of the nation's fight for freedom.

Gandhi took a stubborn stand for the retention of the spinning-wheel on the Indian national flag and threatened that he would not salute a flag of the Indian nation that did not bear it. It was a powerful threat in a country in which every whim and word of his was a commandment and his every fad an article of faith. But the main difficulty in the way of the retention of the spinning-wheel was an heraldic imperfection because a flag had to look the same from either side and obviously the spinning-wheel would not. The situation was becoming rather ridiculous when Gandhi climbed down and agreed to respect a national flag with Asoka's wheel instead of his spinning-wheel.

There were many who found it difficult to salute the flag for other reasons. For decades, the stooges and minions of British imperialism had treated the same Congress flag with contempt and scorned the principles for which it stood.

The rough-shod feet of many insignificant policemen had trampled it underfoot and many policemen had wielded the lathi on the heads of those who had been so ill-advised as to hoist it. Now they had to march past the same flag and salute it.

In the darkest days of the struggle, any head that wore a Gandhi cap was fair game for a hard-hitting minion of the law. Then the Gandhi cap signified revolt against constitutional authority. With independence, that coarse white cap of hand-spun cloth became the badge of authority.

In every government office there were people who had served the British loyally, looking upon Congressmen as upstarts. They honestly believed in the benefits of British administration and looked upon those who fought for freedom as enemies of the peace of the country.

They had ridiculed the movement for freedom and never dreamed that the British would surrender the country to the malcontents. Now they who had believed that Swaraj was a fantasy and a madman's dream which could never be realized found themselves confronted with the reality of freedom. It was not easy for these loyal servants of the British to adjust their minds to this historical phenomenon.

There were houses in the land which had become divided against themselves in the course of the struggle. Old faiths died hard and many of the older generation who had never felt the stirrings of patriotism had found it difficult to accept this young madness for self-government. Freedom was anarchy to them, and many were the fears they had for the future. But in that dawn of freedom, it was difficult even for these men of little faith to fail to respond to the general enthusiasm. The idea of freedom was beautiful and compelling.

But that day, which witnessed the consummation of a long struggle for freedom, saw too the tragedy of a rupture within the nation. A people who had battled together against a common enemy, moved by the same pulsations of patriotism and the same vision of freedom, were now to be divided. A country that was one through long centuries of historical development and by virtue of geographical frontiers was to be artificially bisected into two dominions.

Partition was unnatural. Geographically, the country was indivisible and by historical association the two communities were inseparable. Their cultures had nourished each other so long, that they were indistinguishable. Now a frontier would have to be created, tearing through bonds of association. Not the surgeon's healing knife but the butcher's destructive axe would be in operation. The country would be disrupted, the orderly threads of four hundred million human lives, which were interwoven to form the fabric of India, would be torn.

Like a nightmare, one could see the tragedy of division, the chaos it would bring, and the violence it was likely to entail. All along the frontier people would have to strike their tents, gather up their belongings and emigrate to the side of the frontier to which they were consigned. The frontier question would be a bloody one.

But the uncertainty of the future was overshadowed by the present. We had faith that those who had led us from slavery to freedom would now lead us to peace. We thought over the dangers that were past and lost the fear of the perils ahead.

There was Gandhi who had lighted the path to freedom when all around was dark; and everything, seemed lost.

There were Nehru and Vallabhbhai Patel and many others who had caught the sparks of Gandhi's teachings and in whose hearts burned the same fire, tried, proven leaders of the masses.

There was the Congress which these selfless men had built tier by tier with their sacrifice, an institution of altruistic national service. The Congress which had been the spearhead of our people's struggle for freedom would now guard the freedom we had won. The leadership that had through so many dangers would not fail us.

The faith of our three hundred million people was centred in the Congress.

(Bombay, 14 August 1947)

The Birth of a Nation

WILFRED RUSSEL

Wilfred Russel first came to Bombay in 1935 to join one of those British merchant houses, which had grown to power and strength after the dissolution of the centuries-old East India Company in 1857. He was elected to one of the reserved seats in the Bombay Legislative Assembly in 1937. During the War, he commanded two squadrons of the Royal Indian Air Force, but returned to India in early 1946 to rejoin his firm, Killick Nixon and Company. An observer of the Royal Institute of International Affairs at the Asian Relations Conference held in Delhi in March 1947, he found himself 'inadvertently' mixed up in the strife-ridden states of Kashmir and Punjab. 'This extraordinary succession of events,' he wrote in the prologue to the *Indian Summer*, 'seemed to flow in an unbroken chain from 1945 to 1947, and because, by chance, I was able to witness many of the events at close quarters and observe the people, who were themselves making history, it seemed worthwhile writing down those impressions before the memory of them should fade.'

And Freedom rear'd in that august sunrise Her beautiful, bold brow.

—Alfred Lord Tennyson

There can have been few celebrations of independence in history to compare with those of India and Pakistan for lack of bitterness against the former rulers and probably none in which the latter played such a prominent part themselves. I only saw the celebrations in Karachi but from all accounts the same enthusiasm and relief were evident among all classes of people in India and the delirious reception given to Lord and Lady Mountbatten in Delhi on 15 August and a few days later in Bombay, appears to have surpassed

From *Indian Summer* (Bombay: Thacker & Co. Ltd, 1951), pp. 123-30.

anything that had previously been accorded even to the great political leaders of the country.

We arrived at the Palace Hotel, which by now seemed to be generally known as the 'Spiv Arms' on the evening of 14 August. The hospitable Manager, Monsieur So and So, put us with several American and British correspondents into a large room which had been turned into a dormitory. I don't think any of them had been to Karachi before. In fact, some of the Americans had never heard of the place until the partition of India had brought it suddenly into prominence. All of them, including the British, seemed to be disappointed at the smallness of the town, the large quantities of sand and the general lack of up-to-date amenities. Whether it was this provincial atmosphere or because few of them had studied the Muslim point of view before partition that made them feel the Independence celebrations were a flop is difficult to say in retrospect; the fact remains they all seemed convinced that the sober way in which the Muslims were celebrating their freedom probably meant they did not want it very much, certainly not as much as the Indians they had seen in Delhi who had been stoking up emotionally for some time back. It was a short step from this point of view to the conclusion, which at least one of the Americans reached, that the whole business of partition was unnecessary and should never have been carried out. As I went to sleep in our dormitory, I made a resolution to get up early next day and walk round the bazaar. I felt sure that the Muslims of Karachi were likely to be as happy about their freedom as the Hindus in India, although it was quite possible that they were not being so demonstrative about it—in fact I think the ordinary Muslim in the street had scarcely realized yet that Pakistan had really come about.

On my way out of the hotel early in the morning of 15 August I ran into many old friends in the entrance hall, who were up betimes to squeeze every drop of experience out of this great day. There was no mistaking the enthusiasm among educated Muslims whose anticipation of the day's events reminded me of Speech Days at school. I ran into Sir Firoz Khan Noon who had been India's High Commissioner in London at one time, and more recently Defence Member of the Government of India during the war; he was talking to Begum Shah Nawaz, the educationist and champion of women's rights. Since Pandit Nehru's sister, Mrs. Vijayalakshmi Pandit, had gone to Moscow as India's first Ambassador, there had been talk of Begum Shah Nawaz going in a similar capacity for Pakistan.

Outside in the streets of Karachi there was any amount of enthusiasm among the Muslim populace, although the considerable numbers of Hindus who had lived there peaceably, side by side with the Muslims for generations, were obviously a bit worried and were beginning to look over their shoulders into India. Nevertheless, there was peace and quiet throughout the town. Everywhere the new green and white Pakistan flags were sprouting from rooftops, balconies and windows.

During the morning, while the friendly crowds were drifting through the streets savouring the excitement of this very special holiday, Harrison and I drove round the town with an old Hindu estate agent. As he took us from one property to another, he unraveled from the folds of his flowing gown ancient *sanads* and title deeds issued in the portentous names of many past Governors-General-in-Council and when Harrison pointed out that as from today all these sanads would be out of date, the old man looked at us in astonishment. At this particular moment we happened to be looking at a plot of wasteland where some little boys were playing cricket with a tennis ball and soapbox wickets. It looked as if it would be some time before the imprint of England would be completely effaced from India or Pakistan and the odds seemed to be heavily in favour of Hutton and Compton being remembered considerably longer than the Governors-General-in-Council.

The big moment in Karachi on 15 August 1947 was undoubtedly the parade in the afternoon at which Mr. Jinnah, known as the Quaid-i-Azam, 'the foremost in the land', inspected detachments of the armed forces on the large open space in front of the Governor-General's House. Harrison and I had commandiered the ACC car, an old V.8 which had passed through many cement factories before finishing its career with our agent in Karachi. On this exciting afternoon we drove it to the parade ground about half an hour before Jinnah was due to arrive and by a stroke of luck were able to nose the bonnet right up to the ropes not far from the saluting base. We then scrambled on to the roof, which even at this early stage showed an ominous bulge in its thin skin under our combined weight of twenty-eight stone. Before the parade had begun we had collected at least a dozen stalwart Muslims, with whom we were only too delighted to share our grandstand and before the show was over, I counted no less than twenty bodies. It says much for the emotional quality of the spectacle that the imminent foundering of the firm's car never crossed our minds until the parade was over.

I had somehow expected that a ceremony of this kind would have been a sad experience for an Englishman, however sympathetic he might have been to Indian aspirations. But to my astonishment I found myself gripped by a feeling of intense gladness. It is no indication of a lesser sympathy for India than for Pakistan to confess that a few months later when I saw the last company of the last regiment of British Infantry slow march through the Gateway of India at Bombay to the strains of our National Anthem that I did feel sad. It is extraordinarily difficult to account for this emotional distinction, but certainly in Karachi there seemed to be a quality of companionship and continuity about the proceedings, which was not simply occasioned by the presence of several senior British officers, who had been asked to stay on, but which seemed to spring somehow from the sand of the desert on which we all stood.

And then Mr. Jinnah arrived with his sister Miss Fatima in the state Landau. As he got out of the open coach and began his stately inspection of the troops drawn up in a large hollow square, he could have given points in dignity and deportment to the most stately of British Viceroys. The march past of the troops and of the Royal Pakistan Navy, both freshly parted from their brothers-in-arms who were doing the same thing for the British Governor-General in New Delhi, was carried out with a precision and smartness which augured well for the future, since the stability of this new country would to a large degree depend upon the efficiency of the army. Precisely as the last company passed the saluting base, a squadron of Tempests roared by at a hundred feet and I wondered if any of the young men flying those fighters had been in either of the two Indian Air Force Squadrons I had been lucky enough to command during the war.

When it was all over Mr. Jinnah got into his coach and drove back to the big house, which had formerly housed a succession of British Governors. The proceedings had been so sensible and friendly and apparently inspired by a spirit of real comradeship between the new and the old. As the last hefty Muslim heaved himself off the Ford we stood by with bated breath to see if the poor old car would sink down on its knees and expire. Happily it seemed to have been inspired by the importance of the day with amazing powers of resistance and we were able to drive back safely to the hotel.

Seventeenth August was a Sunday and, as if to underline his friendship for the departing British, Mr. Jinnah made a gesture which was indicative at once of his attitude to the official and unofficial European community of his capital and of his determination that Pakistan should not become an exclusively religious State. The Anglican Archdeacon, it seems, had arranged for a special service of prayer called thanksgiving to be held in the Cathedral on this first Sunday of Independence. He had also composed a special bidding prayer for the occasion in which Mr. Jinnah was naturally mentioned. News of this service apparently reached the Quaid-i-Azam by chance and he at once instructed his Military Secretary to ask the Archdeacon whether he and his sister, also Sir Ghulam Hussain Hidayatullah, the Governor of Sind, might attend the service in State. I managed to get a seat at the back of the nave for this extraordinarily moving service and again I felt even more strongly than on the parade ground the spirit of friendship and of continuity, which seemed to envelop everyone who was connected, however humbly, with the first days of this new dominion.

Mr. Jinnah, who knew only too well the orthodox fervour of many Muslims, might well have been taking a political risk in making this graceful and moving gesture to the Christian community of Karachi. He left after the first hymn and the bidding prayer.

The temptation to stay on in this exhilarating atmosphere was great, but clearly we had to get back to Bombay as quickly as possible to report on the happenings in London. Our stay in Karachi was in fact prolonged by one day owing to the difficulty of arranging interviews with some of the leading Pakistan ministers and officials, whose ideas were necessary to our plans, but who were so enraged at the terms of the Radcliffe Boundary Award on the day it was announced that they were clearly not in the mood to see anybody of the same nationality as the Chairman of that Commission.

As it happened we did run into my companion of the air-conditioned coach, Amin-ud-Dill, during the morning the announcement was made and his wrath was such that we decided to fix our appointments with the Pakistan officials when the storm had passed. The trouble was that the tenuous ethnological borderline dividing Muslims and Hindus in the Punjab ran between the capital city of Lahore and the great trading city of Amritsar, traditional rallying point of the Sikhs. These two towns were only forty miles apart and were linked by the Grand Trunk Road and the main railway line. Sir Cyril Radcliffe had drawn his line between these two major towns and since Lahore would clearly have to be the capital of the new Pakistan province of the West Punjab the Pakistanis were upset because the frontier was to run within a few miles of their provincial capital, which would thus lie only twenty odd miles from their mortal enemies, the Sikhs. Where else it could have been drawn was a mystery, but there was a similar outcry in the Indian press and it seemed that the Radcliffe Award, by and large, was as good a dividing line as anyone could have drawn under the circumstances. By the following day tempers seemed to have calmed down and we did our rounds of the officials and ministers, all of whom were most friendly and interested to hear what people in London were thinking of their new dominion.

We had a pleasant interview with that most pleasant and capable of Premiers, Liaquat Ali Khan, who seemed to remember me from our previous meeting in New Delhi. It was a strange encounter and typical of the pioneering atmosphere of Karachi at that time. He had already moved into the Prime Minister's House, but his furniture and belongings were still lying all round the empty bungalow in packing cases; workmen were swarming all over the house unpacking, painting, hanging up curtains and scrubbing floors, while the Prime Minister of this new State endeavoured to deal with the innumerable problems and people, that were crowding round him on every hand. Under the circumstances it was remarkable that he should see us at all.

We were shown upstairs to a little balcony at the back of the house where there seemed to be a little more peace than on the ground floor. We sat round a packing case, which served as a table and on which we balanced the beautiful model Viking ash tray. This provided a natural opening for the conversation and Liaquat said at once that Pakistan would soon have to get down to the problem of organizing her own internal air services. He also mentioned that Mr. Jinnah would have to have a fast and comfortable aircraft with a long range so that he could visit the farflung outposts of his domains, especially the North-West Frontier and eastern Pakistan, which was separated from Karachi by over a thousand miles of

Indian territory. Within a few months he had a Royal Viking, which had been specially built for him by Vickers Armstrong at Weybridge. It was sad that he was not to use this lovely aircraft more than half a dozen times before it was to bring him down from the hill station at Ziarat to his deathbed in Karachi.

From aircraft the conversation turned to a discussion of Pakistan's economic future. Liaquat was most emphatic that from an economic point of view the new dominion had every chance of survival. After explaining about the static population of the country and its self-sufficiency, he exclaimed:

'Thank God, we have the wheat.' Then he went on: 'But in any case as far as I know there has been no example in history of a State foundering through purely economic causes. We certainly do not intend to be the first!'

We discussed the location of the dominion capital—whether it would be wise from a strategic point of view to have the capital so near the sea or whether it would be feasible to build a new capital somewhere in the interior.

I was continually amazed that this important man was prepared to discuss such things in such a matter of fact way with two Englishmen, who had no official or indeed any other status in his country, but he seemed to be taking us completely into his confidence. Looking back, I think there must have been a reason behind this discussion about the future capital, since Liaquat clearly knew that Harrison had been one of the leading experts in the cement industry of undivided India and that Killicks had many connections with the building interests of Great Britain. In any case he told us that he was going to press for the capital to be retained at Karachi despite the congestion and the strategic arguments against it. He enquired about the time needed to construct a new town, introduce modern hotels and all the paraphernalia of an up-to-date capital city. He also asked if Killicks could do anything at Chittagong about putting up a cement factory on the other side of the subcontinent. Before leaving him we roamed over the whole field of coal, minerals, hydro-electrics and currency. Liaquat made it quite clear that so far as he was concerned Pakistan was to become as economically independent of India as possible. After a stimulating forty minutes with him, we left and prepared to return to Bombay.

Within two hours of landing back at Bombay we were sitting in front of the senior partner's desk; it was exactly a month after the new India had been liberated by her own rulers. When our story had been told I was sent back to finish my holiday in Kashmir. I must confess I looked on this unexpected development as just another stroke of luck in an unusually lucky summer. I had no idea I should be walking into the middle of a civil war.

A Limb Cut Off

This is adapted from an interview with Lakshmi Sahgal by Ritu Menon and Kamla Bhasin

Captain Lakshmi Sahgal of the Rani Jhansi Regiment in the Indian National Army was born in Madras on 24 October 1914 into a highly political, nationalist family. Her father, Dr S. Swaminathan, was a noted criminal lawyer, and her mother, Ammu Swaminathan, an active social worker. The young Lakshmi had her early political education at home, when the family stopped wearing English cotton, boycotted English goods and spoke only Malayalam and Tamil. Lakshmi graduated as a medical doctor was politically active in Madras University, but did not agree with Gandhi's call to students to give up their education and join the Civil Disobedience Movement.

Her growing disillusionment with Gandhi's policy of nonviolent resistance crystallized at the time of the Meerut Conspiracy Case, and through her contact with Comrade Suhasini (Sarojini Naidu's younger sister), an accused in the case. In 1940 she left Madras for Singapore to work there as a doctor, and came into contact with a group of expatriate Indians who would form the core of the future INA. In July 1943, she formed part of the welcome party to receive Subhas Chandra Bose in Singapore, and in the same month, Netaji called upon her to participate in the formation of the Rani Jhansi Regiment. On 12 July, Netaji ceremoniously presented weapons to the 20 women who formed the Regiment there. The Rani Jhansi Regiment was the first and only all-women regiment in modern Indian history. Trained in warfare and weaponry, it participated actively in the INA's struggle for freedom in exile till 1946, when the INA was disbanded and its officers returned to India.

When partition was announced, I felt as if one of my limbs had been cut off. I couldn't feel the joy of Independence. We were not even given a chance to settle down, mentally and physically after our return from Burma and the war to sort out our thoughts and discover what it was all about—there were press interviews, meetings and *dawats*—really it was maddening and at each place I used to be asked about partition, and I always said, it's absolute nonsense. I would just pass it off without realizing how deeply it had already caught on and how serious the problem was, till a year before partition. I had gone to Lahore and my husband's younger brother, who was in his final year at Law College had several Muslim friends. One evening he said to me, 'You know, you've been giving lots of interviews and you've been brushing partition aside, but it's a very serious thing and is bound to happen.'

I said, 'Suresh, how can you say such a thing?'

He replied, 'I have many friends among Muslims, among them intellectuals who are progressive. They all say that the Muslims have been pushed to such a position that nothing short of partition is going to be acceptable, that it's absolutely inevitable.'

They felt that on the whole the national movement had completely bypassed the Muslims. They had not been given a chance to involve themselves as they should have or to join mainstream politics, with the result that they had all come under the extremist and opportunist politics of Muslim leaders who thought they had no chance of survival unless they had a separate organization. In any united nation they would be completely swamped by Hindu leaders. They got around these young Muslim students and pressed their point home with the result that the younger generation were all in favour of partition—many of the women students also were in favour of it. But still, in Punjab, there was no ill-feeling between Hindus and Muslims and Sikhs. That rabid kind of religious fervour was more evident in UP.

This might have been because they were being mobilized as Muslims. You see, we realized that, especially at the later stages, Congress mobilization—as opposed to the INA ideology—had always been around members of the Congress, never around Indians. This Gandhian influence, it worked both ways—on one side he mobilized the largest number of people in India, there is no doubt about that, but he also gave it the aspect of Hindu mobilization. You can't have it both ways—Gandhi used to always say Muslims are like my left hand and Hindus are my right hand, yet he wanted to keep his left and right hands apart from each other. He always acknowledged a kind of separate identity for Muslims—

their ethos, and a Hindu ethos. For instance, he never approved of Muslims and Hindus marrying each other—even Mrs. Vijayalakshmi Pandit's marriage to Syed Hossain was annulled because of Gandhiji's objections. Then there was his great reverence for caste— he didn't want to touch caste.

It seems evident now that as a result partition was inevitable, but there was no need for it because the INA showed that it was not necessary to keep the Hindu and Muslim ethos separate—that we could evolve an Indian ethos if we kept religion out of the whole thing and emphasized the fact that we were Indians and had a common enemy in the British. After driving the British away we had to build this country afresh, together. In the INA this played a very prominent part, but not sufficient emphasis was placed on it in India, specially after 1942, after the Quit India Movement when they all went to jail. They completely lost touch with the masses. In India there was no real ideology at work after that.

Now a great deal of the INA activity was outside the country and that might have made a difference—it is always easier to forge unity outside, because whether you like it or not, you are considered an Indian. Nobody asks you whether you are a Hindu, a Muslim, a Sikh, it's much easier to be united. Within India, it needs more effort, more positive activity. You can't just go on saying 'Hindu-Muslim *Bhai, Bhai*' and stop at that.

I believe that Gandhi was someone who had his convictions— all this Ram Rajya business—but people like Jawaharlal Nehru who were supposedly secular, who were not orthodox, who believed in the unity of Hindus and Muslims, they were not positive enough in this respect. You see, I think very few of us can get away from this kind of thing. That is probably one reason why the INA ideology didn't really take root. The whole INA trial came as a tremendous jolt to the leadership. When they saw the effect it was having in the country, they panicked and said, we must accept independence at all costs—even a truncated independence. That's why the Muslims also felt that we must capitalize on this. Some Muslim officers offered to provide them with legal counsel to argue their case and so on. They tried to take in a little bit of the INA glory but they didn't really succeed because they came into the picture too late. But it had such an impact that both the Congress and the Muslim League felt that the real threat was the INA spirit and ideology. You see, it created tremendous enthusiasm, but it should have been nurtured properly and not allowed to evaporate like the fizz from a bottle of soda. Even though much of the activity was going on outside the country the real enthusiasm started with the trials by which time the war was over and all the INA members were back in the country. Before that we were all dismissed as Japanese puppets! But there was very little time because by then talks were under way about independence and the Congress had practically agreed to partition, the Muslim League also. So this INA enthusiasm was gradually diluted and practically suppressed.

If Netaji had been around, I feel he would definitely have made an effort and rallied as many people around as he could have, and he would have opposed partition tooth and nail. There is no doubt about that. And he would have had a following. Bengal he would have definitely got because they were against partition till the very end. There, both Hindus and Muslims were all for a United Bengal seceding from the partitioned country. So he would have had Bengal, and South India would also have fallen in because there is no such acute Hindu-Muslim antagonism there. Then there was Abdul Ghaffar Khan, and Kashmir—so there was a good chance of it succeeding.

We haven't yet done with communal politics, it's going on in one form or the other. If it's not communal, it's regional or linguistic, because in the 47 years since Independence no really active, positive steps have been taken to change things. After all, there is so much insurgency in the northeast—but 80 per cent of Indians don't even know where it is! So how can you make them feel they are one with us, when we don't even know who they are or what they are? Nothing has been done.

The problem now is how to forge this unity. For one thing, religion in its organized form must be banned. People can practise religion in their homes but not take it out on the streets. Here in Kanpur there are hundreds of temples. They find a stone, the next day you have a temple. And what happens in these temples? They are hotbeds of all this drug-trafficking, drinking and anti-socials. And the same thing with the money coming from the Gulf, Muslims build mosques. Indians, I think, have a very strong dual personality. Even the most senior of our comrades who are party members, our trade union leaders, all of them, as long as they are within the four walls of the mill, fight against the mill-owner or the management. But the moment they go home, they are willing to give dowries for their daughters' weddings, they won't allow an inter-caste marriage. This is one of the strongest factors in our make-up and our religious background. We have not even been able to keep what is good in it and discard all these worn-out shibboleths, all this fundamentalism, feudalism and obscurantism.

Did the INA discuss this? Well, Netaji in his lectures and in the daily national history sessions—that we had as part of our curriculum during training—always used to say how this country was united even before the British came. It was a country where Hinduism was the faith of the country but Hinduism itself was not a religion in the accepted meaning of the term, because it did not believe in proselytizing. And it gave refuge to people who were persecuted for their religious beliefs in all parts of the world. And of course Netaji propounded the theory that it was the British who brought the virus of communalism and religion into the country because they felt this was the only way they could rule. He felt that unless some strong steps were taken after Independence to separate religion completely from politics and from the government and life of the common man this would always be a major problem in the country. It is something we have to actively fight against. Yet he always used to say, don't think I don't believe in religion, I have my own religion, but I believe in it in private, I don't want to force it down anyone else's throat, and I also respect people who have other religious beliefs. Everyone knew that Netaji had studied religion and philosophy but there was no organized religious activity in the INA. Yet on *Diwali*, the Muslim officers organized a *bada khana* and invited everyone. For *Id*, we Hindus organized a feast. Then the Sikhs had a *gurudwara*, there was a Hindu priest and a *mullah*, and those who wanted could go for prayers. On Sundays people went to the gurudwara.

But we did not have any intercommunity marriages. Everybody got married (to each other) afterwards! Now on the class issue because Netaji was always speaking to the soldiers, he had to emphasize the anti-imperialist war against the British, but he used to talk a lot about the *kisans* in India, how they were the backbone of the country, that they had received a very raw deal and that there should be a just division of land. He also spoke of the rights of the workers in factories. And this is why, as I said earlier, the Congress and the Muslims League were afraid of the INA ideology taking over. Because, after all, in a revolutionary movement, people start thinking. For example, the rank and file, the jawans, were all from the peasantry of the country and after joining the revolutionary army and fighting for independence they would not go back to their land under the same conditions as their forefathers lived in—they would definitely ask for a better deal. This kind of consciousness was definitely there.

The riots had already started, so all the functions had to be cancelled. Before that, off and on in Delhi, the Congress had tried to woo me, but I took a very non-committal stance. I tried very hard to contact the communists. I had always been inclined towards communism—I had studied some communist literature and Mrs Naidu's younger sister, Suhasini Jambedkar, was a very close friend of mine. But the communists wouldn't touch me with a barge pole because they said, 'Oh! you're a fascist, we will have nothing to do with the INA.' They wouldn't even talk to me! (Laughs). I said, your ideology couldn't be strong enough, if you think that talking to me will damage it! So this was not possible. I was not at all drawn to the Congress because somehow I felt they were hypocritical. And in any case, I had never agreed with Gandhi's brand of politics. You know when all these people in the INA wanted to meet him, he said that they must first take an oath of non-violence! I said, I am not a violent person, I don't go shooting people but I'm not going to take any oath!

I remember the time of the Meerut Conspiracy Case . . . that's when I got indoctrinated with communism. This Suhasini Nambiar of the Meerut Conspiracy Case came to Madras and was staying in our house under police surveillance. We used to have long discussions. The trouble with Gandhi was that he never took anything to its logical conclusion. He would organize the rural people but the moment they got really militant, he would call the whole thing off and say that they had broken the vow of non-violence. Even if they were provoked beyond endurance, he would call off the agitation. You can't leave a revolution or a movement like this in mid-air. The leadership must also follow the people. For example, I think he was very wrong in calling off civil disobedience because hundreds of Chauri-Chauras could have happened. You can't avoid that in a revolution. One should ask a psychologist about it, but I feel that the so-called non-violent revolution, when people's passions were aroused to a certain extent and then not given free reign, was probably one reason why we became so violent in the communal rioting. . . .

So, I came back in 1946 and left politics. I felt as it is not my scene let me get back to my medical work. Mrs Vijayalakshmi Pandit was Health Minister in UP at that time, so I wrote to her and asked if she could sanction an honorary job in the Women's Hospital in Kanpur. She wrote back to say we have no such provision! So I started my medical work in the municipality. Then the refugees started coming. There was too much pressure on Delhi, and some large settlements had been built for workers in Kanpur which were not being used. This was a good place for refugees to camp. And then, being an industrial city, they thought many of them could set up ancillary industries and begin the process of rehabilitation. There must have been over a lakh of refugees.

For destitute women, there was Mridula Sarabhai's organization. They used to come and take them to camps in Delhi, Jalandhar, etc. and if we knew of any cases we used to write to them and tell hem. I worked on my own, but the All India Women's Conference was also active. I did this work for six months or so. They rehabilitated themselves very quickly. They did not want any charity, they did it on their own. Most of them stayed on in the camps and quarters, started small businesses. Those areas became little replicas of the places they had left behind, where you could get that particular kind of Punjabi food, etc. These localities are still there but many of them were depleted in 1984—a lot of violence took place there because people knew that these were all refugees from 1948—at least 40 per cent were Sikhs.

In the Punjab riots of 1947 the entire blame was put on the Muslims—they were started and sparked off by them. The retaliation from the Hindus came later. This was done to make the Hindus fearful and force them to leave. And the tragedy of it all is that the Muslims have suffered the most in India as a result of Partition. You see what has happened to the poor Muslims who are here— they can't catch up with the mainstream because of lack of education and economically they are much worse than they used to be. The Hindus might not have fled from West Punjab if there had been no violence, so what if Partition was taking place.

People like my father-in-law did not even move his library. He didn't move anything from his house even when the High Court was shifted to Simla as a precaution. If the Naval Mutiny and the Telengana Movement had coincided, the momentum for independence would have been much stronger. . . . Their ultimate aims were more or less the same, but they were so isolated that the impact of one was not felt anywhere else. How many people even know about the Telengana struggle? The Naval Mutiny has practically been forgotten and yet the interesting thing is that the working class in Bombay supported it. Hundreds of workers were killed and put in jail—so it could have become a mass movement. But people like Sardar Patel advised the British to put it down with an iron hand. . . .

In the INA trials, the main one was of General Shah Nawaz, Colonel Sahgal and Major Dhillon. They were the test cases; depending on the verdict, they would go ahead with the others. They were absolutely sure that the verdict would go against them and they would be condemned not only by the military court but by the people. The charges against those three were that they were waging a war against the King of England! But because I was not one of the King's men—I had never taken an oath of allegiance to the King! I was never tried.

There has been a grave misconception in the minds of those in India that our Muslim comrades who were in what became Pakistan played a very sinister role in the carnage that took place. This is absolutely false. When the final decision regarding Partition had taken place, a delegation of senior INA officers under the leadership of Colonel Habib-ur-Rehman (he was the officer who accompanied Netaji on his last ill-fated flight from Saigon), called on Pandit Nehru. They told him that as they believed in the unity of India and did not believe in a state built on the basis of religion, they wanted to stay back and not become citizens of Pakistan. Pandit Nehru refused to consider their honourable offer and advised them to remain in the place where they were born, and serve the new State of Pakistan with loyalty and devotion. It was after this that some officers helped in the evacuation of Muslim refugees stranded in East Punjab, and also advised the army on guerrilla tactics. Never did they indulge in any kind of atrocity.

A Quick Look at Pakistan

A. D. MANI

A. D. Mani (1910-78) was the well-known editor of the daily *Hitavada* from 1936 to 1966. A member of the Rajya Sabha, he represented Madhya Pradesh for two terms, 1960-6 and 1966-72. He was alternate delegate of India at the UN General Assembly from 1952-5; vice-president, Servants of India Conference from 1952-6; and director, Press Trust of India from 1950-78.

On my way to London, I dropped in for a few hours at Karachi to have a glimpse of Pakistan. As my plane droned over the Drigh Road aerodrome, an inexplicable wave of sadness swept over me. I had seen Karachi as a proud province of a United India and now I was going to see it as a part of another state, hostile and unfriendly to India, whatever the protestations of Mr Jinnah and his friends may be. At the aerodrome, I found ample evidence that Karachi was in a turmoil. On all the benches of the windswept and bleak airport, I saw many refugees sitting with mountains of baggage by their side. They were all men and women who were fleeing from the Utopia of the Quaid-i-Azam. They wore hunted looks, and were distraught, pale and worried. I could not resist asking myself: 'Is this the India for which we yearned and dreamed all these years?'

At Karachi, I noticed signs of panic everywhere. The Frere Road, which was a busy thoroughfare in normal times, looked deserted. Literally, deserted. There was not a soul to be seen, not a crow flying over the fine asphalted roadway. My taxiwala explained that it was a Saturday afternoon and people had gone home from their offices. But I insisted that it could not be the proper explanation. It was unthinkable that everybody was back home to enjoy his cup of tea. Then the taxiwala hesitantly told me, '*Log bhag ja raha hai.*' [People

Article 16 September 1947, London. Reprinted from *Of Yanks and Others* (Nagpur: Hitavada Publications Division, 1948), p. 1-11.

are running away] I was told later that the rate of evacuation was about Rs 2,000 a day. There were many houses which had been padlocked and whose door paths were unswept. This was the onetime beautiful city of Karachi, one of the best planned towns, where the Amils and the *Bhai-Bhands* had lent colour and riches to the aerial gateway of India. Quite a number told me that Hindus and Sikhs had left the city by thousands. The Sheikhupura Hindus, the brain of the mercantile community of Sind, had fled to Madras and it appears their leader told friends in Karachi, 'Whatever happens, we are not coming back to Sind. We will go down to Cape Comorin, merge ourselves with the South Indian community, marry there and make our home in a place where there will not be a whiff of Pakistan.' The powerful Bhai Bhand community, the counterpart of the gentlemen from Marwar in Sind, have left *en masse*. Taking advantage of their worldwide connections, they have shifted their capital to Indian centres. When I heard that the Sheikhupuras and the *Bhai-Bhands* had left Sind, I wondered whether there could be a commercial future for Sind. It is these two communities that have built Sind brick by brick, stone by stone. With due respect to the Muslims of Sind, it must be stated in the interests of truth they have not been conspicuously successful in commerce. It is very difficult for them to replace the *Bhai-Bhands*, despite the Isphahani, members of whose family seem to have the run of Karachi at present. The commercial power-station of Sind has been smashed up.

There were also signs at Karachi that law and order in that hitherto peaceful province was being shaken. In a taxi in which I was travelling and which was driven by a Hindu, the car was stopped on the road by some young men who thrust across the road a big bamboo pole. It was lucky that the headlights were not smashed, let alone our heads. I was told further that while the government was governing better than in the Punjab, there was a noticeable anxiety not to hurt the feelings of the Faithful, who had assisted Jinnah in the realization of his dream state of Pakistan. Eastern Punjab refugees who had come to Karachi had forcibly occupied some of the houses abandoned by Hindu refugees and the rent controller till now had not taken action against such unlawful seizures of property. This does not mean that authority had broken down completely. The situation was very much better in Karachi than it had been or ever will be in western Punjab, but there was no knowing when peace will be ruffled in the province, so far governed with consummate strategy by that notorious opportunist Mr Gulam Hussain Hidayatullah. When stories of atrocities poured into Karachi from other parts of India, reprisals were bound to be taken against the minorities. There was an orgy of rioting in Karachi in December 1947. I had heard of one case in which a Sikh was speared to death and curfew was immediately clamped down as a consequence. There was considerable tension in the city, the voltage was high, and people were whispering the explosion may take place any day, but on the day I was there the situation was, in the usual phraseology of Reuters, 'well in hand'.

The authorities of Pakistan will have great difficulty in restoring order in Western Punjab, whatever the situation may be in Karachi. In western Punjab, the fields are remaining unharvested. There has been colossal destruction of property worth crores of rupees. Unofficial estimates place the loss at about Rs 70-80 crores. In the Frontier Province, too, the situation is not free from anxiety. The Khan brothers, though not commanding a majority of the electorate, are definitely creating trouble, and Khan Abdul Qaiyum Khan had been to Karachi with a woeful tale that Dr Khan Saheb had squandered all the money of the government and there was not much money for him to carry on the work of the government. Eastern Pakistan has already raised its wail that the central Pakistan government must come to its help or she would be sunk. Jute prices have gone down and have to be geared up if the province is to balance its budget. The supplicants for the favours of the central government in Pakistan are many. This has created considerable uneasiness in the minds of the Sind Muslims, who with their final and fundamental allegiance to Islam are at heart very parochial. There are vague whispers in Muslim circles in Sind that the presence of Mr Jinnah and his colleagues in the Pakistan government is not something to be talked and boasted about. I was told that Sir Ghulam Hussain is already dropping gentle hints that he would not mind Karachi being denied the privilege of having the Pakistan government and that the government might be shifted to some other place.

Pakistan's financial condition is one which should necessitate the use of one bottle of aspirin for each member of the Pakistan government. Frantic efforts are being made to have the revenue raised, but these efforts only witness the gradual fall in revenue under all heads. The customs revenue of Karachi has registered a

decline, according to knowledgeable circles, and it was explained
to me that trade was being diverted to Jamnagar. Income tax will
also suffer with the mass exodus of Hindu capital. The Pakistan
government is faced with considerable difficulty even in financing
the day-to-day conduct of the administration. To add to all these
difficulties is the report that the Rohri Canal has been breached and
lakhs of rupees have been lost on that account. It is to help him
tide over his financial crisis that Mr Jinnah has asked for the services
of Sir Archibald Rowlands. Sir Archibald Rowlands was Finance
member of the India government at a time when inflation was at
its height and the printing press at Nasik was working a double shift
to print notes. I am not suggesting that he has been sent for only
to advise them to print more notes. But faced with the situation
which obtains today in Pakistan, Sir Archibald Rowlands may have
no other alternative but to increase the quantum of currency. I asked
a few with knowledge of what was going on in the inner counsels
of the Pakistan government whether foreign aid would not be
available. The answer to the query was that soundings had been
taken but the response was not very encouraging. It was plain to
me as a pikestaff that the Pakistan government was in for heavy
weather and that it was heading for the shoals of financial
breakdown. If Pakistan is to be propped up, some form of
international aid is necessary and more necessary is some sort of
understanding with the Indian government to prevent the diversion
of trade from Karachi. There are other problems of Pakistan, which
if left unsolved, might lead to the emergence of a fascist state in
Mr Jinnah's country.

One of the few factors known about Pakistan's new set up is
that the Muslim League leaders have taken care to see that the key
positions are manned by the Punjabis. In Pakistan itself, there are
many leading figures who hail from provinces not belonging strictly
to Pakistan. Mr Chundrigar comes from Bombay, Nawabzada
Liaquat Ali Khan from the UP and there are only two representatives
belonging to the Pakistan area in the cabinet. In the administration
of Pakistan, that is the secretarial appointments, Punjabis have taken
charge of the wheel. There are two reasons to explain this Punjabi
dominance in the administration. The Punjabi is far more educated
than the Sindhi Muslim, or the Frontier Muslim. Secondly, he is
trusted by the League more than the Sindhi Muslim or the Frontier
Muslim. The Sindhi Muslim has been notoriously volatile, changing

sides often and endangering the prestige and the strength of the Muslim League. With the solitary exception of Khizr Hayat Khan Tiwana, the Punjab Muslim has been wholeheartedly behind the League. He has been in fact the core of Muslim League strength during the past five years. He can be trusted to do the job which the League would like him to do and we have seen how well he has done it, with disastrous efficiency, in western Punjab during the last few weeks. In view of the fact that he is far more dependable than the Sind and the Frontier Muslim, he is placed in key positions. The district magistrate of Karachi, the collector of Customs, to mention only two important officers, are Punjab Muslims.

The Sind Muslim and the Frontier Muslim are not altogether happy about this development, and earlier I had written about the gentle hints which Mr Ghulam Hussain has been dropping about the desirability of changing the capital of Pakistan from Karachi to some other place. The conflict between the Punjab Muslim and the non-Punjab Muslim is bound to break out in an acute form, when the economic crisis, consequent on shortage of foodstuffs and consumer goods and inflation will descend on the new state. At present, this antagonism between the two sections is submerged because there is from the League point of view a common enemy to be faced, namely the minorities. The minorities are bound to be liquidated or eliminated or evacuated within a few months' time and when once they are out of the way, the ring will be clear for an internecine battle between these two sections of Muslims.

This is one of the dangerous elements in the situation. Another is that the economic position of Pakistan itself will stimulate the lawless elements of Pakistan (they are as considerable as in Hindustan) into activity. There is bound to be a show down if the Pakistan government is not able to handle the situation fairly. Out in London, I read that there have already been demonstrations in front of Mr Jinnah's residence asking for reprisals against the minorities. The allegiance to the new government is there for the time being because the new state has been in existence only for a month or so, but when disillusionment, poverty, economic despair skim the cream off the new state, there is bound to be an explosion. In this flare up, the Punjabi Muslim will play an important part. He is better disciplined, has a long tradition of military training behind him, is far more intelligent and has a better corps spirit than his Sind or Frontier confrere. Already the unofficial League elements

are holding themselves in readiness. The Muslim League National
Guards are holding their parades in uniform in Karachi, unchecked
by the Pakistan government. The trouble with the Pakistan
government is that the elements of organized administration are not
there. Many of the records have been destroyed in transit from Delhi
to Karachi by armed bands which help up the Pakistan special. There
is a joke in Karachi that in Pakistan they have dispensed with files.
Work is done across the table and if telegrams are addressed to Mr.
Liaquat Ali Khan he puts them in his pockets and they are filed
there! Since the groundwork of orderly administration is absent, it
is difficult for the Pakistan government to deal with new symptoms
of fascist emergence, like the parade of the National Guards.

It is rash to prophesy anything in politics and certainly not in a
country like ours, where changes come and go with the speed of
summer lightning. With a due sense of caution, I must say that I
left Karachi with a vague sense that the new state will one day
witness the birth of authoritarian government. It may be said that
there is already an authoritarian Government, with Mr Jinnah sitting
on the top of the world, issuing directives, but it must be conceded
that Mr Jinnah works through democratic forms and democratic
institutions. Even this cloak of democracy will be off some day and
naked force will prop up authority. It will not surprise me in the
least if as a result of the various explosive elements being detonated,
there is a *coup d'état* in Pakistan.

I asked myself in Karachi where the minorities stood in the
mêlée. I put the question to a number of knowledgeable men in
Karachi. Almost all of them said in one voice: 'There is no place
for the Hindu in Karachi. He must go, the sooner the better.' The
emphasis and the accent were the same, whoever said it. I agree
with this conclusion. The Hindus are in a hopeless minority in
Karachi, they have so far kept themselves afloat and have been sailing
merrily by their superior intelligence and political manoeuvring
power. They have been successful because they worked in an artificial
atmosphere of British protection and stability. But now the situation
has changed. They have nobody to look to protect them except
themselves. Their safety in Karachi is not worth a minute's talking.
I asked Mr Nichaldas Vazirani what advice he would give to the
minorities. He paused for a few seconds, pursed his lips as if to
rehearse what he was going to say and then said: 'My advice is, don't
run away aimlessly.' But, I interrupted, 'What protection can you

give them?' 'You had interrupted me before I was answering your first question fully,' he gently chided me. He went on to say, 'My advice to the minorities is this: There is no point in aimlessly running away. You must find an alternative place of habitation. There is no good running away to this province and that and then finding ultimately that you are not wanted and that you have no roof over your heads. First, find out which place wants you and if you are wanted, then by all means go. If you can go, please go.' I asked Mr Nichaldas what he thought about the Congress functioning as an all-India body in Pakistan. He hesitated to answer first, perhaps his own opinions on the subject were not final and then he said slowly: 'The Congress can function in Pakistan, but we must have complete autonomy and we cannot be bound down by an all-India directive. Local situations must be met by local counsels.' Which I thought was another way of saying that the Congress cannot function in Pakistan, as a coherent all-India body, subject to central directive.

The whole atmosphere and the future for minorities in Mr Jinnah's new state depressed me and as I boarded the York sleeper plane at the airport for London, I turned round to have a good look at the city what I was leaving for a few months. I could not help muttering when I thought about the minorities, 'God bless you.' I assure you I had a lump in my throat when I said that.

I Say Unto Waris Shah

AMRITA PRITAM

Amrita Pritam (b. 1919), the distinguished Punjabi poetess and fiction writer, has been an ardent crusader for humanism as the bedrock of communal relations. Her first collection of poems *Amrit Lehran* was published in 1936 when she was barely 17 years old. Starting as a romantic poet, she matured into a poetess of revolutionary ideas as a result of her involvement with the Progressive Movement in literature. Her *magnum opus*, the long poem *Sunehray*, won the Sahitya Akademi Award.

Aj Akhan Waris Sah Nun (I say unto Waris Shah) is a heart-rending poem written during the riot-torn days that followed the partition of the country. It is addressed to Waris Shah, the celebrated eighteenth century Punjabi poet and author of the immortal *Heer*.

Today I implore Waris Shah
to speak up from his grave
and turn over a page of
the Book of Love.

When a daughter of the fabled Punjab wept
he gave tongue to her silent grief.
Today a million daughters weep
but where is Waris Shah
to give voice to their woes?
Arise, O friend of the distressed!
See the plight of your Punjab.
Corpses lie strewn in the pastures
and the Chenab has turned crimson.

Reprinted from *Modern Indian Literature,* vol. I, ed. K. M. George trans. from Punjabi by N. S. Tasneem (New Delhi: Sahitya Akademi, 1992), pp. 945-7.

Someone has poured poison
into the waters of the five rivers
and these waters are now
irrigating the land with poison.

In this fertile land have sprouted
Coutless poisonous saplings
Scarlet-red has turned the horizon
and sky high has flown the curse.
The poisonous wind,
that passes through every forest,
has changed the bamboo-shoots
into cobras.

The cobras have mesmerized the gullible people
and bit them again and again.
So in no time,
the limbs of Punjab turned bluish.
The songs vanished from the streets
and the thread of the spinning-wheel snapped.
The girls fled the *trinjan** screaming
and the resounding whirr of the spinning-wheel stopped,
Sudden let go the boats
along with the wedding-beds.
The wing has snapped
along with the strong branch of the tree.
The flute,
through which blew the breath of love,
is lost in bewilderment,
The brothers of Ranjha
have forgotten
the art of handling this instrument.
Blood raining on the earth,
Has seeped into the graves.
The princesses, the valley
called Love,
now weep in graveyards.

---

* *trinjan*—the countryard where young girls gather together to spin and sing.

All the villains
now parade
as thieves of love and beauty.

Where shall we seek
another Waris Shah?

Today I implore
Waris Shah
to speak up from his grave
and turn over a page of
the Book of Love.

Glossary

Abba: father.

Achcha: lit. good, well, really.

achkan: man's garment with a coat collar open in the centre and kept in position by the border hem.

adaab: the full expression is 'Adaab Arz', 'I pay my respects'; usual form of greeting for middle-class Muslims and many Hindus in north India; also *Assalaamalikum* (Peace be on you) and *Valaikumassalam* in reply.

Ahir: a caste which specializes in keeping cattle.

Akali Dal: political party in Punjab.

akhara: tight-knit organization of performers and other groups in north India.

Allah-o-Akbar: 'God is Great'; used as an introductory in the Muslim prayers.

alam: flag of Imam Husain, the grandson of Prophet Mohammad, carried in procession during the Moharram observances.

alhamd-illalah: in praise of Allah.

alim (plural *ulama):* scholars, learned men in the Islamic sciences.

Amma; Ammi: mother.

amroods: guava.

angrez: the British; hence *Angrezi sarkar*, the British government.

anjuman: an association, usually of Muslims.

Apa; baji: sister; hence *Apajaan* or *bajijaan*, dear sister, commonly used in north India.

ata: wheat flour.

babu: a term of respect and affection; also used disparagingly by the British for the English-educated Bengalis and for Indian clerks who used English.

badmash: bad character.

Badshah: sultan; emperor; *padshah* in Persian.

bahu: daughter-in-law.

Bajrangbali: Hanuman, the Hindu god.

Bakr Id or Id al-Azha: lit. 'the feast of sacrifice', Muslim festival.

Bande Mataram: 'hail to the mother' (land); national anthem adopted by the Congress but rejected by the Muslim League.

bania: trader, shopkeeper, moneylender.

barhai: carpenter.

basti: locality.

beedi: thin Indian (*cheroot*).

Begum: madam, Mrs, wife, lady.

behenchod: lit. sister fucker.

behenji: sister.

beldar: a digger.

beta: son.

bhai-bands: commonly used to describe friends, comrades and relatives.

Bhai; bhaiya; bhaijan: brother.

bhakt: devotee.

bhangi: sweeper, an expression not in common usage these days.

bhauj: brother's wife.

bhikshu: Hindu or Buddhist ascetic.

bhonsrivala: one who comes out of a cunt.

bibi: honorific for a woman.

bigha: just over half an acre.

biradari: community.

bori: sack.

bua: a suffix meaning 'aunt'.

burqa: veil observed mostly by Muslim women.

Chachajaan: lit. dear uncle.

Chamar: a Hindu low caste.

chapati: a thin, light unleavened bread made of whole-wheat flour and grilled on a hot plate.

charpoy: cot; a bed.

chaukidar: a watchman.

chillum: the earthen smoking pipe.

choti: braid; or tuft of hair.

churidar: tight pyjamas.

dada: normally elder brother, sometimes also used for addressing an elderly man.

dadi: grandmother.

-da, -dada, -dadi: suffixes of respect for elders.

dal: lentil.

dalkhor: vegetarian.

danda: club; a stick.

Dar al-harb: 'the abode of war', territory not under Islamic law.

Dar al-Islam: 'the abode of Islam'.

dargah: Muslim shrine of an holy person.

degchi: pots and pans.

dehat: village.

dhaba: kiosk.

dhoti: wrap-around cloth worn by men.

Diwali; Dipavali: Hindu festival of lights.

dulha: bridegroom.

dulhan: bride.

dupatta: a light mantle hung across the shoulder.

durbar: a public audience.

Fatiha (fateha): opening *surah* (opening chapter of the Quran); also the ceremony in which this *surah* is read with a prayer; prayer said at the grave for the blessings of God for the dead.

fatwa: written opinion on a point of Islamic Law.

fez: Turkish cap.

garhi: fort.

ghat: a river bank.

ghazal: one of the three important poetic forms in Urdu.

ghulam: slave.

ghunghat: veil.

goonda: a fop; thug.

gulli-danda: an Indian game.

guru: teacher, master; preceptor.

gurudwara: Sikh temple.

hadith: account of what the Prophet said or did.

Haj: pilgrimage to Mecca; the fifth pillar of Islam and an incumbent religious duty.

halwa: sweetmeat.

harami; haramzada; haramzadi: bastard.

haramzadgi: behaving like a bastard.

Harijan: 'children of God' name given by Gandhi to low-caste Hindus or untouchable.

hartal: strike, work stoppage.

haveli: a mansion.

hawaldar (havaldar): sergeant of police.

Hazrat (plural: Hazraat): a title of respect; His Holiness, His Highness etc.,

Holi: Hindu festival held in spring.

hookah (huqqa): elaborate smoking-pipe with a water bowl attached at the bottom, through which the smoke is drawn, hubble bubble.

huzoor: a term of respect given to a superior.

hijrat: act of migration.

Id: Muslim festival at the end of the month of fasting (*Ramzan*).

Imam: 'leader', especially prayer-leader in the mosque.

Imambara: 'house of the Imam', place where *tazias* are kept to mourn Husain's martyrdom.

Imam Zamin: money dedicated to the 'protecting Imam', and fastened on the arm of a person about to leave home, as a protection from evil spirits and the difficulties of the way.

Insha-Allah: god-willing (if God please).

Izzat: honour.

jalebees: sweets.

Jamaat: body, group.

janab (janaab): an expression of reverence.

jehad (jihad): religious war undertaken by the Muslims against the unbelievers.

jet (jeth): brother-in-law.

ji: form of respect showing respect and endearment.

Jirga: assembly of tribal chief; elders.

jhonpri: hut; made of thatched roof.

julaha: caste of Muslim weavers.

kafila: caravan.

kafir (plural; *Kuffar):* 'to be non-believing', infidel, impious.

Karbala: the site in Iraq where Husain and his companions were martyred.

karkhandar: artisan.

kebab: prepared from finely ground meat.

khadi: hand-spun cloth.

Khalifa: a successor, a lieutenant, a viceregent or deputy.

Khalsa 'army of the pure'; Sikh brotherhood.

kharaon: footwear made of wood.

khuda: God.

Khuda Hafiz: God (be your) protector.

Khudai Khidmatgar: lit. 'Servant of God'; movement of the charismatic leader Khan Abdul Ghaffar Khan.

khutba: the sermon delivered at the time of Muslim prayers.

kirpan: a sword, scimitar; a sacrificial knife.

kirtan: Hindu devotional song.

kotwal: police officer.

kotwali: police station.

kundis: bolts.

kurmi: an agrarian caste.

kursi: chair.

kurta: a loose collarless shirt, knee-length.

Lajwanti: the touch-me-not plant.

Lakh: unit of one hundred thousand, written 10,00,000.

lambardar: official responsible for collecting revenue; also written as *nambardar.*

langoti: waist-cloth; a strip passed between the legs, and the ends tucked into a waistband before and behind.

langra; lula: one who has lost the use of hands and feet; a cripple.

lota: a jug with a round body and rim with a long pouring spout, used to hold water.

lungi: a coloured cloth worn as a *lung* or *dhoti.*

Mai-baap: mother-and-father; the role of a ruler.

madrasa (plural: madaris): a secondary school or college for Muslims.

Majlis: assembly, organization.

Malik-ul-Maut: angel of death.

mama: maternal uncle.

mami: aunt; wife of a maternal uncle.

mamun: maternal uncle.

mandi: regular market.

mandir: Hindu temple.

Mard-i Momim: man of faith, piety and commitment; frequently used by the Urdu poet Mohammad Iqbal.

marsiya: elegiac poem describing the tragedy of Karbala.

Masi: aunts.

masjid: a mosque, place of worship.

matam: the act of mourning by the Shias, especially breast-beating.

matimili: a term of abuse.

maulana: term generally used for a Muslim doctor of law, a professor, a learned man.

maulvi: from *maula,* 'a lord of master', generally used for a learned man, a prayer leader, a teacher.

mauza: a village, hamlet, township, district.

mazdoor: labourer.

mehndi: henna.

mehr: amount of money paid/pledged to the bride at the time of marriage.

mela: fair, festival.

millat: religious community, especially community of Muslims.

mithai: sweets.

Miyan: a form of address for a young man, a gentleman.

mohalla: urban residential quarter of a city.

moharrir: clerk

mubarak: auspicious, blessed; welcome.

muezzin: the person who calls the Muslims to prayers (*azan*).

muhajirin (singular: *muhajir*): refugees.

Moharram (Muharram): first month of the Muslim lunar calendar, the month in which Husain and his companions were assassinated.

mujahid (plural: *mujahidin*): holy warrior; freedom fighter.

mulla: theologian, scholar, usually denotes a person attached to a mosque.

mumani: maternal uncle's wife.

musammat: ladies.

mushaira: a literary gathering in which Urdu poets recite their verses and the audiences show their appreciation.

musadas: six-lined verse.

Munshi: clerk.

nala: drain or small river.

namaz: the prescribed prayer in Islam.

nani: grandmother.

nara-i takbeer: noise or clamour in praise of Allah; often used as a war-cry.

neem: an Indian tree (Margosa).

noha (nauha): a short lament; usually written and sung to the sufferings of Husain and his companions.

NWFP: North-West Frontier Province.

pagri: turban.

Pakhtun: Pathan.

panchayat: village council.

pandal: a covered stage.

papad: flattened pancake made with gramflour.

paratha: a pancake made with milk and fried in butter or *ghee*.

pativarta: loyalty or fidelity to a husband.

patka: piece of cloth worn around the waist like a girdle.

patwari: the village official dealing with land records.
pillau (pulau): rice and meat dish.
pipal: the holy fig-tree.
Pir: a sufi master on the mystical path.
prabhat-pheris: morning processions in nationalist movement.
pujari: worshipper; a Hindu priest.
purdah: Muslim women are required by religion and custom to live in *purdah* (veil).
puja: Hindu religious worship.
puri: pancakes fried in butter or oil.
qabaristan: Muslim graveyard.
qasba (qasbah): country town.
qaum: used in Urdu to mean community or nation.
qazi (Kazi): a judge trained in Islamic Law.
Quaid-e-Azam: the great leader; title attached to Jinnah.
rais: a 'respectable' person; man of substance.
Rakhi; rakhi bandhan: custom of tying a knot on the wrist of another denoting solicitation of protection; usually a sister from a brother.
rasoi: kitchen.
saala: brother-in-law; also used in a pejorative sense as bastard.
salaar: head, leader.
Sabha: an assembly, congregation.
sadhu: a virtuous or holy man, a saint, sage, devotee; Hindu ascetic.
sahukar: Hindu merchant; banker, moneylender;
sahukari: money-lending.
Syed (saiyid): descendant of the Prophet through his daughter Fatima and her sons Hasan and Husain, the martyrs at Karbala.
salam: greeting.
Saheb (Sahib): an expression of respect and affection; used also as a suffix to, e.g., Mohammad.
sangathan: a movement aimed at unity and self-defence among Hindus.
sanjhle Bhai: the third of four brothers.
Subhanallah: exclamation indicating appreciation of something exciting, beautiful etc.
Sari (saree): length of cotton or silk draped round body; worn as main garment by women.
Sat Sri Akal: sikh greeting.

Satyagraha: 'truth force'; 'soul force'; Gandhi's passive resistance movement.

seer: unit of weight, about a kilogram.

serishtadar: clerk in a court of law.

Shab-i barat: Muslim festival to pray for the dead.

shaheed: martyr.

shahnashin: raised platform in an *imambara* where the *tazias* are arranged.

Shaikh: 'elder' or 'leader'; often used interchangeably with *pir*; also *khwaja* and *auliyas.*

shakkar (shakar): sugar.

shariat: the divine law of Islam.

shehnai: a musical pipe; a flute; a flageolet.

sherbet: a sweet, cool drink.

sherwani (shervani): close fitting men's coat usually up to knee-length.

Shia: 'followers', the followers of *Hazrat* Ali, the first cousin of the Prophet and his son-in-law.

subedar: governor.

subzi: vegetables.

sumbul: spikenard.

Sunni: 'one who follows the trodden path'; applied to the majority of Muslims who acknowledge Abu Bakr, Umar, Usman and Ali, the first four *Khulafa*, as the successors of the Prophet Mohammad.

Swaraj: self-rule; independence.

Syed: descendant of the Prophet of Islam.

tabligh: the Muslim conversion movement.

takht: low wooden platform.

tanzim: consolidation; Muslim movement to counter *sangathan.*

tasbi: rosary.

tazia: lath and paper models of the tombs of Husain and his family carried in procession during Moharram.

tehsil: a country-sized administrative unit, subdivision of a district.

tehmad: a loose lower garment.

teli: Hindu oil-presser caste.

thalis: tray or large plates.

thana: police station.

thanedar: the officer-in-charge of a *thana.*

tika: a small mark of vermilion or sandal paste on the forehead, worn mostly by Hindus.

tilak: mark on the forehead usually made with sandalwood paste.
tola: a certain weight, especially of gold and silver.
tonga: horse-driven two-wheeled carriage.
tongawalla: horse-cart driver.
topi: men's headdress.
-va: suffix attached to names, indicating fondness and familiarity.
ulama (singular: *alim*): commonly applied to Muslim doctors in Islamic law and theology.
U.P.: United Provinces; now Uttar Pradesh.
urs: 'wedding'; term used in India for the festival commemorating the death of a saint.
ustad: Urdu equivalent of guru.
yaar (yar): friend.
yatra: procession, pilgrimage.
Yusuf: the son of Jacob, and, according to the Quran, an inspired prophet.
wazifa: 'to follow'; a scholarship; land bestowed in gift; religious duty, daily worship (of a Muslim).
Zalm-e-Pakhtun: militant wing of *Khudai Khidmatgars.*
zamindar: landholder.
zamindari: the land held by the *zamindar.*
zenana: women's apartments; women, wives.
zindabad: long live!